The Seventh Wave

Sailing the South Pacific

Ray Archer w/c (ext)

The Seventh Wave

Ray Archer

Gordon M. Smart Publications

Canadian Cataloguing in Publication Data

Archer, Ray, 1924 -
The seventh wave

ISBN 0-9692116-6-X

1. Archer, Ray, 1924 - – Journeys–Oceania. 2. Sea Lure (Yacht) 3. Oceania–Description and travel. 4. Sailing–Oceania. I. Title.

DU23.5.A72 1997   919.504   C97-910917-5

Cover design by Lou and Ray Archer

Photos not otherwise credited are by Ray Archer, or the photographer is unknown

Printed and bound in Canada by Morriss Printing Company Ltd., Victoria, British Columbia

Quotations from *South Pacific Handbook*, second edition, 1982, reprinted by permission of Moon Travel Handbooks, Moon Publications, Chico, California

Published by   Gordon M. Smart Publications
                        #215 – 1149 Rockland Ave.
                        Victoria, B.C. V8V 4T5

Distribution and sales: Ray Archer
                        4116 Virginia Crescent
                        North Vancouver, B.C. V7R 3Z1
                        (604) 980-2830

Dedication

To the late Bob Dormer of Ottawa, Ontario and Barrington Passage, Nova Scotia, my partner in the planning, training and sailing for part of this adventure in the South Pacific,

and to Lucienne Archer, my wife of 48 years, who at first did not take the plan seriously, but once it was inevitable became a participant and enthusiastic supporter.

ACKNOWLEDGEMENTS

Thanks to the following people who provided great help and encouragement in the preparation of *The Seventh Wave*, prior to and during publishing:

Dr. Milo (Mike) Tesar of East Lansing, Michigan, who reviewed the first manuscript and provided advice on the next step in the process;

Ann Westlake of Vancouver, a professional editing consultant, for her encouragement and constructive criticism;

Gordon Smart of Victoria, an editor and publisher, for his constructive suggestions and for undertaking publication of the book;

Juanita Manning, for suggesting the book title;

Charlie and Amelia Graham, for reading the manuscript and contributing their suggestions and much encouragement;

My wife, Lucienne Archer, for countless hours reviewing, correcting and researching various aspects of this book;

Special thanks to my faithful crew who provided essential help and good humour, particularly at "happy half-hour" each day on the ocean (one drink only per crewman), and for coming through when the sailing was really difficult.

CONTENTS

INTRODUCTION

Being born and raised on the Canadian prairies at Dauphin, Manitoba, I have always been fascinated by lakes and oceans. Perhaps this is because so little water was accessible when I was growing up, and I was 51 before I learned to swim. Or perhaps there are some nautical genes inherited from a distant relative not yet identified. This fascination, plus a major retirement project, motivated the late Bob Dormer and myself to plan and undertake this ocean adventure. Unfortunately he was to experience only part of it, as he had to return to Canada after only four months.

The Seventh Wave will serve as a guide for future sailors, both inexperienced and experienced, who have a desire to go to sea, in a small yacht, and see the world. It will also serve as a family record of this ocean adventure.

The ocean is normally a pleasant, friendly place when sailing a passage in the recommended months of the year, or can be a raging monster when major storms or hurricanes appear. All ocean sailors have a multitude of problems that must be solved in order to make the next landfall safely. Most problems are of a minor nature if one is prepared through courses, experience or training, but everyone has some major problems that will test the mettle of the bravest. The most experienced sailors are not spared these challenges.

The Seventh Wave is the story of how one retired Royal Canadian Air Force officer, with some boating experience but little sailing experience, managed at, I believe, a reasonably high standard, a two-year adventure that took me and my crew from Vancouver, B.C. Canada to the South Pacific as far as New Zealand and Australia and return, with stops at all the countries in between.

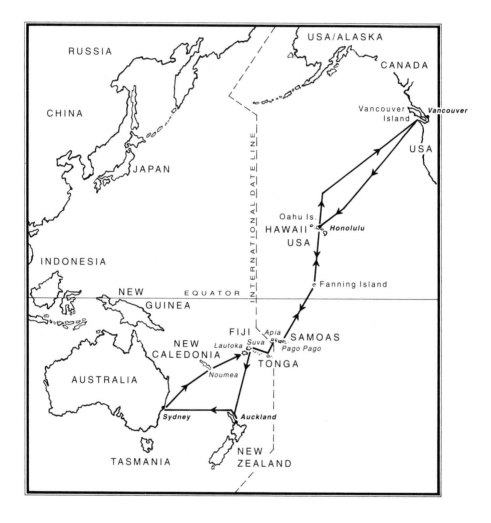

CHAPTER 1

THE SEVENTH WAVE

We were five days out of Sydney, Australia on our return voyage heading for New Caledonia in May 1985. Prior to departure the weather had not been good, with frequent storms coming in from the south and southeast. These storms had a lot of rain and high winds, in some cases approaching hurricane force. Before departure I had watched the weather pattern for several days, and I had chosen a time when no storms had been forecast.

The weather was extremely pleasant. This gave the new crew a chance to get their stomachs in shape, and become familiar with the boat and the watch routine. Also, I had not been at sea for about six weeks, and it always takes a little time to again become accustomed to the swells, the supervision of the crew and the sleeping routine on a rolling, pitching boat. On the fifth day the weather had deteriorated. Black storm clouds were coming up behind us, and the winds were increasing. The ocean swells started to build up, and were soon up to fifteen or twenty feet. The wind was from the southeast, and as we maintained a steady course for New Caledonia the boat was going over the waves at the right angle to reduce the motion, making the boat easier to steer. Also, by reducing sail down to almost bare poles, our boat speed was about 6 knots. This gave the bowsprit time to rise between the swells as we came down the very large waves that continued to build up. I considered this to be the right speed to prevent the bowsprit from going under water and lessen the danger of pitch-poling.

That afternoon Patty was on the helm; James and I were sitting in the cockpit. We each had safety harness on, and the doors to the cabins were closed. A monster wave hit us broadside, and *Sea Lure* heeled at least 60 degrees. She hesitated at the highest point, but fortunately came down the right way. The boat was in a shambles. James and I knew that Patty was off course because of the wave angle, and we called to her to get back on course. This she did immediately, just as a second very large wave hit the stern of the boat with a crash, and the water came right over the boat but did not cause excessive heel.

That night the engine would not start. By now the winds were gusting up to 60 knots on the anemometer, which was as high as it would read, so some of the gusts must have been over 70 knots. This is the beginning of hurricane force, and because *Sea Lure* was running, six knots of boat speed can be added to these wind speeds. Since I was also the engine man, it was up to me to find out what was wrong with the engine and to get it running again. Twenty-four hours later, after much trial and error, I finally decided that the problem was the glow plug switch. It had become saturated with water in the cockpit, and had stopped working. To change the switch it was necessary to wedge myself in the engine room so I wouldn't get hurt, remove the old switch and install a new one. While installing the switch, a crewman had to tighten the nut with a wrench from the cockpit side while I held the switch by hand from the engine room side. I couldn't hold the switch when it was turned, and it touched the next instrument. This in turn caused a short in the electrical system, creating a large flame as the switch wire started to burn. Now we had an engine room fire!

Never in my wildest dreams, eleven years earlier, when planning this ocean adventure, had I imagined I would be caught in this dangerous situation.

* * *

In 1974 I was still in the Royal Canadian Air Force, and stationed at National Defence Headquarters in Ottawa. After two years as a pilot in World War II, and 25 post-war years in finance, logistics and personnel, I was looking forward to retirement in 1975. Retirement was predetermined by my contract with the RCAF, and based on my rank, which was Wing Commander, therefore compulsory retirement was at the age of 51. I planned to move back with my wife and family to Vancouver, B.C. where we had purchased a home in 1962 when stationed at RCAF Sea Island.

I decided that, in order to live retirement life to the fullest, we needed a large boat. Although we had owned a 16-foot runabout in Ontario for five years, I realized that I had to learn more about boating if I was going to operate a boat in the West Coast waters, which at times could be very unforgiving.

In the fall of 1973, I completed my first boating course at the Canadian Power Squadron. The Canadian Power and Sail Squadron, which it is now called, does an outstanding job of teaching amateur boaters how to handle their boats safely on the water, and such things as rules of the road, navigation, tying knots and a host of other subjects. They undoubtedly save numerous lives each year by imparting this knowledge. All students must obtain 80% on the exam at the end of each course, ensuring that graduates know their subject very thoroughly.

Sitting in front of me in the boating class each week were Bob and Marian Dormer. Bob was a senior executive with Bell Telephone and a senior officer in the Army Militia in Ottawa, after serving in air crew with the RCAF during the Second World War. He was an experienced sailor, having owned a small boat for about 20 years. Bob was also an experienced ham radio operator. Marian worked in the Senate in Ottawa and was an executive assistant to a very senior Senator. After comparing notes and answers to homework questions on Power Squadron nights, and many sessions in one of the three Officers' Messes in downtown Ottawa used by the Headquarters Officers, we became very good friends.

Bob and Marian planned to retire in 1980 and move to the Maritimes; Barrington Passage, Nova Scotia. During one of the functions that we all attended, I suggested that sometime after their retirement we both buy large sailboats and sail to meet at the Panama Canal. Bob thought about it for about ten seconds, then we both stood up, shook hands, and agreed that we would meet in the Panama Canal in the 1980's. That moment launched us on a project that lasted for ten years, and finally resulted in our sailing the South Pacific. Bob took part in the first five months of this adventure, and I completed it in two years and four days. The plans for the route we were to follow changed for various reasons, but we both set sail along with a crew of three in my sailboat, *Sea Lure*, from Vancouver, B.C., Canada on 22 June 1984. This was ten years after the idea was first discussed. Our first stop, after refueling and clearing customs in Bellingham, Washington, was Honolulu, Hawaii.

Because of the length of the voyage and the possibility of many problems, we both considered that extensive training courses and ocean experience in sailboats were necessary in order to cope with the unexpected, and, more importantly, to build our confidence. Particularly in my case, as I had not yet learned to sail, and had only spent a limited time in boats on small lakes in Ontario. The most extensive boat trip we had taken was down the Rideau Canal to Kingston, down the St. Lawrence River to Montreal, and up the

Ottawa River to Ottawa, in a 16-foot run-about with an 80 hp engine. Bob and I took many more courses with the Power and Sail Squadron in the areas where we lived, and they included seamanship power, seamanship sail, advanced piloting, junior navigation and navigation. The last two courses covered celestial navigation very extensively. As I would be the engine man and navigator, as well as the captain, I took three engine courses, the last one being diesel engine maintenance and overhaul. These courses were of great value to us and at one time or another over the course of the two-year adventure we used almost all the information we had gained.

Bob had been a radio operator in the RCAF during the war, and had taken a great interest in the ham radio field. He was a very experienced radio operator, and obtained his advanced license shortly before our departure. The ham radio was invaluable from a morale point of view, as all the crew had a chance to talk to the folks back home about once a week. We also ordered parts for the boat to be delivered at our next destination, and we reported each day to the net operated by the ham radio operators for the West Coast of Canada and New Zealand. These operators were prepared to send us medical help from a doctor if required, and also ensure that we were all right by our daily reports. Had there been a real emergency such as abandoning ship etc., the ham radio would have been a great help, as Bob would have reported the latitude and longitude from the previous day. The ham radio operators also recorded our boat speed and course, so it would have been very easy for them to calculate our location to within five or ten miles. This gave me great confidence that we would survive if we lost the yacht, as I had purchased a "Givens" life raft, which is the best available. It had rations, good flares, a water catcher, and all the requirements for five persons to survive for a long period. I also carried an Emergency Personal Identification Radio Beacon for aircraft or ships to home on us.

Additional boating experience was gained on our 34-foot Mariner cruiser, *Blue Dolphin*. It had twin engines and an all-weather bridge, and was an excellent cruiser for the West Coast waters, except that it seldom passed a refueling barge without our having to fill the fuel tanks. It used a gallon a mile at 12 knots. Fortunately, the price of gasoline from 1975 until I sold the cruiser in 1981 was considerably less than in later years. Experience with the West Coast waters in high winds, fog, etc., was gained on this boat, and we did carry out two rescues when small boats foundered. Fortunately both rescues were successful and did provide practice under stressful conditions.

Over this long period of time, Bob and I had not lost sight of our goal and had plodded steadily toward it, much to the chagrin of our wives. They did not take us seriously for the first five years, but after that time they were afraid we might carry out our plan.

By 1982 Bob and Marian had retired and were living in Barrington Passage, Nova Scotia. Bob had not procured a large sailboat. I had sold *Blue Dolphin* and, after a long search, purchased a 40-foot Islander ketch. As the voyage was now going to be made in my boat, I favoured the South Pacific over the Panama, particularly in view of the political situation in that area. Also, two of my friends had just completed a two-year trip to the South Pacific, and it was easier to pick up information on the nine countries I planned to visit. Besides all this, I had personal experience sailing the first 3000 miles to Hawaii in 1978 and I was confident it would be no problem to do it again. I also had some experienced ocean sailors on the crew, i.e. Bob and Larry.

After all our training courses, Bob and I thought some practical experience on the ocean would be in order. Bob made a hair-raising sailboat trip down the St. Lawrence River and around to the Maritimes, and made one or two trips into the Atlantic during very foggy conditions. In 1977 I had the good fortune to sail on the 73-foot West Coast yacht *Greybeard* with the original owner and skipper, the late Lol Killam. It was a December voyage down the Washington, Oregon and California Coasts to San Francisco, and then to Los Angeles. The weather was terrible, with one storm after another, and we were in dense fog about 50% of the time as far as San Francisco. Lol had a crew of 11 sailors, enough for three watches, so I had time to practice navigation when off duty. It was all done with the radio direction finder initially, as we could not see any celestial bodies for navigation with the sextant. This gave me a much-needed opportunity to practice taking radio bearings with my Ray Jefferson radio direction finder. This practice was put to good use during the voyage later, and to this day I still take radio bearings from time to time, particularly in fog, if I'm not sure of my position. Lol had the foot of the mainsail tear the full length and eventually disintegrate in the high winds on the vessel's 98-

foot mast. The main halyard was jammed at the top, and it was too dangerous to send a crewman up in these conditions, so Lol decided to try to wrap this massive piece of dacron around the mast before it caused a knockdown. He masterfully maneuvered the large vessel over mountainous waves, and after about an hour had it completely wrapped around the mast.

He ordered me to navigate during this hectic period, and I did this by recording the headings of the boat and the distance travelled on each heading. There was a compass in the main cabin, so I did the recording where it was nice and dry but extremely rough. A large pot of hot water or food went hurtling across the galley when we went over one of the huge waves, even though the stove was gimballed. Fortunately, I had a good stomach and didn't get sick. I then did a dead reckoning plot on the plotting sheets I had brought along. This was done after converting all the compass headings to true heading based on the TVMDC system, calculating the distance travelled using the knot log, and plotting this information to determine a point on the ocean, recorded as latitude and longitude, that we had reached when the sail was finally wrapped. We then set course from this point. I guess Lol considered it accurate enough, as he set course again based on my calculations and it worked out all right. This was an exciting experience for the entire crew, and it stood me in good stead when I was in the big storm during the South Pacific voyage.

In addition to this experience, I raced on the sailboat *Tarun*, owned and skippered by Peter Hendry of West Vancouver, as the navigator in the Victoria to Maui, Hawaii sailboat race in 1978. All navigation had to be done with the sextant, as satellite navigation systems were not permitted at that time. The daily running fix and occasional two or three body fixes worked out well most of the time. In the last four days, only one minor course change was required to put us over the finish line between the Hawaiian islands of Maui and Molokai. We didn't have any big storms, but line squalls were frequent and we had a serious spinnaker wrap. This was to be expected as we flew the spinnaker night and day, and crewmen do not always react fast enough in emergencies when they are tired.

After the experience on the three ocean trips, I decided that I needed a boat that would accommodate a large crew, i.e. 5 or 6 crewmen including myself. I came to this conclusion after some bad weather sailing on *Greybeard*, when having a large number of crewmen had many advantages under fog and high wind conditions, when emergencies happen. Sometimes they do occur on a long voyage. Also, I considered it important to have enough crew so they would all get sufficient rest, and that a crewman be on the helm at all times – all crewmen to be rotated every hour or half hour and under heavy weather conditions the helmsman to be rotated every twenty minutes. Many ocean sailors will disagree with me, as the majority go with only one or two crewmen, self-steering and the crewperson on duty looks out every 20 minutes, if he/she is not asleep or gets around to it. I was to be thankful for this decision later in the big storm out of Australia, where a good friend lost his 40-foot sloop *Sea Song* partly because he could not cope with the weather conditions with only two crew members.

The search for the suitable boat started in the spring of 1980 and, after looking at a number of boats without success, I had a friend who was a boat broker in Victoria, B.C. start looking for me. I laid out the requirements and he searched for a year. Finally in the spring of 1982, he found an Islander 40-foot ketch (motor sailor) that was eight years old. It was very well constructed with fibreglass with a balsa wood core. The Islander Boat Company of Costa Mesa, California had a good reputation, and built quality boats for the charter and pleasure boat trade. It had Hood furling gear on the bow, an autopilot, a deep freeze, two heads – one with a shower – and an extra 30-gallon tank that could be converted to shower water. It had a centre cockpit, plenty of freeboard and, most importantly, as I had been a power boater, a 75 hp Nissan/Chrysler six cylinder diesel engine with 160 imperial gallon fuel capacity. The fresh water capacity was 200 imperial gallons, which is ample for a long ocean passage, if salt water is used for cooking and doing dishes.

This boat also had some disadvantages, which always seems to be the case when purchasing boats. It had large windows forward and on both sides of the main cabin, and four small windows in the aft cabin. This problem was overcome by having seven custom ¼ inch lexan windows built for the main cabin and placing ¾ inch plywood panels over the four aft cabin windows. The boat was also slow for a 40-footer, but this was not a major consideration, as extra days on a passage were not a problem – I was not in a hurry! It also had too much teak on the railing, etc., which looks great

9

when it is kept up properly, but consumes too many hours of work to keep it in this condition. The ocean swells lift the varnish off the rails, so the teaking must start all over again after each ocean passage.

The deal was put together in May 1982, at the price I had offered after the bowsprit was replaced. The replacement turned out to be a blessing, as several times the boat anchor was caught in coral and great force was exerted on it to break the anchor free.

Two old friends, the late Gard Gardiner from Vancouver and the late Tom Turner of West Vancouver, made the trip to Victoria on 28 May 1982 and we picked up *Sea Lure*. Gard became the first skipper of the boat, as I was still under training. Previously, I had concentrated on navigation, as it was essential to master that for the trip. The sailing part could be learned later, and after taking the seamanship sail course and having completed three ocean voyages in sailboats, I had a good idea what was involved. This approach turned out to be satisfactory. However, Gard Gardiner was a very experienced sailor, having sailed boats on the West Coast for many years, so he was the skipper for the first two or three training trips, then I took over. *Sea Lure* is a most forgiving boat and will usually look after itself no matter what the helmsman does, right or wrong. This suited me just fine. With the full keel and the weight, it is a very steady boat even in a large following sea.

Seven years had gone by since the idea of offshore sailing had been agreed to, so I was anxious to set a departure date as Father Time might catch up to Bob and me if we didn't get moving. One important thing had not been settled: whether we could sail together on a 40-foot sailboat over an extended period of time without serious problems. To determine this, in the spring of 1983 we chartered a 40-foot sloop in the British Virgin Islands for two weeks and six of us flew to these islands via Ottawa, Montreal and San Juan. After checking out the boat thoroughly, we departed in high winds for a destination some 20 miles away. Bob was the skipper and I was the navigator, and we both worked to repair the boat as required. This turned out to be a most compatible arrangement, and we had a great two weeks with enough problems to test our skills, along with many very happy times and good sailing in the trade winds. The passages were short and the area generally sheltered. We wanted to try the open Atlantic and sail to some islands 100 miles distant, but the charter company was not cooperative as the insurance would not cover us, so we didn't press them.

The following summer Bob and Marian flew to Vancouver and sailed on *Sea Lure* with us. They were very impressed with the boat and Bob decided he would accompany me on our great adventure.

It was now possible to set a departure date for our trip. A year was sufficient to get the boat ready, recruit a crew, complete additional training, stock the boat and set sail. I wanted to leave in 1984, late in June, as the Victoria to Maui, Hawaii sailboat race would run again that year, and if we departed a week ahead of the race boats, they would pass us on the way. If we were in trouble, we could call for assistance. I needn't have taken this precaution, as we were so well prepared that we would more likely have been providing assistance to one of the race boats. As it turned out, nobody needed assistance.

Besides, Bob was in favour of a June departure. It fit in well with his activities in Nova Scotia, and Marian was available to fly to Vancouver at the appropriate time to join up with Lou, my wife, so they could meet us in Honolulu, Hawaii when we arrived in July.

The winter of 1983/84 was a hectic time trying to get the boat and everything else ready. The following were the main projects, but many other small items also had to be arranged. I used a PERT (Program Evaluation and Review Technique) chart system to keep track of all the major projects to ensure they moved along to completion by mid-June 1984.

1. Buy a ham radio, install the antenna and test the radio. Fortunately Bob looked after most of this including the purchase of the radio, a Kenwood 401. The companies in Vancouver wanted about $1,000 to install a radio antenna. Bob did it with $25 worth of wire, insulators, etc., and climbed the mast himself. He had started employment some 40 years previously with Bell Telephone as an installer on high poles, so he was quite at home at the top of the mast. The antenna worked very well, and Bob talked to Ian in New Zealand on the ham radio the first day at sea. Ian is part of the Dreamers, Doers, Doners (DDD) ham radio net that operates every day from the West Coast of Canada and New Zealand.

2. Procure, install and test a satellite navigation set. It turned

out to be a Walker 402 I bought from a Canadian who had just completed a similar ocean trip. It was a good set, but we still hadn't worked out the programming when we set sail out the Straits of Juan De Fuca, but we had the instruction book and, with Larry's help, mastered it the second day out. I could have navigated with the sextant again, and had done some recent sight and sight reductions. As it turned out the Sat Nav worked for the first 18 months very well, but stopped working in Hawaii on the way back.

3. Chris Sheffield, a friend from Vancouver and a crewman from Hawaii to Tonga via Fanning Island, American Samoa and Western Samoa, kindly rewired the critical part of the boat wiring and the switch panel. He also installed the extra wiring for the radios, Sat Nav panel lights, and a switch-over so I could use shore power when it was available. After leaving Honolulu it wasn't available. This was a major improvement to the boat, and the electrical system did not fail during any of the critical times in storms, etc. I will always be indebted to Chris for this excellent work.

4. The custom windows were completed just a few days before we were ready to sail, and Wayne, our son, helped me install them. We also installed plywood panels over the windows in the aft cabin of the boat, after the boards were given 12 coats of varnish.

5. I had ordered a new genoa for the furling gear from Leitch & McBride Sail Loft of Vancouver and Sidney, B.C. It was heavier than normal and made of dacron. It was full size, i.e. 150%, and turned out to be an excellent sail. It was the power sail for the 18,000 nautical miles of sailing, except for a few days when it was being sewn after minor tears. During these periods we put up the old genoa, and it still moved the boat at a reasonable speed. Rick McBride, the sail maker, and his folks were personal friends from Canadian Air Force days, as Rick's father Rod and I served together at RCAF station Camp Borden in the early 1950's.

6. I decided that I needed an anemometer, as I had noticed that the one on *Greybeard* was most helpful when determining wind speed and direction, particularly in bad weather or after dark. I bought a Signet anemometer, as it is the old tried and true one that has been in use for many years, and I was not disappointed. I installed it myself, and one and half hours at the top of the mast drilling and tapping holes in a stainless steel plate is not exactly my idea of fun. It performed heroically for the trip, is

still working, and has had absolutely no maintenance. This speaks well for Signet Equipment. It is one of the most useful instruments on *Sea Lure* and we use it all the time. Besides, it is like sailing by instruments and not unlike under-the-hood flying in aircraft. There are really many similarities between the sea and the air, and I suppose that partly accounts for the large number of airmen that get involved in pleasure boating.

7. A six-man life raft had to be procured, and I was fortunate to get a secondhand "Givens" raft. It is the best, as it is self-righting in heavy weather conditions as long as the flap door is kept closed. I had it repacked, and added two long lasting flares at $100 each just in case we needed them. Fortunately we didn't have to inflate the life raft, but had we lost *Sea Lure* at sea I was confident that we could survive for four months with my crew. The raft had a lot of water on board and a water catcher. It had a good supply of food and fishing equipment. The only unknowns were our ability to get into the raft safely, and the sanity of the crew under such conditions. Also, if a shark or other fish seriously punctured the raft, could we repair it quickly? The raft had a double bottom, and we had repair equipment and a pump. Had we been required to abandon ship and go into the raft after only ten minutes to spare, we would have sent several Mayday calls on the two radios to give our location. The homing beacon would have been with us, and the batteries were strong enough to send out an SOS signal for 48 hours for a distance of at least 100 miles. I hoped that a vessel or an aircraft would have heard our Mayday call, and could home on our beacon. When it appeared, we would have shot off one of our long-lasting flares and hoped to be spotted. Prior to departure on every passage the crew were given an extensive briefing, and one of their duties was a specific job when abandoning ship. This helped to establish confidence in the crew.

8. A new VHF radio was procured and worked very well, but the antenna failed several days out of Hawaii on the first leg. Bob rigged a temporary antenna which worked very well. After we arrived in Honolulu, he climbed the mizzen mast and repaired the original antenna, which has been working fine ever since.

9. In case we needed 110-volt power to operate the power equipment on board such as a power drill, or to charge batteries, I bought and installed a Yamaha charger with an exhaust out through the side of the boat and a shutoff valve to keep the sea

water out when it was not running. It was used many times and was a good piece of equipment for a small investment.

10. We needed an inflatable dinghy to go ashore in foreign ports, as there is rarely space at the dock or even a dock available to tie up to after leaving Hawaii, so we would live at anchor most of the time. A small Metzler dinghy with a 5-horse engine did the job. I also carried a second dinghy engine, an Evinrude 2 hp, as a spare. (It was loaned for three months to our friends from England on the catamaran, when their dinghy engine packed up. I retrieved it in New Zealand at the Marina in Half Moon Bay at a prearranged company, and then used it on our dinghy from Fiji onward on our return trip, after the other engine refused to run). We carried the dinghy on the davits when in a country, but deflated it and stowed it in the engine room during passages. The engines had their own custom built containers, so they could not move around in heavy seas.

11. I procured a "Galaxy" compass, which was easy to read and steer by day and night. Lights had to be connected to all instruments for night sailing. Many hours were spent swinging the compass, or "boxing" the compass as the sailors say, but eventually I prepared a deviation table that I had confidence in and it worked out very well. I still use the same table, and it seems to be accurate. A navigator must always have utmost confidence in the vessel's compass, otherwise the skipper is asking for trouble.

12. The stove in the galley is fueled with propane, a most dangerous gas if not treated with care and respect. To provide more safety in this area, I replaced all the lines and the regulator and installed a safety switch with a red light in the galley area. A sniffer and blower had to be installed in the compartment where the three propane bottles were stored and the bottles had to have recessed bases with metal straps to hold them in place when the boat was in motion.

13. Additional items such as a new bunk in the main cabin behind the seats were required. At night when the skipper was occupying his bunk, a crewman had to sleep forward. A new knot log to record the distance travelled, as well as the speed, had to be procured, installed and calibrated on the measured mile. A barometer was acquired, installed and calibrated, and a bimini or canopy to keep the hot sun off the crew when they were in the cockpit and the salt water spray off the helmsman when in heavy seas.

14. The diesel engine needed the injectors reconditioned and tested. A new Racor diesel fuel filter was installed to keep the fuel clean before it went into the engine. Also 24 fuel filters were required to complete the trip, due to the dirty fuel purchased in the South Pacific. The engine also needed a salt water pump and a great range of spares.

15. Obtain all the normal navigation equipment, such as two sextants (one a new German sextant), charts, plotting sheets (HO 229 - four books), pilot books, RDF book for the South Pacific, light lists, etc.

16. I attempted to get insurance for the trip, and we delayed one day on departure to have the boat surveyed, but I was turned down by all companies including Lloyds of London. I guess they considered that an Air Force officer going on such an extensive voyage at sea was too great a risk for them. I was quite happy to keep the many thousands of dollars they would have charged me, and it is surprising how careful a skipper can be when he does not have insurance.

All these projects had to move along at an acceptable rate to be completed in time for the departure. Some of the minor items did not get completed, and this is normal for offshore sailors. As the old saying goes, if you wait to complete everything before departure, you will never leave. So at some point you just leave and try to complete the remaining items as you go along. This actually works out quite well, as long as the major items are completed beforehand. The crew have more to do on the passage if there are still projects to complete.

One question I am asked frequently is: "How do you provision for five people for a month, keep them well fed and not run out of anything?" It's not easy. The system I used is as follows, but I am sure there are many others, particularly for small crews.

I sat down with the crew for about an hour, and we prepared the menu for a week. All crew members had an input, a chance to argue for their preferences, and advised us if they had allergies. This was the only time the menu could be changed. Then we made up a shopping list for the week using a master list, so no items would be forgotten. Next, we multiplied the quantities by four for the long passages or by two or three for the shorter passages. This ensured we had sufficient food on board, but did not have too much, otherwise an inventory count would be required when a crew member dropped off at a port, so he or she would be reimbursed for the food left over. Each crew member put in 1/5 of the money required for the shopping, which normally amounted to $150 for a month, including food, beer, soft drinks, chocolate bars and snacks for the crew on watch. This was considered reasonable by most crew members, as I paid the engine fuel, docking when required, harbour fees, propane for cooking and all other boat expenses. The system worked out very well, but I was once forced to take a crew member who didn't have enough money for food, so I paid his share. He did a few extra duties around the boat, and ran the shuttle service in the dinghy between *Sea Lure* and the shore, as crew members were coming and going at all hours.

Upon arrival in Honolulu on the first leg, it was necessary to do an inventory of all remaining items and cost them, then I had to reimburse the two crew members that dropped off. We had bought too much food in Vancouver before departure, i.e. $1400 total, and about $600 worth was still left upon arrival in Honolulu. So it was necessary for me to reimburse the departing members, and then charge the new crew members for the food on board plus food purchased, less the food left over when they departed. This was time-consuming on the first two legs, but after that we purchased just what we needed and had very little left over at the end of the passages, except for emergency rations that I kept in a separate storage. To keep the cost of food to a minimum, we shopped at the Naval Exchange at Pearl Harbour in Honolulu. Bob and I still had the privilege of shopping at approximately 30% discount, as we were retired officers from the Canadian Forces. Otherwise, I would ask for a discount from one of the largest stores in the harbour where we were provisioning. They normally obliged and delivered the food to the boat, as the purchase was usually $500 or more.

We left Vancouver with much too much food, so we ate steaks, roast beef, chicken, porkchops, etc. with all the trimmings, plus dessert, but still managed to lose weight. Approximately twenty pounds in the case of Bob and myself. Alcohol consumption was reduced to one drink a day just before dinner, as this was the rule when at sea. We had happy half-hour just before dinner. The rule was broken from time to time if we sighted land, or someone had a birthday, and always when we crossed the equator. The beer, wine and liquor were purchased at the duty free shop just before we left a country so the cost was very reasonable. I also carried a stock of hard liquor for emergencies and it was necessary to use some of this stock when a crew member was showing signs of a breakdown.

Storing the food on the boat was a problem at first, and the weight had to be distributed properly to prevent the boat from listing. We stored each type of food in the same area each time, and this information was in the skipper's head, so the crewman doing the cooking would simply ask the skipper where to look for a specific food item. The food shelves at the back of the galley were restocked every week, so it was seldom necessary to go looking for an item.

The watchkeeping and cooking duties were assigned each week by the skipper, and they were coordinated to minimize interference with the sleeping routine. For example, the two crewmen on the midnight to 0600 hours watch made breakfast for themselves and the two crewmen taking over the next watch, and then they went to bed as soon as their watch was completed. The watch taking over washed the dishes and cleaned up the galley. The skipper coordinated his sleeping time with the schedule, or made his own breakfast and washed his own dishes. Serving of meals on time was a great morale booster for the crew, and is recommended. Having every crew member take part in the cooking was also good for morale, as competition for better meals often developed between crew members and we all benefitted. Each crewman was rotated through the three meals a day, and never cooked more than two dinners a week.

Some crewmen had very little experience at cooking big meals for five people and this included the skipper, so crewmen were assigned meals they could cope with more easily.

On the crew there was usually a hobby cook, and he or she gave help to the inexperienced. As the passage progressed, the inexperienced became more confident and sometimes tried exotic dishes. Fresh fish was always on the menu once a week for dinner, and with the exception of the first passage, we always had fresh fish available. The day we caught fish we switched the menu, if necessary, and had it for dinner that day. Fresh fish turned out to be one of our most popular dinners. It was always the skipper's duty to scale, gut and cut up the fish for cooking, and after doing about 40 fish this duty was wearing a little thin. But having fresh tuna or mahimahi grilled in the oven with lemon etc., ready to eat a few hours after it was taken out of the ocean, was worth the cleaning effort. In the area of New Zealand we caught so many tuna, we stopped fishing after we had four extras in the freezer. I didn't believe in fishing unless we could consume the fish ourselves or give it away to friends after arriving at the next country.

During the two-hour briefing of each crew before departure on every leg, I covered the operation of the boat, the watch system, meal system, and man-overboard drill. A great deal of emphasis was placed on safety, even to the point where each crewman was expected to watch his crew mates for unsafe practices, and this included the skipper. When people are tired, or wakened in the middle of the night to do something in a hurry, they may not take proper care. I was advised several times of unsafe acts I was doing, such as walking in the cockpit in socks, etc., and I was glad it was brought to my attention. We did not have a man overboard situation, but had a very close call on one occasion.

The drill for abandoning ship was covered thoroughly. Each crewman had a job to do before entering the life raft, such as sending a Mayday, taking the gallon can of water, getting the food bag that was packed and ready, launching the life raft, assisting other crew members into the raft, etc. Fortunately we did not have to do the drill in an emergency, but it helped to build confidence, particularly with the inexperienced crewmen who had never been on the ocean, and this included over half the 31 crew members who crewed on *Sea Lure* in the two years.

"How do you find crew for the ocean passages?" is a question I am frequently asked. The legs from Vancouver to Honolulu and return were crewed by Canadians whom I had met in Vancouver or talked to on the telephone. Also, two Canadians flew from Vancouver to Honolulu to join the boat – one went as far as Tonga and the other went all the way to New Zealand. They were both Watch Captains, i.e. in charge of watch, and provided much continuity. Although one was a new sailor he picked up the routine quickly, and for the last leg from Fiji to New Zealand I promoted him to Watch Captain, to replace the one who left the boat in Fiji.

CHAPTER 2

IT'S A LONG LONG PASSAGE

Bob Dormer arrived from Barrington Passage, Nova Scotia on 15 June 1984 for the final preparation of the boat, some crew training and the departure parties. He installed the ham radio, hooked up the Sat Nav and did numerous other jobs. The remainder of the crew were all Canadians who lived in the greater Vancouver area, so they had already sailed on the boat and were quite familiar with *Sea Lure*. They were Larry, Laurie and Bill. Larry was an experienced engine man, so that became his secondary duty as he was also a Watch Captain, i.e. in charge of a watch, and Laurie was his assistant. Bob Dormer was the other Watch Captain and Bill was on watch with him. Bill had completed the boating course and had sailed on *Sea Lure* four or five times before, but had never been on the ocean. Laurie had sailed on *Sea Lure* a number of times, but never on the ocean either. He was a hobby cook and very handy at just about everything. He insulated the deep freeze, built the box for the life raft and installed it on the boat, and carried out many repairs as we sailed on the first passage. They were an excellent crew, and I was most fortunate to start out on this two-year adventure with such a competent and good-humoured crew. Laurie and Larry were going for the first leg only, and Bill planned to go to New Zealand, but "mal de mer" over an extended period of time convinced him to change his mind, so he ended up going only as far as Honolulu.

21 June 1984 was set for our departure from Vancouver, with the first stop in Bellingham, Washington to pick up the life raft. After departure from there, the next stop was Honolulu, Hawaii. A great many last-minute things had to be done in the last few days to prepare *Sea Lure*, get the food on board, and do a multitude of other things. It was also party time. Charlie and Amelia Graham had come down from Clinton to see us off, Bob and Ramona Osborne had us and the crew and friends on board *RAO*, their very large cruiser, for lunch and also out for a very special Chinese dinner two nights before our departure. As well, we had a party on *Sea Lure* for the crew and guests. Everything seemed to be shaping up fine for the 21st June departure when I was given dubious last minute advice on getting insurance on *Sea Lure*, even though I had

previously decided that I would go without insurance. The insurance company would not guarantee they could get coverage, and a survey was required including the history of the crew members' ocean sailing experience. In order for all of this to be completed, I had to delay the departure by one day. Actually this was a blessing in disguise, as it gave us one more day to complete preparations, since it was discovered that the meat for the freezer needed to be prefrozen before being put into the freezer so it would remain frozen for the passage to Honolulu. So a rush freezing job in Laurie's freezer took place on this extra day. Numerous friends came down to the boat on the morning of 21 June, but I had to tell them that a 24 hour delay would take place and would they come back the next morning. An old friend, the late Dennis Waddell, who lost his life in an unfortunate boating accident in 1986, carried out the survey in quick order. We corrected several safety items as he recommended, and that probably prevented a major problem at sea. The insurance company representative told us he would advise us in several weeks when we were on the ocean. This exercise was a waste of time, as he came back and told us by ham radio in about 10 days that they could not find an insurance company to cover us. There had been several major losses in the South Pacific and they were not interested. I was back to what I had planned in the first place – no insurance.

On 22 June at about 1000 hours, most of the people that had been there the previous morning came down to *Sea Lure* on "M" float at the Royal Vancouver Yacht Club in Coal Harbour to see us off. Our son Wayne was there, also our youngest daughter Coleen, who brought a bottle of champagne. We all drank a "Bon Voyage" and at 1043 hours we undocked. It was a most unusual feeling for me after so many years of preparation at great expense and effort, and not really knowing what was in store over the next two years. But it was also a great feeling of accomplishment just to get started. My military experience in organization over many years was put to the test. Of course I was still a novice sailor, but I had planned that by the time the experienced sailors on my crew left to return to Canada, I would have enough experience on the ocean to train and guide a new crew, which is the way it worked out. However, there were some difficult moments that tried my patience and ingenuity, especially on the return passage.

Gard and Marg Gardiner, in their cruiser *Wineglass*, took my wife Lou and the Grahams, and they accompanied us out of the harbour and past Point Grey. Many pictures were taken and several appear in this book. Gard had planned to go with me on the adventure for as many passages as he could handle, as he really enjoyed sailing on *Sea Lure*, but he had an unfortunate medical problem in 1983. After that the risk was too great to undertake an ocean voyage, as he might require medical attention on short notice and we might be too far from shore. He did, however, see us off that morning.

We passed the Point Grey Bell Buoy at 1236 hours, stopped at the Point Roberts Marina at 1620 hours to clear Customs by telephone and docked in Bellingham at 2200 hours. There we continued to finish last-minute jobs, bought a few more items, such as an inexpensive winch handle even though we had two good ones on board. Incidentally, we still have that winch handle on board *Sea Lure*. We had installed the satellite navigation system, a Walker 401, only a day or two before departure but had not learned to program it. We had the book of operating instructions, and also talked to the Sat Nav specialist to determine if the set was working properly. After some discussion, he assured us it was O.K., and we just had to follow the instructions in the handbook closely when programming it. I wasn't too concerned, as I knew I could navigate to Hawaii with the sextant if necessary. I had recently taken some sights, reduced and plotted them, so I was up to speed for celestial navigation. The second day out of Bellingham, Larry determined the correct programming method, and from then on the Sat Nav worked. Larry gave me the information and I did the programming each morning.

I found if I turned the set off at night while I was sleeping and programmed it the following morning, it seemed to work better for some strange reason. Unless it was necessary to have it on during the night to give the crew on duty a fix, it was off at night for most of the next 18 months. It gave us 10 to 15 fixes each day that were accurate, and reduced the work for the navigator considerably. I took some sextant sights on each leg and after plotting them, if my running fix was within 2 miles of the Sat Nav fix I would not do any more for that passage. Satellite Navigation and GPS (global position system) is a wonderful invention, and certainly reduces the wear and tear on the ocean navigator plus providing greater accuracy. It is necessary to use the old Sat Navs with caution when doing a landfall, as the headings provided may be off if a satellite has not passed over for several hours and the vessel is experiencing considerable drift or leeway. This problem has been corrected with the new Sat Nav systems which use fixed satellites, and are accurate to several hundred yards all the time, if the power or something else doesn't fail. It is better to do a landfall visually in the daytime, and use the Sat Nav and radio direction finder as back-ups. The first time into a new country can be tricky, as the charts are not always accurate and most of them do not give an ocean view of the mountain, inlets and harbours etc.

After filling the water tanks and fuel tanks in Bellingham, we departed at 1400 hours for Honolulu, made our way through the San Juan Islands to the south end of Lopez Island, and then turned West into the Strait of Juan de Fuca. Unfortunately, I had not anticipated rough water conditions and should have had dinner completed before turning into the strait, as the water was rough with short choppy waves. We made the mistake of cooking chicken in a small shallow pan and the chicken fat overflowed. Laurie and I were cooking supper and ended up skating around on chicken fat that had run over in the oven, down the front of the stove and onto the deck. It was a most dangerous situation, as the fat could have caught fire in the hot oven or one of us could have fallen on the greasy deck in the galley. Fortunately, neither happened. Eventually dinner was served and it turned out all right, but it wasn't a great start, and hopefully the operation would get better. We altered course to starboard to get some shelter from Discovery and Trial Islands, and at 2200 hours we passed Victoria about two miles out heading for Race Passage where we ran into fog.

We did not carry radar, but the fog was not very dense in the beginning. At 0030 we passed through Race Passage in fairly dense fog, and I then set a course for the crew on duty to take us out the Canadian side of the Strait of Juan de Fuca, with plenty of distance away from the outgoing ship traffic lane. I had been out this strait three times before on ocean voyages, and felt confident we could do it again in fog, with relative safety. The watch system was in effect, with two crewmen in the cockpit rotating on the helm, and both watching out for traffic. It was Bob Dormer's watch and he had lots of experience in fog, so I went to bed, as it had been a long day again. I slept for about six hours, quite soundly despite the engine noise, and when I woke up we were almost out of the strait and the fog had lifted. The watch had changed at 0400 with me being barely aware of it, and everything was running smoothly. At 0931 24 June 1984 we set course for Honolulu on the range of the lights on Tatoosh Point and Duntze Rock, where I had set course on previous voyages into the Pacific ocean. The course was 209T, to take us 100 miles away from the coast before turning southwest to head for the high pressure area in the North Pacific that is always north or northeast of Hawaii at that time of year.

Most Canadians think we do not have sharks in our waters. This is not true. The same day we left the Strait of Juan de Fuca, after we had sailed only 19 miles we sighted a large shark. It had a very large tail fin sticking out of the water, and it followed about an eighth of a mile behind the boat. As it is not possible to keep garbage on board for three weeks or more, it is customary to heave the biodegradable garbage over the side as it comes available. Sharks feed on this garbage and will follow a boat for days. The official log of *Sea Lure* indicates that on 26 June the shark was still following about the same distance behind, and on the 27th or 28th the shark finally left us. By then we were more than 300 miles from Canadian waters and hopefully it didn't turn back, so there was then one less shark in Canadian waters courtesy of *Sea Lure*.

On the 25th of June we had our first storm. Fortunately it was not very severe, as the winds reached 38 knots. It was a good storm to break in the crew members who had not been on the ocean before, but not in Bill's case as he was suffering from seasickness. The boat performed beautifully with one reef in the main and the genoa rolled in by one-third. The winds picked up to 30 kts about 0100 hours the following morning. The ocean was just letting us know that it was not going to be a joyride, and that we would have to work to get into the nice weather close to Hawaii. The travelogues, cruise ads etc. show ocean sailors in bathing suits soaking up the sun on the deck. Ocean sailing in the North Pacific, particularly, is not like that at all. The dress of the day and for several weeks is long underwear, warm pants, sweater, floater coat or wet weather gear, toque and warm gloves. This is in June, but in December it calls for more warm gloves, outer rubber and inner wool and constantly damp socks and other clothing. The crew hopes the engine is running so they can dry out their clothes after coming off watch. This is the life we pay a lot of money to enjoy!

Also on 26 June we sighted an aircraft carrier and several

other ships in the distance. I called them on the VHF and talked to the radio operator on the carrier. It turned out to be the Australian carrier *Canberra*; also the Canadian supply ship *Provider* was in the group. They were carrying out maneuvers as part of their annual training exercises. I also had a long chat with the Captain of *Provider*.

In my last year of service with the Canadian Forces, i.e. RCAF, I had the opportunity to spend 5 days on the destroyer *Qu'Appelle* as a guest of the Captain, the late Freddy Choat. We were the same rank at that time, and he was quite happy to have one of the senior career managers from the personnel organization in Ottawa on board. The Captain of *Provider* was a good friend of Freddy's, so he brought me up to date on what he was doing in retirement.

This was also an opportunity for me to get up to date on the location of the centre of the high pressure area north of Hawaii, so he turned me over to his weather man on board and I was given a complete weather briefing, plus information on the high. Although we were a long way from the high, it wasn't too soon to start plotting it on the charts that cover the entire distance from Victoria to Hawaii, and follow its progress from the weather reports I could pick up on *Sea Lure*'s radios.

The Canadian Forces personnel are always most helpful, and do not get the credit they deserve for doing an outstanding job. A month later we met the executive officer from one of the U.S. carriers passing through Honolulu. He had worked with the Canadian Navy a number of times in his career and he called them the true professionals of the world's navies. This remark was completely unsolicited and the West Coast Canadians, particularly from Vancouver, can take note.

On Thursday 28 June we had another storm just to keep us on our toes. It was in the early hours of the morning, and the winds got up to 38 knots again and this time it lasted from 0200 until 1100 hours. Storms were "old hat" for the crew by then, so everything ran smoothly including the reefing of the main.

We were 375 miles out from the Strait of Juan de Fuca when a coast guard aircraft showed up. It was a search and rescue aircraft, and it came in very low over *Sea Lure*, about 200 feet over the mast. It had landing lights on, flaps and wheels down. This made me a little curious, so I called up on the VHF radio channel 16, the emergency channel, to find out what the captain had in mind.

American coast guard aircraft carry the marine emergency channel, and I'm sure the Canadian Forces aircraft carry the same channel, so we were able to communicate very well. He said he was training a new pilot for search and rescue at sea and they were using *Sea Lure* as a target for dropping off supplies, etc. Judging by their speed and height, I'm sure they could have dropped emergency equipment to within 100 feet of the boat if we had required assistance. Fortunately, everything was running smoothly on *Sea Lure* and we didn't have to take advantage of this opportunity. It was nice, however, after 5 days at sea, to know that somebody from the mainland was still interested in us. This reminded me of an incident in the Victoria to Maui yacht race in 1978, when one of the racing boats had its rudder disintegrate. I was on the radio when they called the American Coast Guard and asked for assistance. The radio operator came back and said, "How far are you from the mainland?" The reply was "1000 miles." He then came back and said, "Sorry, you are too far out. We cannot assist you." Had it been a Mayday situation I'm sure they would have found an aircraft with long-range fuel tanks to go to help them.

Incidents like this were a morale booster for the crew, but for Bob and me the sea was our friend and the sooner we were 500 miles away from the coast, where most of the problems take place, the better. This may sound strange to the landlubbers or coastal sailors, but for the offshore sailors I'm sure it has a familiar ring. It is so fantastic out there with no telephones and communication only with the ham radio, a steady swell often for weeks, and steady winds often for many days from the same direction. This was the feeling for which I had spent 10 years of preparation and many dollars to experience.

Today was also our first shower day with fresh water from the shower tank. We could pump water up and fill the deck shower bag with 5 gallons of water, let it warm up on the deck, and then hang it in the aft head. The crew, one at a time, would then sit on the toilet or on the deck and use one gallon each to shower. This was one of the greatest additions I had made to the boat, and is practically unheard of on 40-foot ocean-going yachts. A warm shower after 3 or 4 days of salt water spray is a real treat, and it always gives the crew a great lift. In order for the shower water to drain properly, it was necessary to sail the boat on the port tack, and often we would have to tack to drain the shower and then tack again to get back on course. The water ran into the bilge and was then pumped over the side during the daily bilge pumping sessions. The shower water helped to keep the bilge a little cleaner, as it sloshed around in there for many hours before going over the side.

On Friday 29 June the winds were 20 knots from the west. It was sunny in the afternoon and the boat speed was about 6 knots, which was normal for *Sea Lure*. Unfortunately, we had torn the main during the night, and this was the first of many sail-sewing sessions. I had replaced the genoa, and should have replaced the main and mizzen, but decided to gamble that we could make these two sails do for the voyage. Just in case they didn't, the sail maker in Vancouver, Leitch & McBride, had the measurements for these sails and could have made new sails and shipped them to me at any time. This did not turn out to be necessary, but after many sewing sessions we furled the main when the winds gusted to 25 or 30 knots as the boat would sail just as fast without it but was less stable. Also, after we had sewn the mizzen a few times, we would reef it at about the same wind speeds. On one occasion in the Tasman Sea, when an inexperienced crew managed to tear a seam in the main seven feet long, we ended up having to do 28 feet of sewing as we always double-stitched the repair. Thank goodness for the sail tape that the sail makers insisted that I take along, as we used it all and it made the sewing so much easier. At a time like this, all crew members took turns at sewing when they were on watch but not on the helm, and this sometimes involved 2 or 3 days of sewing. There was space in the forward cabin for the sail when it was not being worked on, so it was not in the way when the normal routine on the boat was taking place. This was a blessing.

Incidentally, the forward cabin is never used for sleeping on the ocean if there are any swells, as the motion of the boat will raise your head up off the pillow and crash it down again – not conducive to sleep even when you are dead tired. I've tried it and am writing from experience. The only time the crew slept in the forward cabin was when the ocean was calm and we were powering. And of course, this is the farthest place away from the engine noise.

It was always necessary to wait until the wind conditions were right to put the repaired sail back in place without a great struggle. Sometimes this meant waiting for a day or two, as we were not racing, and had decided it wasn't necessary to brag about the short time spent on a leg, as most ocean skippers are inclined to do. Incidentally, I have checked several skippers' information on time spent on a passage, and have found in most cases the information was not correct i.e. the boat actually spent more time on the passage or the skipper had a short memory. This may sound like sour grapes, but *Sea Lure* is one of the slower yachts on the ocean except for once or twice when we went all out to get to a destination before another boat, and it was surprising how fast she could actually sail. But our objective was getting there in relative comfort and safety, and if we were a day or two late or even a week, that was not a problem. All crew members had time to spare and knew the game plan before we left the harbour.

The 30th of June was uneventful, but we did finish sewing the main and hoisted it again. The winds were still from the west at 15 knots with a few gusts to 22; we were making reasonable progress, i.e. 113 miles a day, but it was still cold and we were wearing warm clothes.

On 1 July an unusual incident took place, an unnerving one for Bob Dormer. Bob was on the helm during his normal watch, when a cargo ship appeared over the horizon. It was the first vessel we had seen since the navy ships, so we all watched with great interest. It had almost disappeared over the horizon, when suddenly it turned around and started heading directly towards us. The ship was cruising at about 14 knots, and so it took about 15 minutes to get close to us. It started to slow down, but kept coming directly at us. Bob altered course sharply and the ship altered course too, and by then it was only about 250 yards away. By that time we had *Sea Lure*'s engine running and I wasn't too concerned, as I knew I could turn inside the ship with ease, after the experience on the destroyer, if by some strange coincidence the helmsman or captain had gone berserk and was trying to run us down. Bob wasn't sure about the maneuvering of *Sea Lure* with all sails up, and he was showing considerable consternation. The ship was slowing down noticeably, so I decided it was time to call the captain on VHF channel 16 and find out what he had in mind. He came back immediately with the surprising response in broken English, "Can you see me?" I was tempted to say we can't see anything but your ship, but I wasn't sure if the skipper was friendly at this point so I just answered "Yes." The name of the ship was *Golden Luck* and she was of Polish registry. The skipper had a report of a missing yacht from Canada – in fact we had heard the same report – and he was just checking to see if we were the missing yacht. He asked for our name etc., and how we were doing. I assured him everything was just fine and that we were progressing to Honolulu on schedule, even though we did not have a firm schedule. He thanked me for the information and said, "We are off to San Francisco," altered course and left at full speed. We all breathed a sigh of relief, especially Bob, and got back to our normal boat routine.

It turned out that the missing yacht was late arriving in Victoria, and a friend or wife of the skipper had reported the boat missing. It was found a few days later tied up at the dock in Victoria, and the crew did not have enough sense to report to the Coast Guard that the yacht had arrived. The system I used on all legs of the trip was to give Lou, my wife, the estimated date of arrival in the next country, and if I had not called within 24 hours to report my arrival, she would have the applicable Coast Guard check on us. I was invariably late and once four days late, but the Coast Guard always called us on the VHF, or I called them as soon as I arrived in port. Ocean sailors and captains of ships will always do everything possible to help a brother sailor at sea. But it is unnecessary to put sailors to a lot of trouble for nothing (like the captain of *Golden Luck*) but human nature being what it is, I'm sure this will happen over and over again.

3 July was uneventful; the winds veered slightly to the northwest, and were steady at 15 knots. Ideal sailing conditions, but we made only 114.5 miles and our position at 1900 hours was 37.5N latitude and 136.1W longitude. We had sailed 1027.5 miles since setting course at the Straits of Juan de Fuca. We were making steady progress and with a minimum of problems.

4 July at about 0530 hours we had a genoa wrap – not easy to do – but I expect the crew was getting tired, and when the wind dropped the sail was not winched in. It was quite a bad wrap, but not nearly as bad as the spinnaker wrap we had on the yacht *Tarun* on the Victoria to Maui race in 1978. It took us about half an hour to clear this wrap, and tall Laurie Donovan finally stood on the bowsprit rail and reached up and cleared it after other crew members had cleared several wraps. Fortunately, we did not have any sewing to do, and as the sail was new and strong no damage was done. Also, the whisker pole folded that day. It was not strong

enough to stand the strain when we were running, as it was much undersized. Fortunately, I had a second pole on board that was the right size to go inside the original pole, so by doubling the metal thickness we were able to use it again. I tried to buy another pole in Honolulu but was unsuccessful (just as well as I didn't need it). Our mileage that day was 121.3 despite the delay, so it was a good day. The winds were from the northeast and blowing 15 to 20 knots.

6 July was another interesting day, as the racing yacht *Charlie* that was in the Victoria-Maui race came over the horizon leading the fleet. We had heard on the radio that *Charlie* was doing very well, and were surprised to have them come into sight. We were in sight of each other for about four hours, and I had a good chat on the VHF with the skipper. He was hoping to break the record for the first boat in, but I assured him he wouldn't make it, as the record had been set in 1978. I had already calculated his distance to go and average speed, and he was running a couple of days behind. As it turned out he did not break the record, but was still into Lahaina in about 12 days, which is actually very good time. He was really moving when he passed us – I would estimate 10 or more knots – and the winds were light. The record time from Victoria to Maui was broken in 1992 by the same boat that had set it in 1978, a yacht by the name of *Merlin*.

That day we also picked up a life ring. We had passed fenders and life rings before but they were usually so covered with barnacles that they were worthless. This one had been lost recently and it only took about two hours of work to clean it up to an acceptable standard and it is still on *Sea Lure*.

At 0200 hours on 7 July, the Watch Captain Larry woke me up from a deep sleep with the information that the engine had stopped and he could not turn the propeller shaft. I got up, took a flashlight to the stern of the boat and had a look in the water, and sure enough we were trailing about 10 feet of fishing net. It had wrapped around the propeller causing the engine to stop. It had to be a bad wrap to stop the 75 hp six cylinder diesel engine as it has a lot of power. I told Larry we are really a sailboat now and not to worry, as we would correct the problem the next day, and I promptly went back to bed and to sleep. A small problem like that was not serious enough to lose any sleep over. The next day about noon, when the winds were about 10 knots from the east and the ocean had settled down to a nice easy swell, we inflated the dinghy and Laurie and

29

Bob volunteered to go over the side in the dinghy to clear the propeller. We tied a line to the dinghy and the man in the boat had a line on the diver, then they took about three dives each with a snorkel mask and cut off the net plus a fishing line that had previously wrapped in the prop. This exercise took about an hour or more but when completed the engine started as though nothing had happened.

We were now at 30 degrees North latitude and the winds were light, so I started heading in a southerly direction to try to get to the trade winds as soon as possible. They usually appear at about 25 degrees North, and disappear at 25 degrees South latitude. This is a general rule but there are many exceptions. The trade winds are wonderful for the world's ocean sailors, and have been since man first took to sailing vessels. They blow most of the time from 10 to 20 knots and are usually from the east, northeast or southeast and this is true on both sides of the equator. The weather is warm and pleasant most of the time and hurricanes are minimal, although they do occasionally head over in the Hawaii direction just to make the sailor's life a little more interesting.

During the ocean race in 1978 on the *Tarun*, I plotted a hurricane that had originated in the Panama area and made its way eventually to Hawaii. The navigators in the fleet plotted the hurricane as we were given the coordinates of the eye, and each day it was very easy to calculate its average speed and direction. Based on this information over 10 days or so, it was possible to determine the estimated time of arrival of the hurricane in Hawaii. I was also able to calculate that all the yachts in the fleet would be into Lahaina before the arrival of the hurricane, and sure enough, about a day after the last yacht was in, the hurricane arrived. The wind speeds had reduced considerably as it progressed in our direction, so there was very little damage and the yachts, protected by the breakwater at Lahaina, were just fine.

On this passage I was plotting three hurricanes at one time coming out of the same area, and one of the ham operators reported, incorrectly, that we were on a collision course with one of them. This caused a morale problem on board for a few minutes until I showed the plotting sheets to the crew, our latitude and longitude on this big ocean and where the hurricanes were located. They were satisfied and none of the hurricanes came within 1000 miles of *Sea Lure*.

A method I had used on *Tarun* to keep the crew informed on our progress to our destination was to plot our position at 1100 hours each day on a small scale chart that covered the entire ocean from Victoria to Maui. This indicated to them our location, our progress, and the miles to go. I used this system on all long ocean voyages, and would recommend it to other skippers and navigators. New ocean sailors have a great deal of apprehension before signing up on a crew for a voyage and their minds need to be put at ease as often as possible.

We ran the engine at least once a day for an hour even if the winds were good. This was necessary to charge the batteries, as the water pumps, lights, Sat Nav, ham radio, etc. used power, and also to lower the temperature in the freezer and refrigerator so the food would not spoil. I would put the engine on every afternoon for at least an hour, and put it in forward gear so we would gain a mile or two. Also I pumped the bilge at the same time, as the stuffing box was dripping more than necessary. We lived with this problem for the entire trip, and I had the stuffing box repacked after arriving back in Vancouver two years later.

Sunday 8 July was a boat cleanup day, and everyone pitched in. It was also the day we filled the shower bag, placed it on the deck to warm up the water and everyone had a shower, one at a time in the aft head. We each had a gallon of water to shower with and this is adequate if it is used sparingly. It was also the skipper's day to cook the steak dinner with baked potatoes, vegetables, salad etc. Sunday was the one day of the week when we were permitted two drinks before dinner and a glass of wine with dinner. After having been practically dry for the week, most crewmen got quite happy before dinner, but not to the extent that their abilities would be impaired if we had an emergency. All in all, Sunday was the best day of the week and it broke the routine to a large extent. This became even more important after three weeks at sea with nothing but water to look out on. A person begins to wonder if there is any land on this planet or if it is all water!

10 and 11 July were quite uneventful, with the winds from the northeast and east at speeds from 3 to 18 kts but usually in the 10 to 12 range. Our distance travelled was 113 and 122 miles, so we were slightly over our average. On the 10th we retarded our watches one hour to zone description +10, so we would be on the same time as Honolulu. This was accomplished in the watchkeeper's log by

recording 2400 hours twice, and each watch taking 30 minutes extra during their watch. Every skipper has a different way of handling the time changes as he sails into a new time zone, but this was our particular method. On the return trips, we were advancing our watches, so the crew ended up with 3½-hour watches instead of 4 hours.

On Thursday 12 July we sighted a sailboat several miles away, but could not determine the name. It was probably a yacht in the Victoria-Maui race. I called on the radio but there was no answer, so they must have had their radio turned off to save battery power.

We were now at latitude 25N and I noticed that the winds had steadied to 12 to 20 kts. We must now be in the trade winds. Unfortunately we had gone a long way south looking for the trade winds, so now we had to go a long way west to compensate, i.e. from 145W longitude to 156W longitude to get us to Honolulu. A few yachts have been known to miss the Hawaiian Islands completely due to faulty navigation. We were in a location where this would have been possible, except that the Sat Nav was working well, and it gave us a heading for Makapuu point which is close to Honolulu. The radio direction finder was working, and I had been picking up Hawaiian music at night when we were 1000 miles from Hawaii.

I could have taken sights with the sextant if necessary, so there was no danger of us getting lost and missing those beautiful islands. There is a false rumour that a yacht can follow the vapour trail of the jet aircraft flying from the mainland to Honolulu. At this time we were several hundred miles east of the aircraft route, and this is a normal route to Hawaii from Canada. After going around the high pressure area that moves around northeast of Hawaii in the summer months, and staying on the mainland side of the high to get the winds that blow in a clockwise direction in the northern hemisphere, many yacht crews find themselves well east of the Mercator line running from Tatoosh Light at the Strait of Juan de Fuca to Honolulu. I have checked on the vapour trails and they are not normally visible at all, due to the temperature in that part of the world, and even if they were, it is only in the last 50 miles that they could be followed. If you are heading for Hawaii or anywhere else in the ocean, make sure someone knows how to navigate with a sextant, or at least you have a radio direction finder and a satellite navigation system. Loran is O.K. in this part of the world, but in the southern hemisphere it is not used, or was not in 1984 to 1986, and I expect they have gone directly to satellite navigation systems.

13 July was normal except that we sailed 126 miles, which was more than our average, and a good day for *Sea Lure*. 14 July at 0300 the winds picked up to 32 kts and I decided to practice lieing-a-hull, as we had never practiced this before. This is sometimes necessary when the winds and waves get so high that it is not desirable or possible to continue sailing. It is often the solution when a small crew is on board, and there are not enough people to change helmsmen every 20 or 30 minutes in order to keep sailing. We furled the main and genoa and reefed the mizzen. *Sea Lure* was then lieing-a-hull, and I'm sure could have handled winds up to 100 kts. Fortunately we did not have to test this assumption at any time in the next two years. I also noted in the log that Laurie tightened the brake on the drive shaft. The Borge Warner transmission and propeller were not permitted to windmill when the boat was sailing with the engine off, so it was necessary to put the brake on each time the engine went off and release the brake before starting the engine. We put a red cloth on the gear shift each time as a reminder that the brake was on. Incidentally, the brake did not need any adjustment for the rest of the voyage, so Laurie must have tightened it very carefully, which is typical of the quality of his work.

On July 15th, the water line to the forward head burst. This was due to the excessively hot water in the hot water system, caused by a sticking thermostat in the engine. It was not opening sufficiently to allow the water to run faster, which would in turn allow the engine to run at a lower temperature. A section of the plastic hose could not take the heat any longer, and burst at 0200 hours in the morning. These urgent jobs often came up in the middle of the night when I was in a deep sleep, and so in this case I installed a new short hose as a temporary fix. The engine must have been off so the crew could hear the water pump for the internal water system running. We were not so lucky on the passage to American Samoa when we pumped all our fresh water overboard.

Since we had started getting line squalls with wind speeds to 30 kts, we must be approaching the Hawaiian Islands. Also the skipper of a container ship talked to Larry on the VHF when he was only a few miles away. He asked Larry if we would like some ice cream for lunch. He said O.K., so the ship started heading over in our direction, but just before pulling up alongside *Sea Lure* he veered off at high speed. Larry called up on the radio and said, "Where is our ice cream?" The skipper called back and said it would be too dangerous for *Sea Lure* if he came too close, as we might break our mast if the yacht rolled on a wave and hit the hull of the ship. Perhaps he was afraid of being sued. If he had put the ice cream in a plastic bag, well tied, and dropped it in the ocean close to the boat, I'm sure we would have made a supreme effort to pick it up. Ice cream at this stage of our trip would have been a real treat! At least his idea was great, and he was the friendliest skipper of any ship we encountered on the entire trip.

It was Sunday, so we had our usual steak dinner with all the trimmings, plus our two drinks before dinner. There was no comment in the watchkeeper's log so the meal probably was not up to the usual standard, but there was sketch of a wine glass with vapour coming out and "hic" beside it with an exclamation mark, so I presume the wine was really good. Perhaps that watchkeeper had more than one glass!!

Our latitude was 23º 39'N and longitude 152º 12'W at 1920 hours, so we were slowly but surely closing in on Hawaii. However we had 3 days 9 hours to go before docking in the Ala Wai yacht basin in Waikiki. After having completed the voyage in the Victoria-Maui race with Peter Hendry in the *Tarun* in just over 16 days, this was really a slow trip in a slow boat. Twenty days seems to be about my limit on the ocean, as after that time I get irritable, short tempered, etc. I guess boredom or whatever you call it sets in.

Monday 16 July was normal, the winds were from the east 10 to 18 kts and we sailed 116 miles to midnight. The next morning at 0200 hours we had a fairly severe line squall and the boat heeled more than usual. I would estimate 25 to 30 degrees. The other Watch Captain and I woke up with a start and the heel continued. Bob, the Watch Captain on duty, I think was attempting to give us a scare, as he must have known by then that *Sea Lure* would handle much more heel with no problem. Larry leaped out of bed, as he was sleeping in the Watch Captain's bunk on the starboard side, and told Laurie to ease off on the sheet, which he did immediately. *Sea Lure* went back to about 20 degrees of heel, which seemed more normal to us. Later in the voyage we sailed all day at 30 degrees of heel, but for a novice in sailboats it seems most uncomfortable until one gets used to the boat's attitude. Line squalls can be tricky, particularly at night, so the crew must be prepared to take appropriate action quickly to prevent a knockdown. The rest of July 17th was good with some sunny periods.

Wednesday 18 July we sighted land through the cloud cover. It was the island of Maui and a very welcome sight indeed. I had noticed a slight change in the colour of the cloud cover, and knew that Maui, at the higher peaks, would be in sight if the clouds were high or thin enough. Shortly after this at 1200 hours we confirmed it was land and we had a drink to celebrate the event. This became traditional on *Sea Lure*. There was some discussion among the crew as to which Hawaiian Island this was, so I found it necessary to use the radio direction finder and home on a Honolulu radio station to convince one member of the crew that it was really Maui we could see. With a serviceable Sat Nav there was no doubt as to our location, but after so long on the ocean, it is easy to come to a wrong conclusion when doing a landfall. This was my first landfall since 1978.

I had left the VHF radio on as I expected a call from the American Coast Guard from Honolulu, and sure enough it came that afternoon. I had advised my wife, who had been in Honolulu for three days by then with Marian Dormer, Bob's wife, that if no word was heard from us by July 17th to have the coast guard organize a search. She had contacted the coast guard that day, but they convinced her that ocean-going yachts are frequently late on arrival, and to wait another day before doing anything. This worked out very well as we were within VHF radio range on the 18th, and I answered their call immediately. I gave them an ETA of 1100 hours the next day for our arrival at Customs in the Ala Wai yacht basin in Honolulu. We actually arrived at 1030 hours, but this was mainly due to a little power boat race we had with a famous ocean racing yacht by the name of *Shadow*.

The morning of our arrival, at about 0800 hours, we saw a large yacht several miles off our starboard side, obviously heading for Honolulu. There was no wind and we were both powering, so to add some interest for the crew at the end of a very long voyage I decided to have a power boat race with the other yacht as they were about to pass us. *Sea Lure* has a powerful engine, capable of moving the boat at over 8 knots. I kept easing on more power to keep even with the other boat and the other helmsman picked up the challenge immediately, as it was a racing boat and racing is what they do for a living. The other boat was considerably bigger (about 60 feet) and would have a much faster hull speed but *Sea Lure*'s engine was more powerful. Racing boats do not have large engines, as the excessive weight would slow them down when under sail. We raced along together for about an hour, converging on the channel to the Ala Wai yacht basin. We were going over 8 knots which is the hull speed for *Sea Lure* and the other boat was doing exactly the same speed which I found out later was full power for their engine. About two miles from our destination the other boat suddenly slowed right down, so I slowed down a little as Larry, our engine man, was complaining loudly that I would damage the engine exhaust system at such speed. He was quite right, as there was damage done at this time and I was to pay for it later. I was caught up in the spirit of the race at this stage, and wasn't too worried about the exhaust system. After we got about half a mile ahead of the other boat, it suddenly put on great speed again and tried to cut us off at the entrance to the yacht basin. I immediately put on full power and beat them to the finish line.

The next day several of us were sitting at a table in the Hawaii Yacht Club having a drink, when the skipper asked me what kind of engine I had in *Sea Lure*. He said they were going at maximum power when their engine threw a belt. They had to close down to install another belt, and that was when we got ahead of them. They were not used to losing to a much smaller boat even in a power boat race, and didn't take it lightly. We watched the sailboat races with interest as *Shadow* was competing the following week in the famous Hawaii yacht races that take place every second year, starting from Honolulu.

Lou and Marian were at the dock shortly after we came in to customs. They were shocked at the sight of Bob and me, and apparently the first thing we said was "Where is the beer?" We had each lost about 20 lbs., and I was the thinnest I had been since university days in 1948. We looked haggard and tired but otherwise we were fine. Despite the excellent nourishing meals, we had lost a lot of weight and found this happened on all long passages. The body is in motion most of the time, even when sleeping, and this accounts for the weight loss. Also our reduced intake of fluids was another contributing factor.

We were happy to get customs down to the boat to clear us,

move the boat to the Hawaii Yacht Club, take the perishable food out of the freezer, and get a taxi to the apartment, in downtown Waikiki, that we had rented before leaving Vancouver. Lou and Marian had already been staying there for four days. Our shakedown passage had been completed, the yacht was performing better than expected, our fuel consumption was less than expected, and we were in good shape to press on for our great South Pacific adventure after a three week holiday in Hawaii. Some minor repairs to the sails etc. were required, a few boat parts had to be picked up, and a new heat exchanger installed that Lou had brought in her suitcase. With a fresh stock of food and beverages, fuel and water etc. we would be ready to depart on our second passage.

CHAPTER 3

FANNING ISLAND HERE WE COME

We spent three weeks in Hawaii recuperating from the long voyage and seeing the sights of Oahu Island, as several in the group had not been to these islands before. I was able to get my land legs back in half an hour but Bob went on for several days hanging on to things so he wouldn't lose his balance; after that he was fine.

We went out for a crew dinner with the wives and friends, which Bob and I sponsored and it was very much appreciated.

After about two weeks we vacated the apartment in Waikiki, and Bob and I and our wives flew over to the island of Kauai where we spent a week – the Dormers stayed for several days then flew to Maui and the big island of Hawaii for short stays in each place. This was all very pleasant and relaxing, then at the end of the third week Lou and Marian were booked for the return flight to Canada. They had arrived four days before us, so we had four days left in the three-week period to stock the boat etc. before departing for Fanning Island, our next destination.

Laurie and Larry returned to Canada as planned, and Chris and Ed arrived from Canada on schedule to replace them. Bill had planned to go for the entire trip, but since he had suffered from seasickness this was not realistic, so he decided to leave the crew in Honolulu. This meant we were short one crewman. I put an ad on the bulletin board in the two yacht clubs in Waikiki and a Spanish fellow "Raphael" replied. He had sailed with his father in Spain in a large sailboat and he was a keen, experienced sailor. He was short of money, so I agreed to pay for his food if he would do a few extra chores around the boat, and this worked out very well. When we arrived in a country Raphael did not spend as much time ashore as the rest of the crew, so he ended up operating the dinghy at all hours to transport the crew to shore and back. He also did the maintenance on the dinghy engine, refueling etc.

When it came time to stock the boat with food, beverages etc., it turned out that Bob's military identification card was acceptable at the Navy Exchange at Pearl Harbour. We had to rent a car for several days to transport the food to the boat.

After preparing the menu with all crewmen present so they could have their input, we drew up the shopping list with quantities etc. from the master list and went shopping. This way we had everything we needed for cooking gourmet meals and nothing was missing. Also we had approximately the right quantities so not too much was left over at the end of the passage, although I did keep a reserve stock for emergencies, if we were really late on a passage. The total cost was about $750 and it took three or four trips with the car to get everything to the boat. Just storing this quantity of food took two crewmen many hours and we had to ensure each item was in the right place so we could find it easily. Initially we kept a record for the food storage but after the first passage this knowledge was in the skipper's head and the crewmen who did the storage usually knew where to look. We restocked the galley shelves once a week, so after that we rarely had to search for something. Before shopping we took inventory of the food on board and didn't include these items on our shopping list, otherwise we would have ended up with surplus quantities.

The menu ran for one week and then repeated. It was posted in the galley for each passage with the name of the crewman responsible for cooking each meal. It worked out that each crewman cooked four meals a week and never the same meal consecutively. The skipper cooked five meals and always dinner on Sunday. This gave the crew something to do besides steering the boat and making coffee. With some crews it became competitive to see who could cook the best dinners. I prefer this system to having a full-time cook as I have sailed under both systems. Of course on a racing boat when ocean racing, a cook is desirable as every position must be manned to the maximum efficiency.

On 8 August at 1200 hours everything was ready to go. The boat had been refueled several days before and the tanks took 100 American gallons. The boat does not have fuel gauges. We had used only half the fuel on the first passage, and knew how much fuel the engine used at various throttle settings, as I had been keeping detailed records. This meant we would have more than enough fuel for all future passages and could use the engine with reckless abandon. The rule from then on was, if the boat speed dropped to three knots the engine was started and we used power to bring the boat speed up to five or six knots. This helped to reduce the time on all future passages and did not increase my expenses for fuel to a noticeable degree.

It was very rough as usual for the first hour out of Honolulu but then it settled down. I had forgotten to clean the knot log propeller under the boat and it was stuck with barnacles, after sitting in the harbour for three weeks in the warm ocean – so it was shower time again for me. The weather was quite warm so I put on a bathing suit and lifted the plug that goes through the hull, on which the propeller is installed. When this is done the water shoots up about three feet from the pressure under the boat so the trick is to stop the flow by hand while putting in place a stopper plug. After cleaning the little propeller the procedure is reversed and the knot log works again. This instrument is essential for navigation as it gives us boat speed as well as the distance travelled. Later in the voyage I would clean the propeller before leaving the anchorage. This was much easier as it was calm and I could do it at my leisure.

We set course for Fanning Island at 1235 hours and it was 185 true or 176 compass. Fanning Island is approximately 1000 miles almost directly south of Honolulu. A nice passage in warm weather, good trade winds from the east and the boat was performing much better. Most of the time the winds were on the beam, which is the fastest point of sail, and Chris – a racing sailor from Vancouver – was able to trim the sails more effectively.

The following day we sighted three ships; two of them were U.S. Navy vessels. They were probably patrolling off Pearl Harbour to deter Russian submarines that also patrolled frequently in that area, as the cold war was still on.

On 10 August we had a telephone patch with my wife in Vancouver via the ham radio, courtesy of Bob, and also sent a message to my brother in Dauphin, Manitoba via a Vancouver ham operator, to a Winnipeg ham operator, and then to Dauphin. Several days later I received a reply from him via the same net.

The wind was picking up to 20 kts or more in the evening, so we reefed the main in case of higher winds during the night. At noon on 11 August the wind increased to gale force, 30-40 kts from the east, although most of the day it was less. It made for a good day of sailing and we covered 125 miles. 12 August was a Sunday so we went to our Sunday routine with boat cleanup, extra drinks and steak dinner. It must have turned out all right, as the watchkeeper's log at 2000 hours noted that the dinner was "great." By 2100 hours the wind had dropped to 18 kts. It was a really good day but the next day would be even better. The winds were still blowing hard from the east and were constant. The sails must have been trimmed to perfection, as we made 155.6 miles for the day for an average of 6.5 miles per hour. The slow boat was really flying. The boat was lighter by probably a ton due to water, fuel and food consumption, and this does make a difference as racing sailors well know. The weather was warm and pleasant despite the wind and our latitude was now 11 degrees North. The equator was not that far away and we were approaching it quickly. We would, however, have a three-day stop in Fanning Island before finally crossing the equator.

On 14 August we caught our first fish – a twelve-pound tuna. We had been fishing by dragging a line and lure about 75 feet behind the boat since we left Canada. On a number of occasions the lure had been taken and the line broken. Obviously my fishing equipment was not strong enough. When I was in Hawaii I talked to an ocean sailor who had been catching fish successfully, and he advised me to buy a 300 lb. test line and a type of lure that attracted the smaller fish. Also connecting three shock cords together and hooking them to the boat end of the line was necessary, so we would know when a fish took the lure and could pull it in before the hook was pulled out of the fish's mouth. We also stopped the boat when we had a fish on to reduce the drag on the fish. By being careful when pulling in the line, which was not on a reel, it was possible to land 5-20 lb. fish. We, of course, used the net with the long handle, as it was too dangerous to lift the fish out of the water using the hook only. By following these rules very carefully we were able to catch over 40 fish on the entire voyage. They included mahimahi, tuna and several other types that we could not identify. When we violated these rules we didn't catch fish. Each week from then on, we had fresh fish on the menu for dinner one night and we seldom failed to land the fish. The day in the week that one came on board we switched the menu and had fish grilled that night, and it was really delicious. We talked to Larry on the ham radio that night from Vancouver and he reminded us that it was our first fish since leaving Canada. Fortunately it wasn't our last.

That day was also logged as a stormy day, with plenty of rain and wind. At 1800 hours when we were having dinner we were visited by 100 to 150 dolphins. I've never seen such a demonstration before and may never again. They were shooting out of the water in four-dolphin formations on both sides, in front and behind us, and when the water was literally filled with dolphins, more were coming over the waves in all directions to join the ones around the boat. Fortunately they were all friendly. Apparently when they consider themselves in danger they can attack a vessel and sink it. But this is rare. We had dozens of visits by dolphins over the two-year period, and all were friendly and curious. Perhaps the red hull on the vessel attracted them and the engine noise was not a deterrent. Normally they would stay for only about 20 minutes and would leave, as we were moving too slowly. We came to this conclusion because dolphins used to form up on the bow of the *Blue Dolphin* (our previous power boat) in the Gulf of Georgia and stay there for quite some time, but we were then doing about 12 knots which seemed to suit them better.

All in all, it was a most interesting day and we sailed 137 miles. We were fast closing in on Fanning Island with only 3½ days to go. The winds had dropped to the 15-20 kts range from the southeast. The ocean was a little smoother and there was plenty of sunshine. We had a short line squall at 2000 hours but they were few and far between. Near Hawaii we got a lot of them. I did note in the official log that it was a squally night. The distance of 126 miles was acceptable even though we were spoiled with the previous excellent days. On the 15th we caught a small fish, about five pounds, but it was perfectly acceptable to our crew. Our latitude was 05 degrees 08 minutes North and longitude 159 degrees 08 minutes West at 2300 hours and at 0620 hours the following morning we had 40 miles to go to Fanning Island, if the Sat Nav was giving us the right information.

The sailing directions and the Fanning Island chart indicated that a very tall tree would be the first thing to come over the horizon when approaching the island, and it is so tall that it was visible from our vessel 18 miles away. Raphael had very good eyesight and I guess he was always most anxious to sight land, as he was the first one to spot the top of the tree. So at 1215 hours on August 15th we sighted land again, and this called for a drink all around on the captain. This was such a happy and pleasant passage I can say I was honestly sorry to see it end. I was just amazed that the contrast with the previous passage from Canada was so great. Also, *Sea Lure* was performing beautifully and was sailing faster than I thought possible. The crew morale was good and undoubtedly I was becoming a better and more relaxed skipper. The new crew contributed a great deal to better performance of the boat, and the warm weather and good winds were contributing factors.

The next thing that came into sight was a shipwreck on the shore north of English Harbour, the main anchorage in front of the village on Fanning Island. As we sailed closer, we could see that the ship had been wrecked some years before, since it was in poor shape. We heard the story later as to the cause of the shipwreck. About eight years before, on New Year's Day, the crew including the captain were celebrating and I suppose the helmsman was too drunk to know where he was going or the navigator was not operational. The result was they just sailed right into Fanning Island. The tall tree didn't help them that time. They must have been travelling at a good speed as the wreckage was right up on the beach. There was no loss of life but I'm sure the captain lost his job. The local people must have had a field day when they stripped the ship of everything they could move.

A large yacht was also wrecked on the beach not far from the ship. We never did hear the story of the second wreck, but it suggested to me that extreme care must be taken when going in to Fanning Island. Fortunately, I had a good chart of the area, which I had purchased in Vancouver, but the edge of the reef on each side of the channel entrance, running back about a mile, was not marked, and there was just a lighthouse at the entrance to the bay. I had been studying the chart for some time before our arrival and had plotted our compass heading, but it was getting close to dark by the time we'd had a good look at the area, so I decided to anchor for the night in Whalers Cove, about three miles along the coast of the island. We put down two anchors and had a good night. The crew appreciated a full night's sleep and at 1000 hours the next morning we lifted both anchors and powered to the entrance approach to English Harbour. The supply ship that goes to the island every several months had arrived early that morning and the crew and locals were busy unloading. As we approached the entrance and were still 1½ miles out, the captain of the ship called on the VHF and asked us if we would wait for 1½ hours until he finished unloading and came out. I quickly agreed to this, as I could then watch his course on the way out and we would go in on the reciprocal course. As an extra precaution, Raphael was winched up to the spreaders and watched for the reefs. There was no problem, and we anchored in front of the village in the bay at 1215 hours. It was necessary to put down two anchors, one off the bow and one off the stern, as the current reversed each time the tide changed and during the season of high tides the current ran as fast as 6 knots. The two anchors held *Sea Lure* very well and we did not drag. This was our first experience with coral reefs and later on we became more confident. With the "lookout" on the bow and on both sides of the boat, we went through coral passages many times, fortunately with no mishaps. The water is so clear in that part of the world that the coral can been seen fifty feet down, and with a little practice it is possible to accurately determine the depth of the coral and to turn around if a passage is not clear.

Fanning Island is one of the Line Islands and is several hundred miles west of Christmas Island. It is an atoll which is formed from coral over millions of years. The coral is in a circle about ½ mile or less across and runs many miles. In the middle there is shallow ocean water that goes up and down with the tide. These islands and 31 other islands make up the Republic of Kiribati and they stretch over a distance of 4000 km. The natives are quite large, happy people and are very hospitable. They speak Gilbertese and very few on Fanning Island spoke English. Only the customs man, who was also the radio operator, and a schoolteacher, plus an Englishman who owned and operated the only store. I had talked to the customs man on the VHF radio that morning and asked about customs clearance. He advised that after we were anchored in the harbour they would come out by power launch to do our customs clearance. An hour after we anchored he showed up with the schoolteacher and three local men. I suppose they were not taking any chances in case we were unfriendly. We presented several bottles of liquor to them, completed the customs papers, took pictures and had a friendly chat for an hour. They invited us to their village and made us most welcome. The main industry of the atoll was copra, operated by an Australian company who bought all that could be produced. The company also installed large diesel generators, and this was one of the few small islands that had electricity. Several years later the Australian company decided to pull out. The locals then lost their electricity, as they were not able to run the generators and pay for the fuel, so they were back to primitive. This didn't seem to bother them much as they had lived for hundreds of years with no electricity.

About 500 people lived on the island and each family had a house or hut that looked reasonably comfortable. The store was operated by Allen, who had sailed in a very tiny sailboat from Canada to Hawaii then to Fanning Island. His boat was sitting on a cradle close to the shore. Apparently he had been more than a month sailing from Hawaii. He said the winds were poor but I also suspect he got lost as he was navigating with a sextant, and had difficulty getting within 18 miles so he could see the tall tree. In fact, on his boat he would have to be within about 12 or 14 miles to see the tree unless he climbed the mast. He finally made it and decided to stay. He opened the store and stocked what the locals needed and had his stock shipped in on the supply ship. He charged rather high prices and must have made a lot of profit in several years. He also married one of the local girls and they had two children. The few yachtees that came to Fanning Island also purchased items from his store and this was very handy for replacing supplies. Allen was very helpful, particularly two years later when I had quite a serious boat transmission problem.

We all went ashore that afternoon, and stretched our legs by walking several miles along the atoll. One thing I noticed was the presence of very large land crabs that had dug holes in the soil every fifteen or twenty feet. The crabs disappeared down the holes when we came along.

We had a chat with Allen, and it turned out he and Chris had a mutual friend in Vancouver. We also had a tour of his store. Apparently his wife had worked in the store at one time but as they made more money he could afford to hire help. This did give employment for one family on the atoll. He also had a stock of beer and liquor for sale, and I remember that his New Zealand beer, Steinlager, was available at $1 N.Z. per bottle. This was higher than we paid in Canada at that time, and I know his source of supply was very reasonable and ship transportation is not expensive even though the distance was very long. I mention these things because we discussed this subject with the crew on our way to American Samoa, and it was to have disastrous consequences for Allen three or four years later.

We invited Allen and Seto, his wife, for dinner on *Sea Lure* that night or the following night, and enjoyed their company very much. She had learned sufficient English to make herself understood, and I suppose he had learned Gilbertese. We were invited to their house for a drink or dinner, I can't remember which, but I remember distinctly the row of shark teeth he had displayed on the wall of his house. He had a long chain with a hook on the end, and at night he would bait the hook and throw it out as far as he could by hand and leave it. The other end of the chain was well anchored with a steel pin. In the morning when he came out, some days he had a shark on the hook and by the look of the mouth size, some must have weighed several hundred pounds. Needless to say, the crew were careful about swimming in the water although close to shore was quite safe.

The natives live mostly from the sea, as fish, octopus, crayfish etc. are very plentiful. We could often see them go out in their small boats about 5 p.m. to catch their dinner for that evening. Also one of the local men caught a very large octopus and gave us a demonstration on how to kill it. I believe he held the octopus in such a way that it could not attack him, and then he proceeded to strangle it with his hands. It was quite a sight and the octopus put up quite a fight, with its many legs waving and grabbing him in all directions. The end result was a foregone conclusion but it took him five or ten minutes to complete the job.

The following day was Sunday. The natives of Fanning Island are very religious and have their own pastor who conducts the church service each Sunday. Bob, Ed, and Chris went to church while Raphael and I changed the oil and filter on the engine and carried out a few boat repairs. Bob met the pastor, and he invited the crew to have dinner with him that night – it was the experience of a lifetime!

The dinner was held in their council meeting place, which is a building with a cement floor and large posts about 15 feet high around the floor, holding up a thatched roof. The food was placed on mats on the floor, with plenty of room for sitting cross-legged on both sides. The mats are made by the natives and the food is taken from the ocean or is grown on the island. It was a large and varied spread of food – enough for about 12 men. The pastor sat in the middle on one side and seated me next to him, and then Bob. The schoolteacher sat on the other side of the pastor, and acted as interpreter, as the pastor spoke Gilbertese only. The rest of the crew were placed among the local men on both sides of the mats, and one of the elders sat across from me. We were sitting on mats cross-legged and remained in this position for at least 1½ hours. It was not difficult as the experience was unique and I also conversed with the locals through the interpreter. The food was delicious and cooked to perfection – such a treat after the fare on *Sea Lure*. A can of salmon plus a can opener was placed in front of me, for use in the event I did not like their food. Needless to say the can was not opened but I thanked them for their consideration. I was getting an idea of how Captain Cook felt in the 1700's when he was exploring and mapping the various countries that he visited in the Pacific particularly Tahiti. The main difference was that I was quite sure that the crew of *Sea Lure* would not end up in the pot! Apparently, one of the Chiefs in Fiji had intended to kill Captain Cook and his crewmen and eat them but Cook brought so many gifts to present to the chief and his warriors that they decided to spare them. The Fijians, even up until 100 years ago, were still very warlike and practiced cannibalism. Captain Bligh, after he and part of his crew had been set adrift off Tonga, narrowly escaped ending up in the pot when they were making their way past Fiji.

After dinner, the elders of the church held a short meeting, and then we all got up and went to the pail of water to wash our hands. We had been eating with our hands only – no utensils were provided – so it was necessary to wash up. After we left, the women restocked the food plates and then they and the children had their dinner. This is standard procedure in Kiribati. I guess they had not heard of "women's lib." I doubt that the custom has changed at all to this day.

That same afternoon we were invited to a choral competition held in a hall in the same general area. It was a competition held between two schools or church groups, but this was not clear. It involved singing in harmony, with groups of about 20 children, teens and a few adults. Each group was led by an adult, and I noticed that one leader was the schoolteacher/interpreter. Each group evidently had sung together for a long time, as they sang in harmony so well. Both groups put on a small concert two or three times on the stage, and they were judged by several of the senior people on the island. One was the Member of Parliament for Fanning Island in the Kiribati parliament and he was also the speaker of the House at that time. He did the presentation after the judges had made their decision as to who was the best, and I'm sure it must have been a very difficult decision. The prize was a bag of grain, and I suppose it would be divided up among the families of the people who took part in the chorus. It was an outstanding day, and one of the most enjoyable and interesting on the entire voyage. The hospitality of the Fanning Island people was absolutely superb.

After the weekend at Fanning Island we were ready to press on for American Samoa, so on 20 August at 1200 hours we lifted the two anchors and threaded our way through the reefs again.

Prior to departure Raphael took me aside and practically begged me not to depart, as he had heard on the radio about a hurricane in the Hawaii area and he was afraid we would get caught in it. I had plotted the hurricane for several days on our charts and determined it had passed Hawaii and was heading in a northwest direction. This was explained very carefully to Raphael, satisfying him we would not be in danger. In addition, I had been told by the locals that they had never had a hurricane in their area in living memory, so I was doubly confident we would be O.K.

CHAPTER 4

THE SAMOAS

It was nice to get back on the ocean. We were heading for Pago Pago, pronounced "Pango Pango," the capital of American Samoa. Our course was 212T and we had 1280 miles to go according to the Sat Nav, which had proved quite accurate up to this point. The winds were light, 12-15 kts, and mostly from the southeast so we were still on a beam reach. The following day about dinner time the wind increased for about an hour, gusting to 40 kts. With it came very heavy rain. Dinner was delayed, and we sailed right through the large line squall with the help of the engine. By 1930 hours we were on the other side and the winds had subsided to 20 kts – dinner was then served. Raphael probably thought we were heading into the hurricane but he didn't say anything.

At 1126 hours the next day I recorded in the log that the sea was lumpy, winds were 20 kts and we had 22.3 miles to go to the equator. I had never crossed the equator before, so this would be a new experience. Also we might be becalmed in the doldrums at the equator, but I was not concerned as we had lots of fuel and would use the engine if necessary. None of the crew had crossed the equator, at least in a yacht, so it was a great occasion for merriment! Chris prepared a plywood board indicating the equator, the name of the vessel, and a place for the time to be filled in at the moment of crossing, just before taking pictures. We all signed the board, and I still carry it on *Sea Lure* as a memento. At 1632 hours 22 August the Sat Nav switched from latitude North to latitude South, as though it was human, and we were then in the South Pacific.

After all those years of work, preparation, etc. at great expense on the part of Bob and myself, we were finally in the part of the ocean where we would have our best sailing, most hair-raising experiences and the best part of our adventure. The liquor bottles came out, and we had several drinks while congratulating each other and snapping many pictures while we were in this happy mood (one appears in these pages). We didn't bother with the Neptune ceremony, as no one was qualified to carry it out, all of us being first timers.

The crew had purchased two large bunches of bananas, about

200 in all, and many breadfruit on Fanning Island and they were ripening gradually, so we were eating bananas every day from then on and they lasted most of the passage to Pago Pago. Fortunately Raphael had dunked the two bunches of bananas in the salt water before bringing them on board, and a lizard came shooting out of one bunch and up his leg. He quickly disposed of the lizard and we were happy not to have it on board.

The following day the winds were 15-20 kts and we had a good day with no problems. On 24 August we sighted two ships at a distance. They were the first and only ships we saw on this passage, although we were not far from the large tuna boats. Two schools of dolphins came to see us that day and put on a display, but as I recall, the numbers were less than twenty. The next morning at 0300 hours the dolphins visited again, and it was quite a sight to see the florescence caused by their flippers as they made high-speed runs toward the boat then peeled off again. They could be seen for at least 100 feet under water. I missed that show as my sleeping time was about 2200 to 0630 hours, but some nights I was up several times. Under certain circumstances, the Watch Captains were requested to call me, e.g. if a ship was heading for us, was within a mile and they could not determine what action to take, or if some unusual situation came up. After all this time, I would wake up automatically if the sound in the rigging changed very much. Also, the crew shouting and running on the deck would get me up in a hurry. It was usually a small emergency and by the time I dressed it was usually resolved.

One problem that came up on this passage had to do with the food consumption. Some of the young crewmen had very healthy appetites and were in the habit of robbing the refrigerator at all hours. This didn't go over very well on *Sea Lure*, and had to be stopped. We had provisioned for only the meals planned on the menu, and this snacking wasn't fair to the rest of the crew who had paid their share of the food cost, and of course we didn't want to run out before getting to our destination. This caused considerable discussion, and finally my ruling was that the young fellows would clean up all leftover food at the end of each meal, but wouldn't rob the refrigerator at night or any other time. There was a little cheating in the beginning but the Watch Captains monitored the situation, and as the young crewmen were filled up at mealtime, they soon got in the habit of waiting until the next meal. The crewmen doing the cooking would ask each person how much they could eat and then the right quantity was cooked. On the first passage we tried to save leftovers, but after cleaning up spills in the refrigerator several times, I passed the rule that all leftovers would be chucked overboard along with the garbage. There wasn't much left to throw overboard after each meal from then on as it was cleaned up by the young crewmen. Having gone through the same experience on the farm as a young man, I knew what it was like to be filled up at dinner time but hungry several hours later, even though I always ate all I wanted at mealtime.

We had our showers on Saturday as preparation for Sunday, as it was a calm day with light winds, a kind ocean and the engine had been running most of the day. The next day was boat cleanup day as we had been at sea for six days, and the skipper's turn to do the dinner. The watchkeeper's log indicated it was quote "delicious steak" unquote so it must have turned out all right. By this time I had cooked so many steak dinners that my skill was increasing and I could even serve it up rare, medium or well done! For someone who had never cooked before, I was feeling rather good about this situation.

On 27 August, we experienced some sheet lightning, which was unusual for me on the ocean, also more rain from time to time. The ocean was just preparing us for Pago Pago, where it rains almost every day at one time or another.

On the 29th, the water line burst and the engine had a bath. This was caused by malfunctioning of the thermostat in the engine. The engine had been running much hotter than normal due to a sticking thermostat and this gave us lots of hot water, but the heat was too much for the plastic hose in part of the water system, and it finally gave up. At the time it broke the engine was running, so the crew did not hear the water pump running for the boat's internal water system, nor the bilge pump. All our fresh water ran into the bilge and the bilge pump automatically pumped it all over the side. So we now had no fresh water, and we were still four or five days from Pago Pago! This would normally be a serious situation but not in this case. We had 12 gallons of water left in the hot water tank; the shower tank still had some but I preferred not to use it, as it was rather soapy water. Also, we had lots of soft drinks and beer, and used salt water for cooking and doing dishes. After we repaired the water hose and got the water system operational again, it started to rain. We carried tarps for emergencies, so we spread one over the aft cabin and after letting the rain wash it off we caught rainwater – gallons of it! We poured it into pails and then put it into the water tanks. A shortage of water at sea is not always that serious a problem, as it does rain out there frequently and if you have a water catcher, which most yachts and life rafts are fitted with, it is possible to catch enough water to live for a long period of time.

The previous day at 0300 hours the crew saw a loom on the horizon and gave me a call. It was too soon for Pago Pago to appear, so we came to the conclusion it must be one to two large vessels with very powerful lights or floodlights. We continued on our course and did not see the vessels, but after anchoring in Pago we found out that large tuna vessels night fishing caused the loom. The same day we saw something floating on the water and altered course to go over to take a look. It was a buoy with an antenna on it, and as we came close something wiped the program off the Sat Nav. I presumed it was the signal that the antenna was sending or receiving so we didn't go any closer. I was able to reprogram the Sat Nav and it continued to work normally. We never did find out what the buoy was doing. It could have been reporting on sea conditions, temperature etc. or it could have been much more ominous.

The following day was uneventful, and we retarded our watches one hour to zone description +11. I was in the middle of a good sleep the next morning at about 0300 hours when the Watch Captain called to advise that the engine would not start, and as I was the engine man it was up to me to fix the problem. It turned out that the bath the engine had received the previous day did not help the glow plug solenoid, and it had stopped working. I carried spare solenoids, but this particular one is very difficult to change due to its location and the very cramped quarters. Bob gave me a hand and by about 0430 hours we successfully installed a new solenoid and the engine started.

30 August was a squally day with lots of rain. We thought we must be getting close to Pago Pago, as this is typical of their weather. Also, we were picking up the Pago radio station on the broadcast band so there was no doubt we were getting close. The Sat Nav was right on the money and I didn't need to use the radio direction finder to confirm our position. At about 1300 hours the

following day the island of Tutuila, on which Pago Pago is located, came into sight.

The mountain peaks are only around 2000 feet high so are not visible from a great distance. I turned on the VHF radio but the radio operator in Pago was busy with tuna boat traffic. After a long time he answered and gave us instructions to go to the main dock in the Pago harbour and wait for customs. Customs charge overtime for clearance after 1630 hours and I know we docked before that, but it is the practice in Pago for customs to delay so they can collect overtime. It probably goes straight into their pockets. It cost us $30 US plus a bottle of liquor, but they did clear us without any difficulty and we remained at the dock for the night.

Shortly after we docked a catamaran from England rafted beside us, and this started a friendship that lasted a long time. The boat's name was *Peter Peter* and Charlie Prendergast was the skipper and navigator. The vessel had been built in England and Charlie had assisted with the construction and became the first skipper. A well-to-do lawyer in England actually owned the catamaran, but Charlie had organized an around-the-world voyage over a long period of time with a crew. Some of them paid for the trip and sailed only on previously agreed passages, while others worked their way. They seemed to operate on limited funds, and it was necessary for Charlie and the permanent crew to get jobs in some ports in order to pay their expenses. The owner flew to meet them from time to time with his girlfriend, and I suppose he paid the expenses when he was on board, which wasn't very often. They were sailing with the trade winds, and after crossing the Atlantic and stopping in numerous countries they made their way through the Panama Canal and into the South Pacific. They stopped at Tahiti, the Cook Islands and several other places and finally arrived in Pago Pago an hour or so after *Sea Lure*. They spent the night rafted beside us, and in the evening they came up with a proposition that we split 24 cases of local beer at a ridiculously low price. We quickly agreed and all chipped in to pay for the beer. It was delivered by truck shortly after and then the party really got going. Several enterprising fellows in Pago made a business of selling beer and liquor to the yachtees when they came in. The prices were very reasonable, and this was known far and wide by the sailboaters, so we stocked up in Pago. The businessmen charged a small fee for delivering the liquor, and I expect received large tips especially from the tuna boat crews. They were driving fancy half-ton trucks and looked prosperous, so business must have been good. We took on board 2 cases of Beefeater gin and numerous other bottles before departure several days later. Charlie's catamaran was large and the main salon could accommodate about 20 people, so it was used several times for entertaining.

Pago Pago has the worst harbour I have ever encountered. The pollution is very bad, and the hulls of vessels get covered with sludge, oil, etc. in about 10 days. In fact, the boats that stayed there for extended periods had to have their hulls cleaned every 30 days.

It rains and blows almost every day but usually quietens down in the evening. The people are friendly, but often because they are looking for a bottle of liquor or some other favour. The local Samoans were spoiled by the U.S. Navy, who administered the islands from 1900 until 1951. They are lazy and shifty and cannot be taken at their word. Pago Pago was the place where Somerset Maugham got his idea to write the short story "Rain" and I'm not surprised as they get over 500 cm of rainfall yearly. Both times I visited it rained, and the wind blew down through the valley into the harbour. It is also a rough town. The crews from the tuna boats are often in port as they sell their catch of tuna to the fish processing plant by the name of "StarKist."

A number of Korean ships were in port, rafted or docked in various places, and they were all in very poor shape. The last time I was there, in 1985, one of these vessels was half submerged in the harbour and the crew had pumps running so it would not sink. But Pago is not all bad. It is a good place to do vessel repairs, or have parts shipped in from the mainland or from anywhere else, as there is good air service.

The cost of food and liquor is very reasonable, and the hotels and bars are fairly well run. I went for dinner at the main hotel, "The Rainmaker," and the meal was quite good. After dinner one night I went back to the boat in a taxi, as they are very reasonable, and found that Sea Lure had moved about 200 yards. When we moved from the dock the day after arriving, we dropped the anchor in the harbour and we did not set it properly, as it got caught on something that had been dumped into the harbour. It seemed to be well hooked, so I said, "Don't worry, we will solve the problem just before we depart." However, that evening the tide had swung the boat around in the right direction for the anchor to unhook. Fortunately Bob and the crew were on board, and started up the engine before they had dragged very far, then went around and set the anchor properly this time. The boat was about 200 yards from where I left it before going for dinner, so it was still no problem, just a little farther to run in the dinghy.

On the fourth day in Pago, the crew was anxious to leave. I had no objections, but we had to refuel and stock up with groceries, etc. The refueling dock was about a mile away and they were so busy with tuna boats etc., it was necessary to make an appointment, which we did. We filled up with good quality diesel fuel at a reasonable price, then went back and anchored again in the harbour. The groceries were delivered by truck from the grocery store, but when we were ready to transport them to the boat it was raining and blowing as usual, and the crew was a little apprehensive about dumping a load of groceries in the harbour. So we put two crewmen on the dock and two crewmen on *Sea Lure* and I ran back and forth with the dinghy. It took about 10 trips to get everything on board, and some of the boxes and bags were soggy. The following day the liquor was delivered to the boat, and we still had most of our 12 cases of beer, so we departed about 1500 hours. I wasn't familiar with the country clearance certificate that ocean-going vessels must turn in when they arrive in the next country, so I departed without my certificate. We had some discussion among the crew about this requirement, so I thought I had better leave on the VHF radio, and sure enough about 1600 hours a call came for us to return to Pago and pick up our clearance certificate. So back we went, in very rough conditions, to pick it up from the customs man who had carried it down to the dock. It was 1700 hours by that time, so he charged me $25 for overtime. We then departed for the second time. It was getting dark, raining, blowing, and the ocean was very rough. My memories of Pago from this time and the following year are not very good, but I must admit it has its advantages.

The distance from Pago Pago to Apia, on Western Samoa, is 87 miles by *Sea Lure*'s knot log, which was an overnight sail. I was not able to purchase good charts, and therefore did not have a harbour chart for Apia. All night it continued to be rough and I set course to cross the channel, but warned the crew not to run up on the beach of Upolu, the main island and the only one we visited. At 0600 hours we altered course and ran parallel to the shore about 2 miles out, as this was the route to Apia. There were reefs running out on both sides of the channel for about a mile, but there is plenty of room to go into the harbour as long as you don't cut the corner too soon. We were able to eyeball it O.K. and as we were near the inner harbour we got a call from *Cygnus*. This was a beautiful American yacht, a Swan 65.

The hired crew had seen us in Pago, or may have been talking to our crew, so they welcomed us to Apia, as they had arrived the day before, and told us where to find the customs dock. This started an association with the owner and crew of *Cygnus* that lasted until May 1985, as we followed each other around for the next 10 months. They visited the same countries we did, not always for the same period of time, but we met up in Tonga, Fiji, New Zealand and Australia. *Cygnus* was owned by Franz McVay from Los Angeles, California. I still have his personal card and will quote from it: "Cygnus the Swan, a Northern constellation containing the bright star Deneb, which with other stars forms the Northern Cross. Cygnus was known to the ancient Babylonians as the 'bird of the forest' while the Greeks described it as a swan flying southwestward along the milky way. In mythology, the swan is Zeus in quest of the love of Nemesis." Franz was really in love with his yacht to go to this amount of work to have cards printed of this type, but I don't blame him as the yacht was really a beauty. For the uninitiated, the "Swan" is the Rolls Royce of yachts and very expensive. *Sayula II*, a Swan 65 from Mexico, won the first around-the-world Whitbread yacht race in 1973.

Franz had a paid crew – his skipper was from North Vancouver and lived about a mile from my house. He also had an American crewman assisting the skipper. Franz, who was also a fairly experienced sailor, stood watch on long passages with the help of his girlfriend. *Cygnus* was beautifully equipped with all the latest electronic equipment, etc. The night they sailed from Pago and headed for Upolu Island in the bad weather, they just set the radar alarm and when the island was a mile away the alarm rang to tell them to alter course. I still feel better with four eyeballs peering through the rain and haze to determine when to alter course, but guess I'm "old fashioned." *Cygnus* was also very fast and she made passages in much shorter times than *Sea Lure*. The crew had been sailing for several years at that time and sailed for another year at least, probably much longer. More stories of *Cygnus* will be forthcoming.

Customs was very slow in Apia, but in about three hours they cleared us with no trouble after we turned in our clearance certificate from Pago, answered a few questions and completed some papers. Then we were welcome to Western Samoa! Getting out of the dock area is always tricky, as the current swirls in there quite violently. Anchorage is right in front of the town centre, and in front of the famous "Aggie Grey's" hotel. All the yachts anchor there and at times there are up to ten. It is not necessary to put down two anchors, as the weather is much better here and the anchor sets very well in the sand.

Western Samoa was a pleasant change from American Samoa. The harbour and town are very pretty, the people are friendly, mostly honest and hardworking. The contrast is most remarkable. Apia is the capital and about 35,000 people lived there in 1985. Ninety percent of the people are full-blooded Polynesians. They are big, handsome, very proud people, and expect visitors to follow their customs, such as dressing properly when walking down the street. Shorts and bathing suits are not permitted. Their culture has been developed over 2000 years and they are very religious people.

The town square was also in front of *Sea Lure* and not very far away. The local police force carried out a flag-raising ceremony each morning, with a 10-piece marching band and about 20 marching policemen outfitted in their colourful uniforms. Bob was in his element as he was the retired District Commander of the Ottawa Militia District and really enjoyed ceremonial occasions. Every morning when he was on board, he raised the Canadian flag on *Sea Lure* at the same time their flag was raised in the square. He also lowered the flag about sunset each day, so I didn't have to worry about it.

We were there for two Sundays, and the first Sunday about 0900 hours the air suddenly became very smoky, but we didn't know why. Upon inquiring, we found that most families go to church on Sunday, then have a big meal at noon or as soon as the church service is over. The local women would cook the meal on wood stoves before going to church so it would be ready when they returned. This happened both Sundays so I'm sure the information is correct. Because we had good weather there was not enough wind to blow the smoke away. We were not invited for Sunday dinner in this country as we had been in Fanning Island, but I'm sure it could have been arranged. As I recall Bob went to church and met the pastor and had a long conversation with him, in fact, I think he did go to the pastor's house.

The legendary Aggie Grey was at her hotel in 1984 and in 1985 she was still there, but in a wheel chair. It was then a 120 guest room hotel with 13 Samoan fales or bungalows named for the famous people who have stayed there including Gary Cooper and William Holden. It was an interesting place and I moved into the hotel both times we stayed in Apia. The room rate included three Polynesian meals a day served in the very nice dining room. The prices were reasonable in 1984 but had gone up considerably by 1985, although by North American standards they were still reasonable. Several times a week a special dinner show was held in a separate part of the hotel, at a cost of $15 per person. The smorgasbord was excellent and the show was superb. In 1984 Aggie Grey took part in the show and performed her dance after a great fanfare. She was a great lady, and I was saddened to hear of her death in 1988 at the age of 90.

She built her hotel after the war in the Pacific, and gradually expanded it to its present size. It was very well run, her son being the manager at that time. One thing I remember which was unique in my experience, was that a fresh bunch of ripe bananas were hung each morning, in three or four strategic locations around the pool area, where guests could help themselves.

The architecture of the building was taken from the island people, and it was done in a very luxurious style. The pool was large and hexagon shaped. The fales had thatched roofs. Unfortunately I got sick both times I stayed at this hotel, and I don't know the cause, but suspect it was the water or one of the dishes served in the dining room. This is not to detract from the hotel as it was a super place. I probably encountered some virus I could not tolerate, as the other guests were not complaining. I stayed at the hotel five of the eleven days we spent in Apia. Some of the crew travelled on the island and found it very interesting but I was busy at that time. The hotel bar and lounge area became the headquarters for the *Sea Lure* crew and we met there every day, consuming large quantities of beer as well as making plans to restock the boat, and doing various minor repairs.

In Apia we met two sailors from Switzerland. My wife is Swiss and I have been to Switzerland a number of times over the years. How two Swiss fellows could learn to sail, get a boat organized, and sail all the way from the Mediterranean to Western Samoa I found interesting. They had a metal-hulled boat, probably steel, and just two of them sailed the boat. It had obviously taken a beating, but was still seaworthy. About half way through our stay in Apia, they departed on their way to Fiji. I believe they stopped at some other island, as about a month later we met them again at the Suva Yacht Club in Fiji. They were still going strong and came over to *Sea Lure* for several parties. They liked the Canadian whisky, Seagram's VO, and knew that I kept it on board. They had not learned how to drink this potent whisky and invariably would drink too much. At a going -away party for one of my crew in Suva we started out on *Sea Lure*, then went for dinner at the Yacht Club. Half way through the dinner one of the Swiss fellows disappeared, but his partner didn't seem to be worried so I didn't get concerned. When dinner was over, and we were going back to the dinghy to return to *Sea Lure*, we had a look for our Swiss friend and found him sleeping under a tree in front of the club. The Canadian whisky had done him in again! His partner must have looked after him that night and got him back to their boat.

Robert Louis Stevenson helped to make Apia famous, as he loved the Western Samoan people and lived just up the hill in Apia for many years prior to his death. His wishes to be buried at Apia were carried out and his grave is at the top of Mount Vaea. His large home and grave are tourist attractions which hundreds of tourists visit each year.

The second largest hotel after Aggie Grey's was the Tusitala at the other end of the town. It had recently been taken over by the Samoans and was being operated by them. I had dinner there one night and enjoyed it very much.

CHAPTER 5

THE BEAUTIFUL KINGDOM OF TONGA

After 11 wonderful days in Apia we lifted the anchor at 0700 hours on 18 September and departed Western Samoa on a short passage to Tonga. We had a dolphin escort on our way out between the reefs, then we turned port and headed for the passage between Upolu and Savai'i Island and the Apolima Strait which separates the two islands. Shortly after passing through the strait we noticed a whale about ½ mile off our port beam, then shortly after that we spotted two more whales, one off the starboard beam and one off the port quarter. They were very large, about the length of the boat, but I'm not sure what type. We didn't worry, as they kept their distance and didn't seem interested in *Sea Lure*, but they continued to cruise along with us for the next couple of days. I guess they like company or thought we were another whale. But with our engine on part of the time I'm sure they knew the difference. The first day and a half we were doing about 5 kts average and I guess that was a good speed for them, as the next day our speed dropped about 1 kt and they went on ahead of us. They apparently went all the way to Tonga, as yachtees we met in Neiafu, Tonga, said they saw the same whales on their way to Tonga.

On 19 September one of the crew spotted an island off our starboard bow. I knew we would be passing by the island of Tafahi and I had studied the chart previously, but didn't expect we would be able to see it. My first reaction was that we were off course many miles to port, but upon checking the chart again noted that the island was over 3000 feet high, and using the appropriate tables I determined it was actually 27 miles away. Chris was surprised at my reaction, as I did pride myself in good navigation with no surprises. The same day we retarded our watches another hour to +12 zone description, and this meant we were approaching the International Date Line – the first time for me! On 22 September we sighted land – it was Tonga. The time was 1924 hours and following my rule of not doing a landfall at night – a rule I wish I had followed religiously for the rest of the voyage – we turned around and sailed a reciprocal heading at 2100 hours. Our previous compass course had been 200C and we changed to 020C and sailed on this heading until 0400 hours the next morning. The boat speed was only 2 or 3 knots so we did not go very far in the seven hours. Before going to bed I programmed the Sat Nav, but instead of putting a boat speed of 4 knots I programmed 40 knots, and after a couple of hours the Sat Nav was right out of our area. Perhaps this had something to do with the few drinks we had after sighting Tonga. When I got up about five hours later, the Sat Nav was completely confused but the crew disregarded it, as our speed was so slow they knew we couldn't get into much trouble. Needless to say, the crew had a good laugh at my expense.

At about 0800 hours, while sailing along the coast of Tonga, we spotted a yacht anchored in one of the bays. It turned out to be *Drummer*, owned and sailed by Louis and Sylvia Beaurivage from Vancouver. They were to become good yachting friends and our paths crossed many times over the years, when we had good times together. At 1030 hours we docked in Neiafu, the largest town in the Vava'u group of Tongan Islands.

I had planned to arrive in Tonga on Saturday, but discovered that the date changed there and it was actually Sunday. We had lost a day, which we would not gain back for over a year. As the International Date Line runs through Tonga, the locals consider that the time for the world starts in Tonga, and I suppose they are right depending on how you look at it. In our part of the world, Greenwich is much more important from the point of view of calculating time and time zones.

Getting customs officers out on a Sunday isn't easy, in fact getting them out any day is not easy, as they seem to operate by their own rules. Fortunately I still had two cases of gin, and decided to donate two bottles to them. This happened to be the right move, as they cleared us quickly. Some other yachtees are not so generous and don't offer customs officers any liquor. The officers will then go on board the yacht and demand drinks, and sit there most of the day to consume a bottle or more. The rest of the yachtees have then to wait for hours before they can be cleared. They seem to have a free hand to do what they want, and of course when they ask, "How much liquor do you have on board?" they mean "How much liquor do you have for me?"

The following year when I arrived in Neiafu from Fiji I was getting low on liquor, and gave the customs officers ¾ of a bottle and reminded them that I had given them two bottles the last time I checked in to the country. They remembered all right, and said "O.K., no problem." By 1200 hours we were anchored in front of the Paradise Hotel in Neiafu, one of the nicest anchorages with the best facilities to be found on our entire voyage.

Carter Johnson, an American, had built a very nice hotel complex on the bay in Neiafu, with a sheltered anchorage for about 50 yachts. He had built a shelter below the hotel at the water's edge with a concrete floor for dinghies to tie up or the yachts to come in for water, supplies etc. For a charge of approximately $12 per week, we could use the dinghy dock, the hotel pool and showers, or go to the movies once or twice a week for an extra charge of $1; go to the dances in his very large covered dance pavilion for about $2.50. The dances were held six days a week. The six-piece band played both Cook Island and North American music. The dances were very well attended by the locals and the yachtees, and it was a place to meet in the evenings. There was a long bar with seats right across the end of the dance hall, and the cost of beer and other drinks was very reasonable. The hotel also had a very nice dining room where excellent dinners were served for about $15 per person. The hotel had plenty of accommodation for anyone who wanted to rent rooms but Carter's business was slow at that particular time. His advertising was poor, as he did not understand the value of advertising.

The air transportation to Neiafu was inadequate, with only three or four flights a week from Nuku'alofa, the capital, and few connections with other countries. A Canadian twin-engine Otter aircraft, owned by the Tongan Airline, came in to the airport at Neiafu but the service was unreliable due to weather and mechanical delays. Navigational aids at the airport were practically non-existent, and the pilot had to fly by the seat of his pants. There was no control tower so the flying was all VFR.

Not long after we anchored, Louis and Sylvia Beaurivage in *Drummer* arrived at customs. I don't think they donated any liquor to the customs officials, so had to go through the routine of the customs party going on board for most of the afternoon. Finally, when they were finished with customs, we met them. I had read articles that Sylvia had written for the "Blue Water Cruising Club" in Vancouver and was amazed to meet them. They had sailed from Vancouver several years before and had gone south down the American coast, I believe, and then to the Marquesas, Cook

Islands, etc. and finally to Tonga. They are great people, and Sylvia, who is an entertainer, sings and plays the guitar. My crew and I went to dances with them, out for dinner together, usually at a dining place right across the road from the Paradise Hotel. For $4 per person we could reserve a few hours ahead of time, then go for a home-cooked dinner. We all sat at long tables in a "fale" with about 10 people per table, with great platters of local food served hot from the oven. There was plenty of fish, vegetables, pork, melons, etc. and the meal was finished off with a special dessert made that day by the family. There was always enough food for everyone to stuff themselves, and the conversation was most interesting, as yachtees from all over the world usually attended. We went there for dinner once or twice a week both times we stayed at Neiafu.

Captain Cook visited these islands, and found the people to be so friendly that he named the country the "Friendly Isles" and we found them to be the same way. It is a kingdom that has not been formally taken over by a European country although it was a protectorate of England from 1900 to 1970 to ensure the Germans would not conquer it.

"In 1616 two Dutchmen, Schouten and LeMaire, first discovered the Islands of Tonga. When Captain Cook visited Tonga in 1773, 1774 and 1777 he and his crew were received with lavish friendliness – pyramids of food were offered to Cook and his men. Some say the islanders intended to roast Cook and his crew and eat them as part of the feast, but Cook's profuse thanks at his reception prompted them to change their minds. Preserved to this day in the premier's office in Nuku'alofa are segments of a scarlet broadcloth which Capt. Cook presented to the paramount chief of all Tonga. Cook also gave him a male tortoise from the Galapagos Islands which was left to wander blind in the queen's garden right up to 1966, when it died at the ripe old age of over 200."[1]

Tonga has 169 islands of which under 40 are inhabited. They stretch over 300 miles in a north to south direction and are divided into three main groups: Tongatapu, on which the capital is located, Ha'apai Group about 75 miles to the north, and then Vava'u about another 100 miles to the north. Tonga is farther from the equator than either the Samoas or Fiji and the temperature is more

---

[1] *South Pacific Handbook*, second edition, 1982, p. 133

moderate with ranges from 25.9C (78.6F) in summer to 21.3C (70.3F) in winter (July and August). Approximately 100,000 people live in Tonga, and even though they are backward by our standards, they have retained the best of modern civilization and are in no hurry to change. For instance there are no poor people in Tonga. Each family operates as a unit, and the money earned by the family members is pooled and used to feed and clothe the family. They did not have television in 1985, have the lowest crime rate, I believe, in the world and also the lowest death rate (1.7 per 1000 in 1976). Guns are not carried, even by the security guards protecting the Queen. Murder is very rare; however, one did take place prior to our arrival. A court found the suspect guilty and the death penalty was imposed after the King finally ruled on the case.

Queen Salote, who ruled Tonga from 1918 until her death in 1965, made Tonga known and famous in the Western world, when she attended the coronation of Queen Elizabeth II, the current Queen of England. Queen Salote was about six feet tall, which was typical of Tongan nobility. The Tongan people are fairly tall and large, at one time were quite warlike, and had many battles with the Fijians in early times. But because of their nature, I suspect that the warring was more in self-defence, as the Fijians are much more aggressive.

Their principal resource is agriculture, and copra, bananas, watermelons, and in recent years wood carvings, are their main exports to New Zealand, Holland and Australia. Fishing is a large industry but it is mostly for home consumption. Also we noticed that pork was available at the market in Neiafu.

The Tongans are very religious people and most of the Christian denominations are represented. Their banking is quite primitive and they do not have an American Express office, which is probably to their credit. The first time we visited, we did not have sufficient traveller's cheques that they would accept, so we had to wire our banks in Canada for bank drafts to be forwarded. After about a week Bob received a reply from his bank and fortunately was sent enough funds for both of us, as I never did get a reply from my bank in Vancouver. I checked with them on my next visit to Canada, and they advised that the wire never did reach them. This is typical of communications in Tonga. It was possible to get through on the telephone to North America if the line was serviceable but so often it was out of order.

On our way into Neiafu we saw our friends on *Cygnus* several miles away, and we talked to them on the VHF radio. They advised they were visiting some of the islands, and would be in Neiafu in several days. After they anchored in front of the Paradise Hotel the owner, Franz, came up the steps to the hotel and found me swimming in the hotel pool. He was slightly astonished as he told me later that when he left Western Samoa – Aggie Grey's hotel – I was swimming in the hotel pool there, and now I was in the pool again but in a different country. We had a good laugh over this and needless to say I was enjoying myself.

Tonga was the best of the nine countries that I visited with *Sea Lure* on this two-year adventure. I spent 17 days in the Vava'u area on this visit, and enjoyed it so much that I decided I would spend a month in Tonga on the return voyage in 1985. The anchorages at more than 42 islands, bays etc. within 30 miles of Neiafu have some of the most enjoyable places I have ever found. The local Yacht Charter Company published a small chart from a 1898 British survey that was available to the yachtees for $1.00, and it indicated all the anchorages and points of interest. It was designed for their charter customers, but they were quite happy to sell copies to us. Each place had a number, so we then visited these places and talked to our friends by radio or in person, using the numbers to identify where we were going or where we had stayed. It was sailing by numbers, the first and only time I have seen this system, and it was very efficient. Number 8 (Nuku Island) was our favourite anchorage and we stayed there twice on this visit and two or three times on the next visit.

If I ever get a chance to go back to Tonga and charter a yacht I will head first of all for Nuku Island. It had a number of reefs on the southwest side, but the water is so clear in that part of the world that a person can see the reefs and avoid them. In fact it is possible to see down 50 feet or more, and when anchoring we could see the anchor's position when we were setting it. Our anchorage was about 200 yards from the shore, and we would go in the dinghy to sunbathe, swim and generally relax. No one lived on the island but it was close to a village on a neighboring island, and someone kept three or four roosters on Nuku. The water was quite shallow out some distance on the east side, and at times the distinct colours of light blue, darker blue and finally mauve appeared at one time when the light was right – the fantastic colors of that part of the rainbow. We normally had the island to ourselves as there were rarely more than three yachts anchored in this area, and very often only *Sea Lure.*

Tonga was as far as Chris Sheffield planned to go on *Sea Lure*, and it was time for him to see the Vava'u area, take the ferry to Nuku'alofa, and fly back to Vancouver. He would go via Nandi, which is the international airport in Fiji. Chris had been an outstanding crewman and Watch Captain, with his knowledge of sailing, cooking, and many other attributes especially his outstanding good humour. We had a small going-away party for him, and were not aware until then that he could sing and play guitar. In fact, I think he said he had done some entertaining in Vancouver a few years before, and I am not surprised. The following day we saw him off on the overnight vessel that sails between the islands in Tonga.

With the departure of Chris, I was a crewman short for the passage to Fiji so we set out to find more crew. I needed only one but it turned out that two female crewpersons, Carol and Doddie, had sailed from Australia on a French yacht and had run out of time for the trip to Tahiti, even though they had paid the skipper $1000 each, and had to make their own way back to Sydney, Australia. They were cousins, and Doddie had been a part-time sailing instructor in Sydney while Carol had picked up a lot of knowledge about ocean sailing on the Frenchman's yacht. Also, they had survived two knockdowns on his yacht, so in that regard they were more experienced than my crew. After a tryout on *Sea Lure*, I determined that they would sail all right with my crew and not create unnecessary problems. I found their knowledge of sailing to be first class, so I decided to take them both, as there was space on the yacht. I only needed one but they were reluctant to split up at this stage of their trip, so I took them both. Also the passage to Fiji was only four days, and Doddie planned to fly back to Sydney from Fiji. This meant I would have an extra crewperson for only a short time.

The Tongan feasts were very popular events, and most visitors took part in at least one feast while staying in Neiafu. Two or three organizations competed fiercely for the business, and I found out later that the major income for a whole village depended on how well the feasts were patronized. The two main organizers, Klappies and Isaiah, came around to the boat promoting their feasts and offered a special rate if I had three or more customers. The cost on that basis was only $8 each for transportation to the site and return, all the food you could eat, and a Tongan dance show put on by the women from the village in very colourful dress. All my crew decided to go and also Louis and Sylvia Beaurivage on *Drummer*. So rather than go in the bus, we decided to take the two yachts to No. 11, which was the bay on Pangaimotu Island where the feast was held, about 10 miles away. We lifted the anchor after lunch, and did some sailing and powering before anchoring in the appointed bay. There a fale had been built for eating, there was a good swimming beach, a suitable place to set up the beer bar, and a place for the dancers. The fale was made of posts every 8 or 10 feet with a thatched roof that was rainproof. It was just wide enough for the spread of food in the middle and a row of people on each side sitting on mats. The food at the feast consisted of melons, many kinds of fish, squid, octopus, crayfish, noodles, coconut milk, pork and chicken etc. prepared by the women from the village. They placed the food on the mats before we sat down. It was wonderful tasty food prepared to perfection, and there was more than we could eat. For anyone going to Tonga I would certainly recommend they partake of a feast.

The night of our first feast, on Saturday 29 September 1984, was rainy and windy. We were able to get the crew ashore in the dinghy with no problem, and the feast and dancing went quite well despite the conditions, but soon after dinner we decided to go back to the boat where it was dry and warmer so we all ended up on my boat, including Louis and Sylvia. We finished off the party there in good style, and remained anchored that night and the following day. By then the weather had cleared up and it was again warm and pleasant.

On Monday 1 October at 1000 hours we moved to No. 21 Taunga Island and anchored for swimming. Later that day we powered to No. 17 Nuapapu Island for night anchoring and snorkeling in the coral gardens.

The following day Bob and I did some engine maintenance, fuel filters changed and the glow plug switch changed again as the engine refused to start. The instrument panel on the boat is poorly located low down in the cockpit, in an area where the water runs off the canopy, down onto the seat and from there over the instrument panel, and invariably some water runs into the glow plug switch. This causes corrosion in the switch and it has to be changed frequently. I always carry spare switches and it is not difficult or time consuming to change a switch. I went through about 6 switches during the two years and still change it at least once a year when doing about 40 days of coastal sailing out of Vancouver. For those not familiar with diesel engines, glow plugs are installed in each cylinder of the engine. Fifteen or twenty seconds of intense heat from these glow plugs and the engine is warm enough to start. Without heat there is no chance of the engine starting when it is cold, so they are an essential part of the engine operation. It was possible to extend the life of the switch by putting light oil into it and activating it 10 or 15 times in a row, but I didn't get around to it very often. Later that day we powered to No. 8 Nuku Island, my favourite, and spent the night anchored among the coral reefs just off Nuku. The following day we powered to No. 6 Kapa Island, where we anchored and took the dinghy to the swallows' caves. The next day we returned to Neiafu and anchored again in front of the Paradise Hotel. This is the type of cruising, with a little sailing, it is possible to do in Tonga in the Vava'u group of islands. It is very sheltered and safe as long as the charts are followed carefully, and only the recommended places used for anchoring. It reminded me a lot of the British Virgin Islands in the Caribbean, only the distances in Tonga are shorter and the sharks are not as plentiful. In fact, I didn't see a shark during the time in Tonga and they are never mentioned in conversation, but they are plentiful in Fiji only 400 miles away, so I'm sure there must be some in Tonga.

Ninety miles southwest of Nieafu is the island of Tofua. It was made famous by the movie *Mutiny on the Bounty*. "On 28 April 1789 Fletcher Christian and his mutineers lowered Capt. William Bligh and 18 loyal members of the crew of the *Bounty* into a rowboat, beginning perhaps the longest voyage (6,500 km) in an open boat in maritime history, from Tongan waters to the Island of Timor in the Dutch East Indies – a fantastic accomplishment of endurance and seamanship. The overgrown grave of John Norton, the quarter-master of the *Bounty*, is still found on Tofua. Norton was killed by the Tongans after he and Bligh and the others had been set adrift by the mutineers."[2]

I had hoped to sail to Tofua in 1985 on our way to Nuku'alofa to meet our oldest daughter Denise, who was six months pregnant

[2] *South Pacific Handbook*, second edition, 1982, p. 147

68

with her second child, but we decided it would be too dangerous for her on the yacht if the winds were high. Instead we flew down to meet her on the Tongan Airline and then the three of us flew back to *Sea Lure*, still anchored in Neiafu.

This area of the South Pacific is still active with volcanoes on the ocean floor and new islands are being formed. Sighting of lava bubbling on the ocean surface or being spewed high into the air has been reported by mariners to the authorities, and a list of these locations indicated by latitude and longitude was posted on the Yacht Club bulletin board in Suva, Fiji. I plotted these places on the chart so I could avoid them when determining our course. This was no guarantee that a new one would not erupt right under the boat on the course I had chosen. I was always concerned that *Sea Lure* would go high and dry on one of these unmarked islands. Before dark, while in this part of the world, I would carefully check our route for the coming night to ensure no islands would be in our way. The crew was also briefed to keep a sharp lookout all night, and if anything looked suspiciously like an island or atoll that I be called immediately. Fortunately I was never called at night for this reason, nor came upon an island unexpectedly in the daytime, so this speaks well for the accuracy of the charts we were using.

Louis and Sylvia probably became our best friends on the voyage over the two years. Louis had worked for B.C. Telephone for some years before becoming interested in sailing on the west coast of B.C. when he lived in the Vancouver area. He had a strong desire to sail the Pacific Ocean, and got lucky on the stock market where he made sufficient money to buy *Drummer*, a double-ender sloop 36 or 37 feet long. After they were married, I believe, they lived on board for a year preparing the boat and sailing the coast for experience for their offshore adventures. In 1982 or 1983 they left Vancouver and sailed down the coast of Washington, Oregon and California and eventually to Mexico. I believe they wintered in Mexico then headed off into the South Pacific, stopping at the usual places such as the Marquesas and Tahiti. Louis was bilingual and could speak French, so they got along very well in Papeete. I'm quite sure they spent the summer of 1984 in that area, and from there made their way to the Samoas with possibly a stop at Rarotonga in the Cook Islands. They had a satellite navigation system on board but it finally stopped working when they were in the Samoan Islands, so they were using celestial navigation to find their way. Sylvia was the navigator and had taken the celestial course, but I suppose she did not keep it up as there is a tendency not to bother with the manual system when the Sat Nav has worked so well for so long. When we first saw them anchored in a bay in Tonga not far from Neiafu they had just completed a rather difficult voyage from American Samoa. Sylvia had a problem with the plotting and calculations, but they had made it all right. Several days after meeting them, they discussed this navigation problem and I decided to have a look at her plotting sheets and the reduction of the sights. It turned out that she had made an error of a full degree, which resulted in a 60-mile error on the ocean, and this can be quite serious depending on the circumstances. Once this was corrected everything else fell into place, and she must have made out all right from then on, as they sailed to Nuku'alofa, about 300 miles south, and from there to New Zealand – the Bay of Islands – and did it all by celestial navigation. They had their Sat Nav repaired in New Zealand, so they probably also used a radio direction finder to make their way to that destination.

We went to several feasts together and often to the dances in Neiafu at the Paradise Hotel. Sylvia liked to dance and since Louis was not too excited about dancing this worked out quite well for me. Occasionally one of the local men would try to horn in and dance with Sylvia, too often by Louis' calculation, and he would get upset, but this did not happen often. Back at the boat Sylvia would play the guitar and sing which made for a very pleasant time. We also went back and forth between our boats for dinner several times, and exchanged a lot of sailing and other stories. We followed each other around for the next year, meeting up in New Zealand several times and again back in Tonga the following August.

CHAPTER 6

FIJI BEFORE THE HURRICANES

On Monday 8 October after 15 days in Tonga and shopping for our supplies, duty free liquor, and clearing customs, we reluctantly left the harbour at 0940 hours. We departed on the same route we had taken when arriving in Tonga, except that when we passed Hunga Island we set a course of 271 degrees true for Suva, Fiji via the Oneata Pass. This was the most direct route, but few yachtees went this route as the southern course around some large islands and then northwest to Suva was preferred. My chart was not very detailed, but I considered it safe enough for a good passage, and I decided to go through the pass in the daylight so we could thread our way through the reefs if necessary. As it turned out there was no problem, with lots of sea room to spare, and this shortened our passage to Fiji by probably a day. At 1700 hours Late Island was off our port beam about 6 miles and we were right on course. That night was uneventful, and the following day the wind was 10 to 20 knots with gusts to 25 in the evening. The mileage for the day was 121 so this was quite acceptable.

The following day 10 October at 1300 hours we were in Oneata Pass, and cleared it with lots of room on both sides. There is no reason for yachts not to use this pass as long as they are able to find it easily. It is not marked at all with navigation aids, so celestial or Sat Nav navigation must be accurate. The winds had dropped and were 10 to 15 kts, but we made only 108.5 miles for the day. At 2200 hours the watchkeeper's log indicated that an island was visible on a bearing of 320C, and the island was Vanua Vatu. I was asleep at the time, but the crew had been briefed that it would be visible and at midnight the moon was full and very bright. Too bad I missed it. The following day was quite uneventful, but the winds had dropped and the engine was on for most of the day. At 1745 hours Ngau Island peak was off our starboard beam, about 20 miles away. Its height is over 2000 feet so was visible for a long distance. The Sat Nav fix over this period and later indicated we had severe leeway to port, so I presume a current runs north to south along the east coast of Fiji. This worked in our favour as we needed to be well south of Suva before turning north, as it is very shallow with lots of reefs. I was called at 0200 hours the next morning as the lights of Suva had come into sight. We altered course to 290C from 265C, which compensated for our drift to port, and continued on. At daybreak we could see a ship high and dry several miles out of the Suva harbour. Obviously the navigator got mixed up and put the ship up on the reef; presumably it had been there for some time. Carol and Doddie had been into the Suva harbour before on the Frenchman's yacht, and knew that we had to keep the ship on our starboard, so we continued west until we were directly south of the city. The lead-in lights and range markers are visible from a long distance, and they took us through between the two reefs that mark the entrance to the Suva harbour. There is plenty of water in the channel and the reefs are about ½ mile apart so as long as you stay on the range markers there is no problem.

At 0830 hours we were in the Suva Harbour, anchored in the medical examination area, which is off the main dock. We had called the port authorities, and they advised us to wait until a doctor came on board to check out the crew before we were permitted to dock. It was a long, slow procedure to get cleared in Fiji. It was 1430 hours before we had seen the doctor and the agricultural inspector after tying up to the dock, and we still had to see customs and immigration. They did let the crew leave *Sea Lure* while we were waiting.

Finally after six hours they found everything in order, and we were authorized to go to the Suva Yacht Club and anchor out front along with about 25 other ocean-going yachts. It is very shallow in this area, is not well sheltered and at times the winds get over 30 kts, therefore it was important to set the anchor properly so we would not drag up on the mud just to the right of the club. Finally everything was organized, and I went ashore in the dinghy to register at the club to ensure we were welcome. The fee here was $14 Fijian for a week, and this included the crew. We could use the showers and bar facilities, come in with the boat for water, fuel and repairs, and have dinner in their dining room for a very reasonable price. It consisted of mostly Chinese and Fijian food.

The yacht club had parties from time to time and we were welcome to attend for a small charge. Their lounge and bar was quite large, and it was a favourite meeting place for the many yachtees. The number was growing each day as more arrived for the final stop before the dash to New Zealand just ahead of the

THE *SEA LURE*

PREPARING FOR
DEPARTURE

THE DEPARTURE

COLEEN ARCHER,
DAUGHTER

WITH
CHAMPAGNE

THE *GOLDEN LUCK*

LOU ARCHER IN HAWAII

THE CREW ON
THE COLD OCEAN

BILL, LARRY,
SKIPPER, BOB,
LAURIE

L. Donovan

CUSTOMS
CLEARANCE
AT FANNING ISLAND

C. Sheffield

SUNDAY DINNER
WITH THE PADRE

FANNING ISLAND

C. Sheffield

SHIPWRECK AT
FANNING ISLAND

C. Sheffield

FANNING ISLAND
– ENGLISH BAY

C. Sheffield

RAPHAEL
AT FANNING ISLAND

C. Sheffield

CHRIS SHEFFIELD
AND BOB DORMER

STOCKING BOAT
AT
FANNING ISLAND

C. Sheffield

PETER PETER

IN
AMERICAN SAMOA

C. Sheffield

TONGAN FIRE-EATER

C. Sheffield

BOB, ED,
RAPHAEL
IN TONGA

C. Sheffield

CYGNUS – SWAN 65

C. Sheffield

FIJI –
BOB'S FAREWELL
PARTY

M. Broda

SEA LURE

ROYAL SUVA
YACHT CLUB

NATIVE IN
OUTRIGGER CANOE

WELLINGTON

CAPITAL OF
NEW ZEALAND

CROSSING THE EQUATOR
RAPHAEL, ED, THE SKIPPER, BOB

C. Sheffield

CAPE BRETT – ENTRANCE TO THE BAY OF ISLANDS
NEW ZEALAND

LOU AND NEW ZEALAND
FRIENDS

SEA LURE IN FRONT OF STONE STORE
NEW ZEALAND

MILFORD SOUND –
NEW ZEALAND

MILFORD SOUND – NEW ZEALAND

LAND OF 23 MILLION SHEEP

FRIENDLY DOLPHINS

C. Sheffield

hurricane season. The day we left for New Zealand there must have been 30 yachts anchored out front of the club, and 10 others had left a few days previously.

Doddie Baker was leaving the crew the morning after our arrival, so that night we had a small going-away party for her on board, and then went for dinner in the club. A couple from Edmonton who sailed the North and South Pacific for several years joined us for Doddie's party. We had met them before in American Samoa, and I believe that Doddie had met them in Suva when she was there with the Frenchman, so they were invited to the party. It was all very pleasant and a suitable send-off for a good sailor. She caught the bus the next morning for Nandi and then flew to Australia. There was a hotel around the bay from the club and I think it was that night after dinner that Raphael and I took a taxi to the dancing lounge in the hotel, and let off steam. Bob was also going back to Canada the next day, and Ed and Carol were not sure at that time if they were going to New Zealand with us, so Raphael and I decided we would sail *Sea Lure* to New Zealand by ourselves if necessary. As it turned out we had more than enough crew for that passage.

The following day was Bob's last day on *Sea Lure* after 4½ months, so we had to have a going-away party for my partner in this great ocean adventure. He had been on board since our departure from Vancouver, and I couldn't have picked a better partner for this, at times, stressful sailing voyage. We were completely compatible when it came to sailing, socializing, repairing the boat and in most other ways. He was a good sailor and ideally suited for this type of activity. I suppose our Air Force background was a large contributing factor. Although I was much less experienced as a sailor, I was the captain of *Sea Lure* and he never questioned my authority. I did call on him for advice from time to time, in the early stages of the trip, but as time passed this became less frequent. When we had sailed in the British Virgin Islands on a chartered sailboat for two weeks, he was the skipper and I was the mate and our operation was just as compatible.

That night we had numerous drinks on *Sea Lure* and the two Swiss boys we had met in Western Samoa joined us. We then went for dinner at the club, and after a few more drinks and dinner I made a speech and presented Bob with a bottle of Cognac. The following morning I helped carry his bags to the bus depot close to

73

the club, where he also caught the bus to Nandi. It was a 50 or 60 mile drive over poor roads in a rickety bus, which apparently was an adventure in itself. Bob then caught Canadian Pacific Airlines, as it was called in 1984, and flew back to Vancouver and from there to Toronto and Barrington Passage, Nova Scotia, where he and Marian had retired. His total flight must have been nearly half way around the world. It had been a long time since we left Vancouver, his elderly mother was sick in hospital, and Marian was anxious that he come home healthy, so he decided it was time to go. I was sorry to see him leave. The boat operation never ran as smoothly after he left. He was the one to keep the wheels greased in the interaction of five people confined to a 40-foot boat for extended periods of time. I'm sure he had experience in the military and/or at Bell Telephone doing the same type of work when he was second in command.

Fiji is a friendly and most interesting country, much more advanced than Tonga. The Fiji School of Medicine, the University of the South Pacific, the Fiji Institute of Technology and the Pacific Theological College were all established since the turn of the century. The country consists of over 330 islands, but more than 90% of the 650,000 inhabitants live on the two largest islands, Viti Levu and Vanua Levu. The population is about ½ Fijian and ½ East Indian, but the Indian population is growing faster, so the Fijians are a minority in their own land. I suppose this is part of the reason for the quiet, bloodless revolution several years ago, when the Fijians took over the governing of the country. In fact there were signs of the Fijian unrest when we were there, but they no longer are the fierce people they had been in earlier times.

"The first European visitor was Abel Tasman; he sighted the islands in 1643 but didn't land. In 1779 Cook's ship anchored off Vatoa (Turtle Island) in southern Lau. In 1789, after the *Bounty* mutiny, Capt.William Bligh was chased by canoe-loads of hostile natives as he and his crew rowed in between the two big islands of Fiji on their way to Timor. The sea between the Yasawas and Vanua Levu is still known as Bligh Water. Bligh's careful observations gave Europeans an accurate picture of Fiji for the first time. Several months after Bligh went through on the westward path of the trade winds, Fletcher Christian took the HMS *Bounty* into Lau on his eastward journey which ultimately led him to Pitcairn Island."[3] Bligh had been a senior navigator

---

[3] *South Pacific Handbook*, second edition, 1982, p. 192

with Captain Cook when he was exploring and mapping the west coast of Canada, and undoubtedly was with Cook when he visited Tonga and Fiji, so when he was set adrift he had some knowledge of the area and also knew that the natives of Fiji were cannibals. He had a close call when chased by the natives, but fortunately was able to get away. Perhaps darkness or rain squalls worked in his favour. We'll never know for sure unless he maintained a log and it is still intact somewhere in England.

The Fijians practiced cannibalism for hundreds of years. "Pre-European times were marked by cannibalism and continual warfare which became even more ferocious with the beginning of the musket trade. Long known to the world as the 'Cannibal Islands,' the Fijian feudal native aristocracy practiced customs that today seem cruel, callous and barbarous. In this tyrannical medieval society, people were buried alive under the posts of new houses, war canoes were launched over the living bodies of young girls, widows of chiefs were strangled to keep their masters company in the spirit world. These feudal islanders were, however, guardians of the highest material cultures of the Pacific. They could build great ocean-going double canoes up to 30 metres long, construct and adorn large well-built thatched houses... and make skillfully plaited mats, pottery and wooden bowls."[4] Fortunately the natives were friendly now and not inclined to put us in the pot for dinner!

The missionaries had difficulty coping with the fierce Fijians and it was not too many years before Christianity was finally introduced and in 1867, the year of Canadian confederation, a white missionary was killed and eaten by the Fijians. Cakobau, a very important chief, changed from being a cannibal, accepted religion, and was instrumental in spreading it throughout the country. The English had many dealings with him and in 1874 he formally ceded the island of Viti Levu to Queen Victoria and this soon included all the other islands so for the next 96 years they came under British rule. On October 10, 1970 Fiji became a fully independent nation. The development of the country in many ways was undoubtedly the result of British rule and influence.

From 1859 on, workers were required to plant the cotton fields and grow the sugar cane etc. The Fijians were not interested in this type of work, so labourers were brought in from the Solomon Islands and eventually from India. When the workers' contracts

---

[4] *South Pacific Handbook*, second edition, 1982, p. 191

75

were completed many of them did not go home, and as a result the Indian population started to grow. Over the next hundred years it has grown until it now exceeds the Fijian population. The Indians are industrious, good businessmen, and operate the majority of the business establishments. They have contributed a great deal to the development of the country but are resented by the Fijians. In fact, Indian people are not permitted to live in the Yasawa chain of islands on the west side of Fiji.

The Fijians are great military fighters and took part in the Pacific campaign against the Japanese in World War II. After the war they fought the communists in Malaya and still contribute to the United Nations peace-keeping forces in the world.

The land in Fiji is owned mostly by the Fijians and the Indians are permitted to lease the farm land. The lease is normally for 30 years, but it is not always satisfactory for the Indians. When we first docked in Suva I met a distinguished-looking elderly Fijian who was very friendly, and insisted on calling me "Captain." In the next few days, when downtown, I would see this gentleman from time to time and he was always very friendly and went out of his way to talk to me. He eventually invited me to accompany him to a church service in his village, and to have dinner at his house. After meeting him at the appointed time the following Sunday in downtown Suva, we took a taxi to his village which was about 15 miles out in the country. He was obviously one of the larger property owners as he had 15 to 20 families living in his village, each in their own house. In the village was a small well-kept church that would accommodate about 75 people. The people of the village were quite religious and the church was almost filled. A minister carried out the service, and the choir sang very beautifully. Because the old gentleman was the chief and the land owner, he had a special chair at the front of the congregation right next to the pulpit. After he had seated me in an appropriate place in a pew, he went up to the front and occupied his chair for the entire service. He was treated as a very senior elder of the church, and the people must have held him in high esteem. After the church service we went to his home for dinner. He may have had a drinking problem and he was divorced, so he was living with his niece and her husband, but I believe he owned the house so I guess they were living with him. We had a very nice Fijian dinner, which I enjoyed, and afterwards they presented me with a large woven mat as a gift. I invited them to *Sea Lure* that evening and then took them to dinner at the Yacht Club. The old gentleman was trying to convince me to provide the money to build one more house in his village, and he said he would live in it when I was not using it. However, I declined his offer, which seemed to be very one-sided in his favour.

The Suva Yacht Club was only about 1½ miles from downtown Suva and the bus service never seemed to run at the right time, so we would catch a taxi. The taxis were deadheading back to town from hotels, schools etc. and we would hail them down. The charge was only 25¢ each, but the driver usually had four or five passengers, and I guess he considered this small amount of money better than nothing. The downtown area was quite developed with high-rise buildings, restaurants and clubs, and very commercialized, with the East Indians peddling their wares in every other store and sometimes on the street. They had plenty of electronics, watches etc. but it was necessary to barter and the quality of the merchandise was often inferior.

In order to be accepted in New Zealand as visitors we needed a visa and this was also true of Australia. There is a New Zealand consulate in Suva so the crew including myself had to go for photographs, complete all the forms, pay a fee and then wait about 4 days until the visa was ready. This was completed with no problems so when we were ready to depart for New Zealand our papers were in order.

After 8 days in Suva we decided that we should see some of the outer islands, so the morning of 20 October *Sea Lure* headed for the island of Mbengga with Ed Nash, Raphael, Carol and myself on board. The island is southwest of Suva, about 25 miles. We eyeballed our way through Sulphur passage at Nanuku Reef, about a mile from the island, with no problem and by 1500 hours we were anchored in Malumii Bay. The weather was turning wet with winds over 30 kts, so we powered down into the bay to get maximum shelter before dropping the hook. It turned out to be a very good anchorage, and it was most pleasant in the bay while blustery outside. The temperatures were still good and it was warm enough for light clothing.

The end of October was coming up soon, which meant summer in the southern hemisphere was approaching. The advantage of a voyage such as this was that we followed the sun, so we had summer all the time, which normally meant warm temperatures. However, this was also the time for the hurricanes in that part of the world, so we could not delay too long before getting to New Zealand. The meteorology people were advising that the conditions a thousand miles west of us were conducive to the formation of hurricanes, and it was a matter of a few weeks or so before one would start moving east, possibly in our direction. As it turned out, nothing serious happened in this area for several months and we all had plenty of time. *Cygnus* was in Fiji at the same time but we didn't see much of them as they were at the outer islands and I think had gone around to Lautoka. They did not go to the Bay of Islands in New Zealand until early December, and didn't have any particular problems.

The following day the weather cleared up, but we decided to stay another day. In the afternoon a fisherman came along in a small boat with two lobsters or crayfish to sell. One was very large and the other medium-sized. He didn't want money, but outboard engine oil for the engine on his boat. I guess it must have been in short supply or expensive in Fiji too, so we traded 1½ liters of oil for the two crayfish. For dinner that night we boiled up the crayfish and had a delicious meal with all the trimmings. I think it was a combined effort as it was necessary to boil the seafood just the right number of minutes so it would not be tough.

The following day we decided to sail to Kandavu Island, which is just west of the Great Astrolabe Reef directly south of Suva. After threading our way out through the reef again at Nanuku reef, the way we had come in, we set course for Ono Island, the large one just north of Kandavu. The winds were about 20 kts and we had a beautiful sail the 45 miles to Ono and arrived there just at dusk and anchored in Mbualu Bay just after dark. The depth sounder does not work in the dark as it must have a light shining on it, so I didn't venture too close to the shore before dropping the anchor.

The night was uneventful, and in the morning after breakfast we lifted the anchor and powered along the west side of Ono Island, around the north end of the island, and over to Mbulia Island. From there we powered southeast about 1½ miles and day anchored in the coral just behind the Great Astrolabe Reef. The water was shallow so we dropped the dinghy in the water and went snorkeling. It was the best snorkeling I have ever experienced – I don't know how it could be any better! There were forests of coral with valleys on the ocean floor, thousands of coloured fish of all descriptions swimming around us, and the sights were magnificent. I had my underwater camera, and took some pictures that turned out well as there was plenty of light on this sunny day. The two boys snorkeled for over a mile from *Sea Lure* and a shark followed them around, but it was just inquisitive and didn't cause them any trouble. We stayed here for five hours just enjoying the snorkeling, and without a doubt it was one of the most memorable days I spent during the two-year voyage. After we anchored on the south side of Mbulia Island the two boys went to a kava party on the Island, to which they had been invited by one of the local boys out at the reef.

The most formal kava ceremony is held normally for high chiefs or on very special occasions. "*Yanggona* (kava) comes from the green root (*waka*) of the pepper plant (*Macropiper methysticum*) and this, its ceremonial preparation, is the most honoured feature of the formal life of Fijians, Tongans and Samoans. It is performed with the utmost gravity according to a sacramental ritual. New mats are first spread on the floor of a big house on which is placed a hand-carved wooden bowl nearly a meter wide called a *tanoa*. Cowrie shells decorating long coconut fiber cords fastened to the bowl lead to the guests of honor. As many as 70 men take their places before the bowl. The officiants are decked out in adornments of *tapa*, fiber and croton leaves, their torsos smeared with glistening coconut oil, their faces usually blackened. The *yanggona* root is first pounded or grated into a powder in the *tambili* (a mortar). Formerly it was chewed. Next it's mixed with water in the *tanoa*. The pulp is shaped into a ball, then kneaded and strained through hibiscus fibers to squeeze out the juices into the *tanoa*. When the drink attains the right consistency, the master of ceremonies shouts '*Lomba!*' (Squeeze!), then '*Talo!*' (Pour it out!) to the cupbearer who approaches the bowl with half a coconut shell (*mbilo*) which he then carries full to the guest of honor. After the guest drains his bowl, the master of ceremonies calls '*Mbiu!*' (Throw!), the drinker then spins his empty *mbilo* as vigorously as he can on the mat like a top and then everyone cries '*Matha!*' (It is dry!)."[5] This ceremony is not unlike the "Toast to the Queen" ceremony at a formal mess dinner held on special occasions in the Officers' Mess in the Canadian Military Forces. The result after the drinking of the toast or kava is similar too!

---

[5] *South Pacific Handbook*, second edition, 1982, p. 195

The kava party the boys attended was informal, and they were simply sitting on the mat beside the kava bowl, which is placed on the floor in the centre of the room, and then drinking the kava "bottoms up" when the half coconut shell was presented to them. This may happen at 10 or 15 minute intervals depending on how exuberant the local boys are feeling, or perhaps how much kava they have drunk that day. Regardless, our crewmen came back to *Sea Lure* happy and full of stories about the visit to the village and the kava party.

The following day I decided to power to the Island of Ndravuni, only about 6 miles away, and anchored at the northwest corner of the island between the reefs. I took the little yellow dinghy and shortly after pulling it up on the beach, one of the young men from the village came down to meet me. He was very friendly and helpful, and offered to take me to see the chief. I had a short chat with the chief and he welcomed me to the village. I found out later that I should have presented about 5 pounds of kava root to him. It was about a year later, before we sailed for two weeks in the Yasawa Islands, when getting a permit to sail in that area, that I was briefed by the Fijian authorities on their customs. It is ancient custom that the chief be presented with kava root before you are welcomed to his village. In this case the chief didn't seem to mind, and assigned the young fellow who had met me to give me a guided tour of the village and take me to the kava party. This may have been a continuation of the kava party the crew attended the day before. The village was very modern, and the houses were even luxurious with many hi-fi's, stereos, etc. My guide and the boys at the kava party said their island was the wealthiest island in Fiji, and I certainly believed them. When asked how this came about, they said a cruise ship from Australia by the name of *Fairstar* came to their island for a full day once a month, so the hundreds of passengers could see an authentic Fijian village. They held a feast for the guests with dancers, etc. and then sold carvings, mats and other things made by the villagers. This brought in a great deal of revenue; they did tell me how much on a yearly basis, so this made the village very wealthy.

During the tour of the village we stopped at the kava party. There was a large bowl on a mat on the floor and two young men were sitting on the mat beside the bowl and a third was lying on the mat. Obviously he had too much to drink, and had passed out or gone to sleep or both. We were made welcome, and one of the boys dipped a half coconut shell of kava, handed it to me and said "bottoms up," or something to that effect, and having taken part in the beer drinking contests in the Canadian Air Force, I had no problem. After ten or fifteen minutes of lively conversation, as they all spoke English fluently, he handed me another half coconut shellfull of kava, which I drank. After some more conversation, it was time to return to *Sea Lure*. By that time the kava was having some effect as my jaws were going numb. The effect is quite different from alcohol, i.e. our strong whisky, rum, gin etc. This amount did not impair my reactions and I did not have any difficulty getting back to the boat in the dinghy, however I am sure many more drinks would have had much more serious consequences.

After getting back to the boat I decided to sail to Suva that night, to arrive in the morning if we could get through the reef before dark. At 1715 hours we lifted the anchor and powered to Herald Pass, about three miles away, as fast as possible. It was just getting dark when we were about to go through the pass, and I saw another yacht approaching the same pass from the other direction, so I decided to wait until it came through. The pass was marked with several sticks to indicate the edge of the reefs, so I watched its route coming through and went back out on his path without any problem, and at 1815 we set course for Suva. The distance was about 45 or 50 miles, and I had calculated that we would be approaching the reefs just south of Suva about daybreak. The winds were good that night off our starboard beam, and we were doing about 6½ knots when the helmsman advised he could see a red light dead ahead. We watched the light for a few minutes; it remained straight ahead and we were gaining on it. It was obviously not the port light of a vessel, as it would have crossed our route. I came to the conclusion it was one of the small fish boats from the islands going into Suva to sell fish, and it did not have running lights on the boat. I called for a course change of 20 degrees port, so we would not run over the vessel, and then I turned on our spreader lights that light up the entire yacht. Shortly after this we saw the red light off our starboard bow, and we must have passed it a few minutes later. We never did see the vessel in the dark, and came to the conclusion that the skipper of the small boat must have had a flashlight with a red lens. He was living dangerously, as we would have run into him if my helmsman hadn't seen the red light. This type of incident is common in this part of the world so crewmen must be on the lookout all the time.

The winds remained 15-20 kts all night. By 0200 the range lights between the reefs south of Suva were visible, and for the next three hours the helmsmen steered by the lights. We had leeway to port due to the wind and Ed had a little difficulty staying on the range, but this was not serious, as the reefs did not appear until about four miles south of Suva. At about 0600 a cruise ship called the Suva harbour master on the VHF to advise of their arrival time and asking for docking instructions. We were well ahead of the ship so would be through the reef in plenty of time. At 0800 we docked at customs, and they did a quickie clearance on us as we had not left the country. But they do have very positive control of all visitors arriving and leaving Fiji, and I was to find out more about this later. By 1000 hours we were anchored again in front of the Suva Yacht Club.

The hurricane season was fast approaching, and by now about 30 or 40 yachts were anchored in front of the club waiting for the right time to make the dash to New Zealand, a distance of about 1000 miles. Ed, Raphael and Carol had decided to go with me to New Zealand, and this meant I was one crewman short for my normal crew, so I went searching for a crewperson. I got word that a New Zealand couple were looking for a yacht for the trip, so I found out what boat they were staying on and invited them over for a discussion. Martyn and his girlfriend Trudy came over later that day. I showed them my method of operation, the safety equipment, radios etc. and he decided that they would go with us, even though they had promised to go on another yacht with an American couple. The American yacht had gone out to the Fiji islands, and came back a day before their planned departure for New Zealand, the same day as we were departing. The skipper and his wife were very upset that Martyn had changed his mind, as they now didn't have enough time to pick up crew and depart as planned. I felt a little concerned as I had met the American couple in Tonga and again here, but their problem was with Martyn, so I didn't get involved in the discussions. They still had a very competent crewman who had sailed with them for many months, and they had self-steering on their yacht, and that is how they finally sailed to New Zealand. Had they really wanted additional crew they could have delayed a few days and picked up more crew, as there were other people looking for transportation to New Zealand. This American – I can't remember his name – seemed to be having a bad time, as he was getting sails repaired in every port. When he arrived in New Zealand he sold his boat, paid about 50% New Zealand tax, and he and his wife flew back to the U.S. Their sailing companion transferred to another yacht.

Charlie and his crew with the catamaran from England, whom we had last seen in Pago, were anchored close by so we had a happy reunion. Their dinghy engine had packed up and they were now rowing their big dinghy back and forth to shore. We had on board a spare 2 hp Evinrude outboard engine, so I loaned it to Charlie on the condition that he would leave it in New Zealand at Half Moon Bay, where I had the name of the marina owner, so I could pick it up three months later. This worked out very well for Charlie. The engine pushed his dinghy with four or five people on board slowly, but it certainly beat rowing.

Cygnus, the Swan 65, and the same crew arrived in from the islands the day after I came back. We had a small get-together with Franz and his crew and dinner in the yacht club. I invited them back to *Sea Lure* later that night and went back early to prepare for their arrival. I had tied the dinghy but not very securely. Franz and his crew did not show up, and after an hour or so I went to bed. In the morning when I got up I checked for the dinghy, but it was nowhere in sight. Charlie was close enough that I could shout, and he brought his dinghy over to *Sea Lure* so we could search for the little yellow dinghy. Unfortunately my engine on Charlie's dinghy had its water passage clogged, and the cooling system was not working, so it soon got very hot and nearly started a fire. I was able to get it stopped, and one of the locals towed me over to the boat where Martyn was staying. He took me in a high-speed runabout they used to go ashore and we started to search the harbour. We came around a corner where a large ocean-going ship was unloading, and there was the dinghy. We arrived just in the nick of time, as the crew had put the oars away and were just about to load the dinghy on the ship. I suppose they would have sold it after they left the country, as the law in Fiji for theft was very severe. For a $20 reward they returned the dinghy, 5 hp outboard engine and all accessories to me, and I breathed a sigh of relief. From then on for the rest of the trip and to this day I double-tie the dinghy at night, one line on each end.

During this time I first met Charlie Vaughan, the owner and skipper of *Bastante*, and a retired colonel from the U.S. Army. His trade had also been logistics, so we had a lot in common. He was looking for crew for the passage to New Zealand and ended up with a doctor, who was sick all the way, and a female crewperson who drove him to distraction. I got to know Charlie very well in the Bay of Islands in New Zealand, and we had many laughs together mostly about sailing the oceans with pick up crews.

I also met the crew of a large American cruiser (power boat) who had attempted to cruise the South Pacific in that type of boat. I think they had holes in their heads, but they had survived this far at least. They must have had special fuel tanks installed for the two large diesel engines on board, as refueling docks are few and far between in some parts of the Pacific. The skipper of this vessel had very bad luck and was not on board at that time. He and the crew had gone out for dinner in Suva, and they had taken a young woman from one of the sailboats with them. Apparently the skipper and the young woman had eaten the same dish which I think was a salad. They were both deathly ill shortly after the dinner and were hospitalized. The woman survived for about two weeks and then died in hospital. He survived the initial attack and was then flown back to the United States, and the last I heard he was still living but not in very good shape. The cause of the attack I don't suppose was definitely confirmed, but an Australian doctor advised that, judging by their symptoms, he expected it was caused by rat droppings in the lettuce. People in that part of the world said that they had been trained as children to always wash and clean the lettuce very carefully before eating it, and probably because this was overlooked it was the reason for the illness. Many of these countries are not very clean and rats are common, especially in the market areas where the restaurants and many of the locals buy their food.

After the skipper had gone back to the mainland, the remainder of the crew was going to continue the voyage in his boat. The boat was very well equipped and had a weather fax on board. Each day they would take a weather map off the fax and post it on the bulletin board in the Yacht Club. Usually there was a low-pressure area west of us, and the winds were reported from the east at about 30 kts. This would then start rumours circulating that it was too dangerous to leave for New Zealand. Some skippers ignored the rumours and three or four yachts left every day, but others got caught up in the rumour mill.

Sea Lure was stocked with food, water and fuel for the voyage, and on Sunday 28 October it was decided we would leave the next day. That night, at the bar, one of the crewmen from the power vessel pleaded with me not to leave the following day as he thought we would have extreme difficulties. I took him over to the weather chart on the bulletin board and asked him to show me on the chart why I shouldn't leave, and of course he was unable to make a case. He undoubtedly didn't know how to read a weather chart, and was interpreting the information based on their power boat. A 40-foot sailboat is much more seaworthy and suitable for heavy seas. We didn't change our plans and made final preparation for departure at noon the following day.

Over the course of the night Raphael had made arrangements to go with an Australian sailor on his yacht to Australia. Now that Martyn and Trudy were going with me, I had one more crewperson than I needed. The Australian was having trouble getting crew, so Raphael decided he would like to transfer to another boat as he knew he was not letting me down. Fijian immigration keep a very close accounting of all visitors entering and leaving the country, and when crewmen transfer from one vessel to another both skippers must be present, and must sign the transfer papers. The next morning about 0900 hours we all went to immigration to complete Raphael's transfer. Previously we had completed the transfer of Martyn and Trudy to my yacht, and immigration were quite concerned about the departure of Bob and Doddie shortly after our arrival. We should have advised immigration at that time, but fortunately I was able to give the airline flight details for both of them. Immigration confirmed later that they had checked the departure details at Nandi to confirm my information.

Raphael had advised me late the night before that he would be leaving the boat, and there was not enough time to organize a farewell party for him. I felt bad about that, as he had been such a good and loyal crewman and deserved a better send-off, but there was not time, so a farewell speech was the best we could do the next morning.

CHAPTER 7

SUMMER IN NEW ZEALAND

On Monday 29 October at about 1130 hours we lifted the anchor and powered out of the Suva Harbour between the reefs, and set course for a point about 6 miles off Cape Washington, which is on the southwestern point of Kandavu Island. We would be passing through this area in the middle of the night, and I wanted to be sure we were well clear of the islands and reefs. I noticed on my plotting charts that we had a great deal of starboard leeway, that we were well to the port of our intended course and passed within a mile of the reef at Mbengga Island. It was daylight so I must have been watching our distance off. The winds were 15 to 22 kts from the southeast, our course was 208 Compass so the wind was on the port beam, our most efficient point of sail, and our progress was more than satisfactory.

At midnight, Cape Washington was off our port beam about six miles. I called for a course change to 191C and went to bed. I noted that the log read 985 miles to go to the Bay of Islands, New Zealand. The seas were quite rough as the wind had been blowing for some days, which wasn't conducive to sleeping, but after one is dead tired it takes a lot of bouncing around to keep you awake. Trudy was sick, and she and Martyn were on the same watch, so I expect Martyn took part of her shift at the helm, and in the daytime I tried to give her a break as often as possible. After several days her stomach settled down and she was O.K. I also expect she was frightened in the beginning, but concealed it very well. She soon became a good crewperson and also took her turn in the galley.

The following day, 30 October, the winds were still 25-30 knots from the same direction. We had the main and genoa reefed, mainly to cut down the 20-25 degree heel, and also to ensure we didn't rip the main. It had been sewn again in Suva and I was nursing it along, hoping to complete the voyage without spending $2000 on a new one and having it shipped from Vancouver. The seas remained rough, and I recall bracing myself against the table leg to hold myself in the navigator's position in the dining area. The boat does not have a navigator's position, so I used the table for navigation between meals and vacated it at mealtime. The Sat

Nav and ham radio were within reach of this position, so I became quite used to it. As ocean sailors know, when you have a Sat Nav much less time is spent navigating, however I still completed an hourly plot from the watchkeeper's log and had a dead reckoning position almost hourly. If the Sat Nav failed I could go straight on to celestial navigation with the sextant, or if we had to ditch, the radio operators could give an accurate latitude and longitude from the official log for the purposes of the search. The first thing I did after rising around 0600 each morning was to bring the official log up to date from the watchkeeper's log, convert the average heading for each hour from compass to true, then plot the true heading with distance travelled on the plotting sheets. These were specially printed plotting sheets based on the mercator projection, and each one covered 3 or 4 degrees of latitude. The longitude I put in as required. This provided accurate navigation, and with half a dozen fixes every 24 hours we knew our location most of the time.

The following day the conditions were about the same, but with our reefed sails our daily progress was not exceptional – about 114 miles per day. Fishing was good that day and we landed a 25 lb. mahimahi. This was the first of many fish we caught on this passage. We grilled the fish for dinner that night and according to the watchkeeper's log it was a "feast." In the late evening the winds went up to 28 kts and it was raining. It rained off and on all night, but late the next morning the sun came out and it was hot. Summer was approaching and the days were getting warmer, but the nights were still chilly. In the evening the winds started to drop a little, and we soon shook out all reefs and hoisted the mizzen. This was the first time that the winds had subsided at all since leaving Suva, and these were the conditions the crewman on the American cruiser was worried about. There is no doubt a cruiser would have taken a terrible pounding in these high seas, but for *Sea Lure* it was good sailing, in fact, very good sailing conditions even if the rail was in the water at times.

The next morning, 2 November, the winds dropped to 10-15 kts and in the evening down to 10 kts so we started the engine to get some more boat speed. At 2000 hours we had a ship off our starboard beam – the first ship we had seen on this passage – and I talked to the captain on the radio. He was going from Auckland, New Zealand to Suva, Fiji and I asked him for a weather report which he gave me – the report was good with fine weather and light winds ahead. The wind direction had now switched around to the northeast. At 0350 the next morning the knot log stopped working, and the Watch Captain on duty had the foresight not to wake me up at that time to fix it, as this was not a major problem. The next morning at about 0900 I cleared it of weeds or whatever the cause, and we estimated our distance traveled. With the help of the Sat Nav we could do this very accurately. The weather had now warmed up considerably and the sea had settled down so much that it was sunbathing and picture-taking weather. Martyn was quite surprised, as the weather can be foul at this time of the year when approaching New Zealand, but we were lucky and it was absolutely beautiful. The following day was Sunday 4 November and the skipper's day to again cook a steak dinner. Also, it was a marvellous day with light winds, so it was pleasant to clean up the boat, have a shower, enjoy the extended "happy hour" with interesting conversation, then crack open one or two bottles of wine to wash down the dinner. I couldn't think of a nicer way of spending a Sunday when only two sailing days from New Zealand and the Bay of Islands.

Since Bob had gone home, we did not have a licensed ham radio operator on board so we did not report in to the DDD net each day, however, we listened out at the appointed time. We also listened to Tony's net and the South Pacific net. The DDD net or the South Pacific net reported that the yacht *Bergere Azur* was missing. This was a Canadian yacht owned by Bernie and Norma Comat from Montreal and West Vancouver, whom we had met in Pago Pago. They had been sailing for some years, and Bernie found employment in engineering in various countries so they would sail to the job and live on board. They were on their way to some country northwest of Australia this time, and left Pago after us for Western Samoa. The Australian coast guard was carrying out a search and we were anxiously awaiting the results. After several days or more of searching the search was called off, although the boat was still missing. About 5½ months later I met a Canadian yachtee who was the last one to see *Bergere Azur* before it went missing, and he was also the one who requested that the coast guard carry out a search.

The following day Monday 5 November at 1500 hours "George" quit. George was the automatic pilot, almost as good as another crew member and he didn't require any food! He had worked intermittently over the voyage to this point, so now we had to go completely on manual steering. With four crew members plus myself this was not a problem, since we had been manned from the start, not depending on "George." We must have had clear skies at night, as the crew were now steering by the stars. This is possible as long as you don't stay on the same star too long. The occasional glance back to the compass will tell you if you are on course, or if it is time to pick another star to steer by, or just use the compass. At 0400 hours the same day the engine stopped for the first time on the passage. After troubleshooting for some time, I came to the conclusion that I had bought dirty fuel in Suva, as the racor filter was plugged up and the sight glass had lots of dirt in it. This was the beginning of a lot of trouble I had with dirty fuel in that part of the world. It was necessary to flush the sight glass, replace the filter, prime the engine and then it started. I carried a large supply of racor filters and before the voyage was completed I would use 24 of them. Up to this time I had used only 3 and the voyage was nearly half finished. Dirty diesel fuel is a real hazard, as the operators do not clean their tanks regularly, and it is possible to damage a diesel engine with dirty fuel. Some yachtees attempted to strain their fuel before putting it in the tanks, but I always found this to be impractical as there were usually other boats waiting to fill up, and there just wasn't time to go through the tedious process of straining the fuel. My procedure was to change the filters when the sight glass started to show excessive dirt and then pump *Sea Lure*'s fuel tanks if necessary. This worked rather well, as both tanks sloped down at one end and there was an access hole that had a fuel-tight cover directly above the lowest point. Using one of the standard hand pumps and putting the plastic hose down the inside of a metal pipe it was possible to draw all the sludge and dirt out of the tank until clean fuel appeared. At the worst, I removed two four-gallon pails of dirt from each tank before clean fuel finally appeared. I suppose this is one of the reasons some ocean-going yachts carry many jerry cans of fuel tied on the deck. I prefer my method, especially in heavy weather when jerry cans might break loose. Had I pumped my tanks a little sooner each time I took on dirty fuel, I would have reduced the pumping by 50 percent.

Tuesday 6 November was our greatest fishing day, the best of the entire voyage, although we had other days that were almost as good. At 0600 the shock cords on the fishing line started to rattle –

this would always wake me up. A few minutes later we landed a 15 lb. tuna. We must have been crossing a school of tuna, as a few minutes later we hooked another but this one shook the hook out of its mouth and got away. At 1030 we landed another tuna – it was a little smaller than the first one. At 1200 we landed a third tuna and after that we stopped fishing for the day. We had so many tuna on board that the freezer was running short of space, and we didn't need this many fish to satisfy the menu requirements, so I decided to give the last two to Martyn and Trudy as they would be at home in New Zealand in several days. Dinner was good that night with fresh tuna grilled in the oven, as we always switched the menu to have the tuna the day it was caught and before it was frozen.

That night at midnight we advanced our clocks another hour to coincide with daylight saving time in New Zealand, so we had 2400 hours twice and each watch took an extra 30 minutes, which worked out to 4½ hours per watch. On Wednesday the 7 November at 1100 hours we sighted land, and even though the sun wasn't quite over the yardarm, we celebrated the occasion by having a drink. At that time of day I'm sure my drink must have been a beer. The winds had been very light (2 to 8 knots) and the engine had been running steadily for about 18 hours or more at low RPM to give us boat speed of about 5 to 6 knots. We corrected our course so we would come through the centre channel into the Bay of Islands. The destination for the Sat Nav was the latitude and longitude for Cape Brett, which was 35 degrees 10.5 minutes South and 174 degrees 20.0 minutes West. The entrance to the channel into the Bay of Islands was 174 degrees 10.0 minutes West, so I reprogrammed the Sat Nav for this destination and it immediately gave me a corrected course, which was 201 true and 185 compass to allow for leeway to port. I gave the helmsman a course of 180 compass and this brought us into the middle of the channel.

This was Martyn's cruising and sailing area, so he took over the helm and in the next three hours gave us a tour of the Red Hen Island, Russell and all of the Opua Harbour. At 1830 hours we docked at the main dock for customs clearance. The current was very strong in the dock area, and it took full power to turn the bow around against the current to bring us along the inside of the dock. So many yachts were now arriving in Opua, up to 20 a day, that the customs official from Whangarei had moved to Opua in order to give faster service with no overtime charges for the yachtees. That year, 1984, over 250 yachts arrived in the Bay of Islands to stay there or somewhere in New Zealand for four months to avoid the hurricanes. In the summer months hurricanes are common north of Australia, and frequently go through part of Fiji. It is quite rare that a severe hurricane hits New Zealand, perhaps one in ten years or so. So it is a suitable country in which to take refuge and also it is a good place to get a yacht repaired, updated etc. as the New Zealanders are great boating people and very skilled in this type of work.

Our time into New Zealand from Fiji was 9 days 6 hours, which was quite satisfactory as the distance was about 1040 miles. This was the mid-point of my voyage, and I was inclined to celebrating a little after docking. No one else in the crew was in the mood to celebrate so I had my own party. They obviously did not realize the significance of sailing a third of the way around the world, after so many years of preparation. The statistics up to this point in the voyage were as follows:

Distance sailed	7515 nautical miles
Time on voyage	4 months 16 days
Days at sea	64
Engine hours powering	404
Total number of crew members	11

Customs clearance was not as easy here, as the customs officer searched the boat and found some stereo equipment, speakers etc. that Martyn had brought along but had not declared on his customs forms. This caused some consternation for a few minutes but was quickly straightened out. The government of New Zealand is trying to keep out the cheap equipment sold in Fiji to protect the local businesses, therefore this accounted for their actions.

The following morning after breakfast we powered to Paihia to cash traveller's cheques at the bank. It is very shallow in the Bay of Islands area, and the channel into Piahia is very narrow and only about 10 feet deep, but with Martyn's help we made it in and out with no trouble. From there we went to Apple Tree Cove, where Martyn and Trudy lived in a nice house, and tied up to a buoy that belonged to his brother. We spent a very enjoyable night at their home and the following two days anchored in the bay close by. On Sunday 11 November, with Martyn as pilot, we all powered up the Kerikeri River to the Stone Store. It is a winding river, marked by buoys, and at high tide *Sea Lure* had about 2 feet of water to spare at the lowest point. It runs for about four miles, and then there are pilings to tie up to, or other yachts to raft beside. This time we rafted beside a 40-foot yacht belonging to John Wood. John was one of those typically friendly and most helpful fellows from New Zealand, and he offered advice, drove us in his car and did many other things to make our life more pleasant. John was quite a sailor too, and we were to meet up again in Pago Pago, almost a year later on our return trip.

The Stone Store was directly ahead of *Sea Lure*. This is the oldest store in New Zealand and it is kept in good repair. There is a museum on the upper floor with various displays of New Zealand history, which is quite extensive. To see it all properly takes about two hours. The charge for the museum was about $1.50 NZ per person. In the lower part of the store David Stretton-Pow and his girlfriend Jackie operated quite a large store. Shortly after this time David and Jackie were married and they still live at Kerikeri. I believe David rented the Stone Store building from the government or county, and operated both the museum and store. Not far away he owned a tea room that served meals and sold delicatessen foods. It was quite large and probably seated 40 to 50 people. David also had his living quarters in part of the building.

This part of Kerikeri is about a mile from the town of Kerikeri. It is an historical area as it also has the oldest house in New Zealand, built in 1822, known as "Kemp House." There is a dam in the river with a small waterfall – in all a very pretty area. John Wood and his family lived in a lovely home overlooking this area and very close to the store. We had met David and Jackie at Martyn's home as David had rented it during Martyn's absence for many months, and soon we became very good friends. We spent many happy times together on *Sea Lure*, having large dinners in his tea room, and several months later they took us on a full day's outing and picnic on a beautiful beach on private property not far from Kerikeri.

Ed and Carol were leaving the crew shortly, so I decided to take them out for dinner at a very good restaurant/dining room in Kerikeri. We walked up to the restaurant on the Tuesday night, had a first-class dinner with wine etc. and then walked back to *Sea Lure*. They left the following day 14 November. Ed flew back to Canada and Carol flew to Sydney, Australia. I was sorry to see them go as my entire crew had departed and I was operating *Sea Lure* single-handed. However, with my new-found friends, and the arrival of the boats and crews I had met previously there were still lots of people to party with, and I had a very pleasant time over the next few weeks before returning to Canada by air.

New Zealand is a very interesting country, and the people are exceptionally friendly and kind and make everyone feel so much at home. The country was first inhabited about 900 A.D. by Polynesian Maori people from Tahiti or Rarotonga. They must have arrived in their very large outrigger canoes, and navigated by the stars and sun, as I'm sure they wanted to know how to return to their homeland in case they were unable to find new land during their travels. I'm certain they had a considerably better idea of ocean navigation than they get credit for. Life was more difficult in this area than in the tropics, and the Maoris became more vigorous and hardworking. They were also quite warlike and I'm positive they practiced cannibalism during this period. Captain Cook first visited New Zealand in 1768, and it is possible that William Bligh was with Cook at that time, although this was 21 years before Bligh was set adrift in Tonga so perhaps this was a little early for Bligh to be transferred to Cook's ship. Following Cook came the seal hunters in 1790 to 1820, the whalers in 1800 to 1840, then the gold seekers after 1861. But the gold was soon depleted and sheep farming became the main occupation of the country and still is to this day. With refrigerated transportation after 1882, they started to ship lamb and mutton throughout the world.

New Zealand is larger than Britain, but the population is only three million. Racism is not at all noticeable and the Maoris are treated very well. They demanded and got almost equal status in the early days and many Maoris occupy important positions in Government, the Senate, etc., and there has been considerable inter-marriage between the whites and the Maoris. In fact I sailed in the Victoria-Maui race in 1978 with an offspring of one of these unions from New Zealand.

"Maori art is outstanding for its huge, deeply-cut plank woodcarvings incorporating the same curvilinear designs used in their facial tattoos. Nowhere else in Polynesia was woodcarving done on so monumental a scale. Maori artists once made excellent small greenstone carvings. The tilted face (*manaia*) of the *tikis* was a unique characteristic of this art."[6]

---

[6] *South Pacific Handbook*, second edition, 1982, p. 511

Mammals were non-existent in New Zealand until imported from other countries. There are some birds, and the kiwi bird that has a long beak and a round feathery body but cannot fly, is the best known. New Zealanders are often called Kiwis. There are also other flightless birds in contrast to our birds in North America.

New Zealand has all the modern methods of transportation at a high standard, and Air New Zealand runs flights to many parts of the world. I flew with them on two or three occasions, and was always most impressed with their service, food quality and reliability. Buses, trains and ferries are also of high standard and very comfortable. During February the following year (1985) my wife and I travelled extensively in the South and North Islands, therefore, I will have more to say about those areas.

The day after Ed and Carol left, I powered and sailed back to Opua and docked to fill the tanks with water. From there, I sailed to Russell Harbour, which is only about 3.5 miles, and anchored for the night. The next morning when I woke up, Charlie on his English catamaran *Peter Peter* was anchored beside me. What a happy event to see them again! That morning the winds went up to 30 kts, and I was concerned that I would drag the Danforth 40, as my rule of thumb is that when the winds exceed 25 kts it is time to drop a second anchor. Charlie was close enough that I could shout, so when I had the Bruce anchor with the 225 feet of gold braid line plus some chain ready, he and a crewman came over in their dinghy with my little two horse Evinrude engine (borrowed earlier) still pushing it, and took my anchor out over the bow about 150 feet and heaved it overboard. I set this anchor by hand with a little help from *Sea Lure*, and then I was secure and good for winds up to 40 kts. That afternoon we hoisted more than a few with Charlie and his crew, and discussed our voyage from Suva. They too had been checked very carefully by customs, and had a second visit from the customs officials with a drug-sniffing dog in tow. Nothing was found on board. I suppose the long-haired Englishman and crew looked suspicious to the customs people, so they must be given full marks for thoroughness.

An Australian by the name of Ken was anchored in his yacht close by, and as usual yachtees are friendly and get to know each other quickly because we have a special bond. I needed a crewman on board the following day, as I planned to go into Kerikeri again, but this time to anchor bow and stern in a hole that has at least 5.5

feet of water at low tide in front of the Stone Store. John Wood had pointed out the spot where I could anchor in mid-stream where other yachts had done it before, so being the adventurous type I was game to try it - consequently the extra crewman was required. The next day at about 1800 hours, we arrived at the anchoring spot. We tossed out the stern anchor at the appropriate place and Ken payed out the line. When about 175 feet of line was out and *Sea Lure* was getting close to the pile of rocks just below the surface, we cleated the line and set the stern anchor. I had to drop the Danforth anchor off the bow. We payed out chain for about 50 feet while Ken then took up the slack on the stern anchor. When the bow anchor was set, and several times it ran over the rocks for quite a distance before it finally caught, we tightened the chain with the winch, pulled on the line on the stern until it was tight. We were then anchored in a spot where there was only space for one yacht, directly in front of David's Tea Room and the Stone Store. This was an even better anchorage than the one in front of the Paradise Hotel in Neiafu, Tonga. How lucky could I get! I have included a picture of *Sea Lure* taken by my friend Les, the owner and skipper of *Sea Song*, from the sundeck of David's Tea Room. I anchored here four more times in the course of the next several months. It was always such a pleasant place and I didn't have any trouble with dragging anchors.

The 22 November 1985 was American Thanksgiving, and we got word that skippers of many American yachts now in the Opua and Russell area were planning a large Thanksgiving dinner in the Opua Yacht Club, to be held in the afternoon and early evening. David wanted to go out on *Sea Lure* for a day of sailing, so we decided he should go with me to Opua for the dinner, stay on board for the night, and return home the following day. We lifted the two anchors at 1000 hours that morning, had a good day of sailing and about 1600 hours anchored at Opua, close to the Yacht Club. After paying for our share of the dinner we proceeded to have a very fine time. At least 100 yachtees and their friends took part – there was enough turkey and trimmings for everyone, with some left over. It was also very well organized and stretched into a party that lasted for many hours.

During the course of the dinner we met Les and Melody. Les, the owner of the 40-foot yacht *Sea Song*, came from California. In private life he was a lawyer with a practice in Los Angeles. He had sailed all the way from home with a small crew and had arrived in Opua within the week. Melody was from Victoria, B.C. and had joined the crew along the way, possibly in the Samoas or Fiji. They were interested in going to Kerikeri and didn't know the route, so we agreed they would follow us the next morning after it was determined they could just scrape over the bottom at high tide the next day, as *Sea Song* drew over 6 feet. High tide was at 0800 hours the next morning, so we agreed on a 0700 start, which would get us to the shallowest place just at high tide. We left the Yacht Club together and when they went to get their dinghy, they found it under water due to the way it had been tied and the rising water at high tide. Their engine wouldn't run, so David and I agreed to take them to their boat, towing their dinghy, and help them with their dunked engine. I carried a hair dryer on board to be used to heat the diesel engine in emergencies if the glow plugs would not work, so we decided to get it to dry out Les' dinghy engine. When there is salt water in any engine it is most important to get the water out as quickly as possible and then get it running, otherwise serious damage can take place. I picked up the dryer from our boat, and Les had a small gasoline-driven generator on board that put out 110 volts. After about an hour of drying, and removing the spark plug from the engine, it agreed to start and Les' problem was solved. The next morning we left on schedule, went up the Kerikeri River without going aground, and were anchored in front of the Stone Store again at 1000 hours. Les tied *Sea Song* to the pilings. This was the beginning of a very good friendship. Les lost *Sea Song* in May of the following year and narrowly missed losing his life on a passage from New Zealand to Fiji.

Charlie Vaughan, the skipper of *Bastante*, had arrived with his crew from Suva a few days after our arrival. I had spoken to him for a short while at the Thanksgiving dinner, and the next time I saw him was up the Kerikeri River in the Stone Store area. In fact, I think he was picking up photographs in Kerikeri the same time as I picked up some pictures. He was a comical fellow and a very experienced ocean sailor. I think I mentioned before that he had retired from the U.S. army as a senior officer. We had both been in the same trade, but in different countries, and each had 20 – 30 years of permanent force experience. We did have a lot in common besides ocean sailing and we communicated very well. He came to *Sea Lure* several times in Kerikeri, and told me about his very unpleasant passage from Suva. I think he had only two other crew people on board and could manage with such a small crew as he had self-steering plus an autopilot. One of the crewmen was a doctor, but he suffered from severe seasickness and it was rough coming down from Suva. I think he was sick most of the time. The female crewperson had some ocean experience, but apparently she was an incessant talker and drove Charlie to distraction after a few days. He said if the doctor hadn't been sick he would have had him do some suturing, in particular, the crewperson's mouth! They made it to New Zealand all right, and Charlie was competent enough and knew his boat so well that he could have single-handed without much problem. In fact, at one time he talked of single-handing on the return voyage, but after much discussion, he decided it was better to have one or two on board so he could get some rest without worrying about being run down by a ship.

During this time we had news of a ship that docked in Australia, and the crew found parts of a sailboat still caught in the ships rudder. They had undoubtedly run over a sailboat and were completely unaware that it had happened. This is one of the reasons that yachts do occasionally disappear at sea, never to be heard of again. This also made most of us ocean sailors much more conscious of having a crewman looking out at all times. With my large crew it was possible to always have someone on the helm looking out for other vessels. Even this was a false hope once in a while, as I did have helmsmen asleep at the wheel, and others not looking out for an hour at a time when the autopilot was working. One of the difficulties of having a small crew and self-steering was that someone was supposed to look out every 20 minutes, but were they doing it or did they fall asleep? At least three or four times on the voyage *Sea Lure* was on a collision course with a ship, and we had to alter course to miss it. I suspect that in most of these cases the officers on the bridge of the ship did not see us. On one occasion a ship was passing us on the port side – about 1.5 miles away. We had our running lights on, and I talked to the Captain on the radio and asked him if he could see our red port light. I described where we were located in relation to his ship, and after awhile he came back and said, "No, I can't see you." We then turned on our large hand-held spotlight and shone it towards the ship to which he replied; "Now I can see you." The running lights on *Sea Lure* were too small, and should have been replaced with larger ones before the voyage, but this was not done. After this incident, I always assumed that the personnel on board a ship could not see us at night, and that we must always take evasive action.

I met Charlie several times in the Kerikeri area over the next few weeks. Once he was aground just off the channel of the Kerikeri River, and was waiting for the tide to lift his boat off. Fortunately, there was enough room for me to get past his yacht. We were to meet again in Auckland, in Half Moon Bay, several months later, and then again at the Great Barrier Islands out of Auckland, just prior to my departure for Australia. He didn't go to Australia but returned to the U.S. mainland via several other countries.

Another time, when we were both anchored or tied up in front of the Stone Store, we met in the store. It had been raining for several days, and the forecast was for more rain. The dam, not far from where *Sea Lure* was anchored in mid channel, had been known to burst after excessive rainfall. If it did burst, I wasn't sure the bow anchor on *Sea Lure* would hold the vessel against the sudden rush of all this water. After long discussions I decided to leave and go back to Opua before the dam broke, and tie up to a buoy I had rented right in the harbour. As it turned out, the rain did not continue for long and the dam held. I think Charlie had *Bastante* tied to one or two pilings and stayed on in Kerikeri.

Louis and Sylvia Beaurivage on *Drummer* had still not arrived in Opua, but we had word they were on their way from Nuku'alofa, Tonga. I knew they still didn't have a serviceable Sat Nav, and there was always a possibility they were having trouble again with the celestial navigation. Finally about 4 December they arrived in Opua. The weather had been bad during their passage, especially when they were close to New Zealand, and I think it was then they had another equipment failure. I believe it was a backstay problem and they had to "heave to" for several days within 50 miles of the Bay of Islands, waiting for the weather to improve. But they finally made it, and anchored close to where I had our boat tied to buoy No. 466. If they hadn't arrived shortly after, we would have asked the New Zealand Coast Guard to carry out a search, or is it the New Zealand Air Force that is responsible for search and rescue in that country? Lou and Sylvia had left it a little late to go into New Zealand, as the weather was deteriorating and hurricanes were now forming northwest off Australia and moving in an easterly direction. We watched the weather report on television with interest these days to see where the hurricanes were heading, as *Cygnus* still hadn't arrived, and there were other yachts still making the passage from Suva. We didn't worry too much about *Cygnus* as they had such a seaworthy, well-equipped boat with a very professional crew. They did arrive about two days later, after making the passage from Suva in about seven days.

During this time several yachts arrived with engines that were not running, but the Bay of Islands was a good place to sail into and then drop anchor close to the dock at Opua. There was also plenty of room to tack up the channel if necessary – there were so many yachts in the area that arranging for a tow would not be a problem. The engine on *Drummer* was not functioning very well, but Lou was able to nurse it along and keep it running. I believe the engine had a complete overhaul in Opua in the course of the next four months.

During the next ten days I had a very pleasant time around Opua, and went up the Kerikeri River once more. Louis went with me this time to handle the stern anchor, and again it worked out very well. The centre channel on two anchors seemed to be our reserved spot, as each time the spot was clear and no other skipper bothered to anchor in this place – which was very thoughtful of them.

Some time before this, I had planned to return to Vancouver for Christmas and to stay until the end of January before returning to New Zealand, so I needed a secure place to leave the boat. A number of buoys were available for rent, so I decided to rent one for the six weeks, tie *Sea Lure* securely, and hope for the best. The buoys were very sturdy and built with a large amount of cement, etc., and one was available for this period at a reasonable price – approximately $50 NZ per month. I was also able to make arrangements with the maintenance people to have them attach a second two-inch line to the buoy so I could double tie *Sea Lure* – one line to the bow cleat and one line to the anchor winch. I was hopeful that if a hurricane came along, the buoy and the two lines would hold the vessel. If it didn't, I would have to live with the consequences. With no insurance, a skipper is particularly careful at a time like this to try to anticipate all possible problems. As it turned out, no hurricanes came to New Zealand that year, although one hit Fiji again, and *Sea Lure* was still riding just fine when Lou, my wife, and I came from Canada on 2 February 1985.

To fly from New Zealand to Canada, it was necessary to take the bus from Opua, a 5-hour bus ride, stay overnight in Auckland then fly out the following morning. After stowing the life raft and dinghy on board and preparing the boat as well as possible, i.e., shutting off all the through-hull valves, pumping the bilge for the last time and checking the automatic bilge pump switch to make sure it was working, with apprehension I prepared to leave. The yacht had looked after me so well for all these months, and I was hopeful she would be all right, even though she would be ignored for the next six weeks. Early on the arranged morning, Louis came over in his dinghy and took me ashore with my bags. It was just a short walk up the hill to the bus stop, and in due course the bus came along on schedule and I made my way to Auckland. It was only about ten days until Christmas, and I was anxious to get back to Vancouver to see my family and spend Christmas with them.

The air flight from New Zealand to Vancouver is very long – sixteen hours of flying time plus time spent in terminals. I flew Air New Zealand via Tahiti to Los Angeles and Canadian Pacific from Los Angeles to Vancouver. The flight, though much too long, was very pleasant. I arrived in Vancouver the same day I left New Zealand, as I gained a day when crossing the International Date Line. I was most happy to see my family – Wayne our son, Coleen our youngest daughter, and my wife Lou. The oldest daughter Denise lived in Ottawa with her family so I did not see them on this visit, but she flew to Tonga some months later and spent several weeks with us on the boat in Neiafu.

I spent a very pleasant six weeks in Vancouver over Christmas and New Year's. This time I didn't have a boat to check on every week or so, although I did wonder how it was doing in Opua, and I called up once on the telephone to make sure it was still at its mooring buoy. The New Zealand women in the office assured me that it was still there and appeared to be okay.

Twice more during the voyage I left *Sea Lure* for extended periods of time and flew back to Canada, but I found that by being very careful about all arrangements, and making sure the boat was closed up carefully with all equipment inside and out of sight and the sea cocks closed, the boat was fine in all instances. I was always apprehensive about the engine not starting after extended periods of time, but in all cases the engine started, perhaps with a little more cranking, but I always made sure the batteries were well charged up. This was important, as it was not possible to plug into shore power because the voltage was not compatible and I did not have a converter.

If the batteries are new when you start out on a voyage such as this and the alternator is working all right, it is not normally necessary to buy a converter. Docks are few and far between in the South Pacific so most of the time it is impossible to get any kind of shore power. 110 volt was available in Hawaii, but after that it was not available at all, except from the small Yamaha battery charger I carried on board. It had 12 and 110 volt and was gasoline-driven but took hours and hours of running to charge up a battery. Twice the batteries did get very low, once in New Zealand at Half Moon Bay, and once in Lanai, Hawaii. Both times it was possible to send two of the four batteries out to a battery shop or garage and get them charged up. This was faster and more satisfactory, but in both cases I had to find someone with a car or truck to take them down to the shop, then pick them up in a day or two. Fortunately most of the locals or yachtees were most helpful and went out of their way. This of course is a reciprocal arrangement, as I always did the same thing when a yachtee needed assistance.

CHAPTER 8

TRAVELLING IN NEW ZEALAND

On the 2 February 1985, we returned to *Sea Lure* in Opua, New Zealand. My wife Lou and I flew from Vancouver via Los Angeles on Canadian Pacific Airlines, then to Auckland via Honolulu on Air New Zealand. I had bought my return ticket in Kerikeri for $1400 Cdn dollars and Lou had to pay about $2000 for a ticket purchased in Vancouver for the same trip. That was the difference in price in 1985, but I think this difference has narrowed considerably in recent years.

After staying in Auckland for a day or two, where we purchased a new boat ladder, we made our way to Opua, by bus. It was a pleasant ride in a very modern bus, with a lunch stop in Whangarei. We arrived in Opua in late afternoon, and had time to buy some groceries before hiring a young New Zealand lad to run us out to *Sea Lure*. She was still riding very peacefully on the mooring buoy with the two stout lines in place, which fortunately weren't even twisted around each other. Everything was in order except for one thing. When we had loaded the groceries in Suva I did not take the precaution of dunking the items in salt water and throwing the boxes away, and we had taken on board cockroach eggs that are laid on the glue on the boxes from the stores. So we had cockroaches on board, and these little beggars are very hard to get rid of. I tried spraying them, trapping them and every other trick I could think of, but nothing worked. I carried them as passengers for the next 1.5 years with much consternation, and finally froze them out back in Canada in November 1986 when we had a really cold spell. I turned off all the heat on *Sea Lure* and the freezing temperature killed them all, also destroyed the eggs. Eleven years later, not a single cockroach has appeared, so I'm sure the colder Canadian temperature, even in Vancouver, did the job.

Sea Lure was in good shape, and it didn't take long to put the life raft back in its box, hook it up, and put everything else back in place. The next morning we let the two mooring lines go and went to the Opua dock for fuel and water, and then sailed and powered to the Stone Store up the Kerikeri River. With Lou's help we anchored in my favourite place, in centre channel with two anchors down, one off the bow and one off the stern.

David and Jackie were still at the store and tea room, and Les and Melody on *Sea Song* were also still there. I don't think they had left after following me up the Kerikeri River on 23 November. Or if they did, they quickly went back to this beautiful place with all the friendly people. The next five days were very pleasant indeed. The six of us got together each day, and had dinner each night on a rotation basis, with one couple hosting. These were gourmet dinners that lasted two or three hours, and the last night before we left, David and Jackie had a very nice dinner for about eight people in their tea room. Martyn, who had sailed with us from Suva, was able to make it so we had a great get-together. The next day David and Jackie took a day off from work and we all went to a private beach some 10 or 15 miles away. The farmer was a friend of David's, and we had permission to use his private beach with the fantastic swimming area. We were the only ones there that day, and I will always be indebted to David and Jackie for treating us to such a great day.

Our long range plan was to sail to Auckland, which was a four-day sail if we anchored at night, but before doing that I wanted to sail to Whangaroa, which was about 20 miles north of the Bay of Islands. In order to do all this sailing in windy conditions, we needed some crew people. I had met John and Emma, Californians who were on an extended holiday and had some sailing experience, at Kerikeri before Christmas and they indicated interest in the trip. They were still in Kerikeri, and had bought a very small sailboat in which they had been exploring the Bay of Islands area. They agreed to sell their boat and go with us on *Sea Lure* as far as Auckland and possibly farther. So on 8 February the four of us set out after saying good-bye to our friends in Kerikeri. We powered out the Kerikeri River and then had to sail to Opua, which was out of our way, to retrieve our new ladder. We had inadvertently left the ladder in Auckland, but a kind American family had brought it to Opua. We finally got out of the Bay of Islands about 1400 hours and still had 20 miles to go. Conditions got windy with some rain, and it was far from pleasant. I hadn't been on the ocean for 2.5 months and, with a new crew, things were not going smoothly. It was a long, hard day, but at 1930 hours we arrived at the main harbour in Whangaroa and dropped our anchor in front of the Marlin Hotel.

While we were cooking dinner, I noticed that the anchor was dragging a little, but we were moving parallel to the shore and no yachts were in our way, so I didn't bother checking. By the time we went to bed we had dragged about ¼ of a mile, but still parallel to the shore, and the chart indicated no rocks or reefs. I should have looked into the problem at that time, but I was too tired so went to bed. About an hour later, when John was getting restless, I decided to get up to see how we were doing. To my surprise we had now dragged about ¾ of a mile, so it was high time I took some action before we went aground. With great effort I got the second 40 lb. Danforth anchor out of the storage with 250 ft. of line and took it up to the bow and threw it over. The boat was now dragging so fast that when the anchor dug into the sand the line almost pulled me off the boat. I let out plenty of scope and cleated it. We were not moving now, and I knew this second anchor had set properly, so I went back to bed and had a good sleep. The next morning when we got up, we were a long way from the hotel and the other boats, but we had not dragged. After breakfast we lifted both anchors and very soon found out why we had dragged. When John lowered the main anchor on my orders, I had not gone astern soon enough and the chain had dropped right on top of the anchor before it had a chance to set, causing the chain to wrap around both flukes. It was impossible for the anchor to set in the mud. The Danforth anchor is the best all-round anchor, and has only let me down when I didn't give it half a chance to perform. This was a good lesson and I knew better. However, when a person is tired mistakes do happen more frequently. We powered back to where we were the night before and anchored again, this time properly.

Whangaroa is a very pretty, well-sheltered harbour. The resort town is famous for big game fish and the fishing club is right there. The big game fish is the marlin, and some of them weigh over 600 lbs.

St. Paul Mountain or rock is 212 meters directly behind the village, and after a 20-minute hike it provides a very picturesque view of the area, including the passageway to the harbour from the ocean. We spent three nights and two days anchored here and enjoyed the area very much. The food was good in the Marlin Hotel where we had dinner one night. The weather was very pleasant, and we were sheltered from the wind that comes up most summer afternoons in New Zealand. It also blows all night on occasion.

When we were in Sydney, Australia, I talked to a sailor who had a personal experience with a yacht that had run into a disaster right in this area several years before. The New Zealand yacht was returning to New Zealand, probably from Fiji or Tonga, when they ran into very bad weather that is often present in this area in the summer months. It was a large yacht with a crew of six, and was equipped with a Satellite Navigation system similar to *Sea Lure*. The skipper had some serious boat problem all night, and the Australian was on the ham radio with him most of the night trying to help with the problem. Towards morning, the decision was made to go into Whangaroa in the dark, using the Sat Nav to find the entrance to the pass from the ocean. The entrance is about ¼ mile across and requires serious navigation in the daytime.

It is a mistake to try to make a landfall at night, as I found out later. It is also a mistake to rely on a Sat Nav for a landfall, particularly with the older type Sat Navs that get their position from a satellite passing over at infrequent intervals. In that part of the world the satellites bunch up and you may get two or three fixes in several hours, then nothing for three hours. Unless the satellite has gone over close to the time of landfall the Sat Nav will be in error, and then there is often coastal current that will create a lot of leeway or drift.

In this case the Sat Nav gave the skipper a heading that was about a mile south of the passage entrance. Even though there is a flashing white, red light on a tall beacon on the south side of the entrance, I guess he could not see it in the bad weather. The yacht went up on a reef and four members of the crew did not make it to shore. The skipper and his girlfriend swam and walked to shore and he left her on a rock while he went for help, as I presume she had been injured. When he returned with help she was gone, and it was assumed that a large wave had washed her off the rock and she was also drowned. The skipper was the only one to survive. He lost his yacht and his entire crew. These waters are treacherous in the frequent high winds and mistakes can be costly.

At 0710, 11 February, we lifted the anchor in Whangaroa, powered the 2.5 miles out the pass to the ocean, and set the sails. We were on our way to Auckland. It didn't take us very long to go the 20 miles to the Bay of Islands, but this time we didn't go into the bay, instead keeping on past Cape Brett and along the coast of the North Island. It was surprisingly rough as the winds were 20 to

30 kts in the afternoon and the waves were short and choppy. It reminded me of the Gulf of Georgia back in British Columbia, Canada, when the winds get over 30 kts for an extended period of time. It's hard on the stomach if anyone is inclined to get sick. I was getting accustomed to the ocean again, and the crew was now working out very well. Also, the weather was warm, and late that afternoon we found a protected place behind an island at Whangamumu Harbour. It had been an old whaling station and after dinner we had time to explore around the area with the dinghy before dark. The nights were usually calm and warm, so we all had a good rest before pressing on early the next morning. That day was windier and rougher than the previous day. We made it down past Bream Head, and found a nice bay opposite Marsden Point by the name of Urquharts Bay. This is well up the channel that runs to Whangarei, and I was able to use this anchorage six weeks later, following a dangerous approach into this area after midnight, a few days before heading off to Australia.

The next morning we left our anchorage early, and headed down past Bream Bay, Beam Tail and Cape Rodney, Takatu Point, Maori Rock and finally to Kawau Island. We had been using the engine when the winds were not favourable, but dirt in the fuel caused problems again and the engine stopped running. We were close to shore but had the sails up, so the crew continued to sail while I changed the fuel filter again and primed the engine, then away it went. Had the engine refused to go, it would have been very easy to sail into the harbour where we planned to spend the night and just drop anchor, but this was not necessary. On the inside of Kawau Island is Bon Accord Bay, a very nice sheltered harbour. It is a popular place and a number of other boats were also anchored for the night.

We had a pleasant night in Bon Accord Bay, but the next morning after starting the engine and lifting the anchor the engine stopped again. This time it was not dirty fuel, but fuel starvation. We quickly dropped the anchor again and then went searching for the engine trouble. After much checking and switching to the port fuel tank, as the starboard tank was empty, it was discovered that the fuel shut-off valve on the top of the tank had been turned to the off position inadvertently. As soon as this was corrected, the engine fired up and away we went.

We also discovered later that a large growth of barnacles etc., had accumulated on the bottom of the boat and this caused higher fuel consumption. During the six weeks riding at the buoy while I was away in Canada, the growth had accumulated even more. Part of this problem was caused by not having the bottom painted with a good quality anti-fouling paint before departure from Canada. A very heavy coat of the best anti-fouling paint available should be put on before a voyage such as this, as the growth builds up much more quickly in the warm water. For the return trip I put on two coats of good New Zealand anti-fouling paint, and on the way back it was only necessary to have the bottom under water cleaned with pressure equipment before the last leg from Hawaii to Vancouver – 16 months after the painting had been completed. The buildup of growth on the way down was extreme and had accumulated in only eight months. This shows the difference in the quality of paints and one coat versus two.

Finally, at 0930 hours, we got underway. We had to hurry as we planned to find Half Moon Bay, which is about 12 miles south of the port of Auckland, and tie up at the dock, as this was the place *Sea Lure* would remain on the "hardstand" for a month while we toured New Zealand. We used the engine to increase our boat speed, and had to head out to mid-channel to make the passage down Hauraki Gulf, between Wellington Rocks and Ballons Rock in the Whangapraoa Pass, and finally down the Rangitoto dredged channel keeping Rangitoto Island on our port side. The winds were favourable and the day warm and sunny so we made good time. It was simple down that far as we had good charts, but from there on I had only a photocopy of a small chart taken from a travel book from Canada, and it was not very helpful. We were looking for the channel into Half Moon Bay, but ended up in a channel about two miles south of it. After going up the wrong channel for about 20 minutes and realizing something was not right, we came close to a local sailor who was working on his boat, and he quickly gave us the information we needed. By 1800 hours we were tied to the dock in Bucklands Bay at the upper end of Half Moon Bay, and ready to be lifted out of the water the following day. It was a good time to get docked, as I found out later that the port fuel tank was also almost empty and I had used my five gallons of reserve fuel from the spare container.

The following morning, with a great deal of difficulty due to the strong tidal current in the marina, we moved over to the dock to have our boat lifted out of the water, as per the arrangements we had made several weeks before when passing through Auckland. At that time we had made a special trip out to Bucklands Bay, and made specific arrangements with the booking office for boat bottom clearing and move to the hardstand on Friday 15 February. In our absence, arrangements had been changed arbitrarily and now we had to wait until the following Monday. After considerable fuss on my part, they allocated us to a moorage where the owner was away for the weekend and we tied up there until the following Monday morning. The delay turned out to be a blessing in disguise, as it was necessary to loosen the shrouds and the back stays, so the forestay could be unhooked and swung back to the front of the cabin. Otherwise the boat would not fit on the portable lifter used to lift it out of the water, hold it while the bottom was cleaned, then transport it to the village where all the ocean yachts were located on a hardstand quite close to the lifting area.

Approximately fifty ocean sailing yachts were located on the hardstand. In fact, so many that it was like a village, and one of the most popular places in New Zealand to have boat work carried out. A number of boat repair and painting businesses were located right in the marina to service the ocean yachtees plus the local boat owners. One Canadian kept his large yacht in the marina on the hardstand for six months of the year, and flew down during our winter to sail New Zealand waters and live on board for the other six months. Not a bad idea. I expect his wife was a New Zealander. I never did meet the fellow, but often admired his beautiful 45-foot yacht, which he kept in excellent condition.

Charlie Vaughan and *Bastante* were on the hardstand — he had been there for several weeks or more getting some major modification carried out on his boat. This was the place to do it, as the New Zealand boat builders' skill level is particularly high, their material and labour rates were reasonable, and the American dollar was worth two New Zealand dollars at that time. Also, the Canadian dollar was worth 1.50 New Zealand dollars. There were other yachtees we had met casually also on the hardstand, so there were people to visit and lots to talk about.

For a charge of about $2 NZ per day we had a space on the hardstand, the use of the washroom, a temporary membership to the Bucklands Yacht Club for a few extra dollars, and many other conveniences. The bus stop was close by, but the bus to Auckland did not run often and took about 45 minutes. The Yacht Club was almost new and served very good meals, buffet style, at a reasonable price. There was a large bar area as well as games rooms, reading room etc., and the people were very pleasant and helpful. We went there for dinner often and it was a favourite place for the yachtees to get together.

After we tied up in the slip allocated to us for the weekend, I went to the store to buy some items and on my way back I saw John and Emma helping my wife, Lou, up out of the water beside the boat. As I mentioned before, the current was very strong in the marina area, and the boat had not been tied close enough to the dock. She had attempted to pull the boat in closer, but the current was so strong it flipped her into the water. On the way down she had bashed her elbow on the dock. She is a strong swimmer, but it is difficult to climb back on the dock, particularly with an injured arm, so John and Emma came to the rescue. After she changed into dry clothing I took her to the doctor's office that was also in the complex, in a small shopping centre just across the road from the marina. An X-ray confirmed that nothing was broken but the arm was badly bruised. We had planned to travel the North and South Islands for several weeks, so it was fortunate the injury was not more serious and that she was able to travel three or four days later. John and Emma decided that they had enough sailing and would proceed on their travels by air, etc., so they bade us farewell and had a friend pick them up at the marina. No going-away party this time, as they had only sailed for five days on *Sea Lure*. We spent the weekend quietly, as the weather was wet and it was a good time to recuperate.

At 0645 hours on Monday we went around to the lift area. The two large belts were placed under *Sea Lure* and she was lifted out of the water. The bottom was a real mess with more barnacles than one could count, and the two cleaning operators had to use scraping boards before the high-power pressure washer could be used to finish the job. There was an extra charge for this service, but I had no objections as it was a difficult job. It would have been much easier if I had used good anti-fouling paint in the first place. After the cleaning was completed, the operators moved *Sea Lure* on the mobile lifter to a clear spot on the hardstand. The boat was now about 12 feet from the ground and it was necessary to borrow a ladder to get up onto it, so the first order of business was to construct a ladder. Fortunately I carried 2 x 4 and 2 x 6 pieces of lumber long enough to build a ladder, and also a power saw which ran after I fired up the generator on the boat. I also carried spike nails etc., so the rest of the day was spent building the ladder from the resources on the boat, and late that afternoon I returned the borrowed ladder. We quickly settled into living on board on the hardstand and it wasn't really a hardship at all. We didn't have shore power so we had to use the batteries sparingly and then charge them with the Yamaha generator. We made many trips to the central bathroom at all hours – that ladder sure came in handy!

After a few days of studying travel brochures that we had picked up in downtown Auckland on our several trips there, we decided to buy two travel passes for two weeks that would be good on the New Zealand trains, buses and ferry between the North and South Islands. Several days later we set out from Auckland by bus.

"The first humans to reach New Zealand were Polynesian Maoris from Tahiti or Rarotonga about 900 A.D. One still hears the story of the legendary arrival of the Great Fleet of Migration in 1350 A.D. but this is now considered pure legend without any archeological support. Life in New Zealand was more difficult than that in the tropics and the Maoris evolved a more vigorous aggressive, energetic way of life. Large houses were built of timber and the huge *totara* and *kauri* logs permitted the carving of giant single canoes. Fortified villages called *pa* were created with elaborate defensive systems. Warfare and cannibalism were rife."[7]

"After Captain Cook made New Zealand known to the world in 1768, man's voracious assault on the environment which began with the *moa* hunters moved into high gear. First came the seal hunters (1790 - 1820), followed by whalers (1800 - 1840), each pursuing their prey to the verge of extinction. The *kauri* forests of the northern half of the North Island were cut clean and the insatiable exploitation continued by digging into the very ground in search of *kauri* gum. There was a rush to obtain choice land for farming after New Zealand came under full British rule in 1840. The mid-nineteenth century saw a series of Maori uprisings on the North Island to protest the forced sale of their lands."[8]

"In a land area larger than Britain, there are only three

---

[7] *South Pacific Handbook*, second edition, 1982, p. 509
[8] *South Pacific Handbook*, second edition, 1982, p. 510

million people. New Zealanders pride themselves on the fact that there has never been any official racism in their country, except against the Chinese. Maoris are accepted everywhere and given equal or better opportunities than whites. What isn't as evident is that the Maoris were only given the opportunity to adopt the white man's civilization after their own had been destroyed."[9]

It is true that there is no or very little racism that is so evident in Canada and Australia, but my theory is that the Maori were more warlike and demanded equal rights, and a lot of Englishmen were killed before they accomplished this end result. One of the chiefs on the North Island was very warlike, and after he obtained the muzzle-loader rifles he attacked other tribes as well as the white man. Also, Maori did not trust the missionaries and some of them were killed.

The first part of our sight-seeing trip on the North Island was by bus from Auckland to Rotorua. The buses are modern, clean and well maintained, and travelling on them is pleasant. Smoking was not permitted even in 1985, and this suited us just fine as we are non-smokers. Rotorua is approximately 150 miles southeast of Auckland and is known as a thermal region. There is a strong sulphur smell in the air, and most of the motels have swimming pools heated by the warm water flowing up from the earth. Steam and water erupts from the earth in a number of places in town. A person adjusts to the smell of the sulphur springs quickly, and it is then not objectionable. We found a nice motel and planned to stay only two days, but liked the area so well we stayed an extra day. Rotorua is a town of about two or three thousand people. It is well kept and the people are friendly. The second day we took a bus tour to the Waitomo Caves to see the glow worms. This is spectacular as groups of tourists are taken by boat into the cave where it is dark, and thousands of worms glow from the ceiling of the cave only about eight feet above the heads of the people. I had seen glow worms before but never such an outstanding display.

Late that afternoon we went back to Rotorua and our motel, and that evening we went out for dinner at the Geyser Springs Hotel. This particular hotel is a short distance out of the town, and geysers of hot water shoot out of the ground in a number of places directly in front of the hotel. We went to the dining room and were

---

[9] *South Pacific Handbook*, second edition, 1982, p. 510

advised that all the tables were full, but just to wait in the lobby for 20 minutes and a table would then be ready. They brought us a menu and after studying it, we decided to order a rack of lamb for two as this hotel was famous for this dish. In 20 minutes the waiter came to get us in the lobby and seated us at a nice table for two. After we had an appetizer, our rack of lamb, which had been put in the oven to roast after we ordered, was served with great style. The lamb was carved at the table, served with all the extras, and was absolutely delicious; the best I have ever eaten or ever expect to eat, and with a bottle of good red wine it was a most memorable meal. When the lamb was brought from the kitchen on the platter I counted four waiters and waitresses serving the meal and looking after all the details. The occasion was so special we had a photograph taken by the professional photographer who was present at the hotel, but unfortunately it has been misplaced. I do not recall the price of the meal, but it was reasonable.

The following night we went back to the same hotel for dinner, but ordered something else on the menu. It was good, but not up to the standard of the previous night. I suppose everything was just right for a special occasion the night before, and having to wait for the lamb whetted our appetites even more. Without a doubt, it will always be remembered as one of the most outstanding restaurant meals we have ever eaten. We have given the name of this hotel to many of our friends and acquaintances who were going to New Zealand, and I hope they enjoyed it as much as we did.

After the third night in Rotorua we took the bus to Wellington, the capital of New Zealand. It is known as the windiest city in the world and I can believe it. It reminded me of Winnipeg, Manitoba, Canada, but with even more wind. Wellington is at the southern tip of the North Island, and I suppose the wind funnels through Cook Strait, which is between the North and South Island and runs in a southeast-northwest direction, the same direction as the trade winds on many days of the year. Extremely high winds, up to hurricane force, are known to blow in this area, and a very serious accident happened with the large ferryboat that runs between the North and South Island. The ferry should not have been operating, or perhaps the weather forecasting had not been accurate, and the ferry was caught in extremely high winds when entering the Wellington harbour. The captain lost control of the ferry and the wind sent it aground in the harbour, with disastrous results. The ferry must have broken up as 10 - 20 passengers drowned trying to get to shore. I believe this accident happened around 1980.

Wellington is a large seaport, with most of the problems of this type of place. Accommodation was not that easy to find, but we eventually found a fairly good place in the downtown area at a reasonable price. We spent two nights there before going to the South Island and one night on our return trip.

There are a number of interesting things to see in Wellington – this includes the Parliament buildings and the cable car up to the botanical gardens from Lambton Quay. When we were strolling around the gardens I noticed a sign "Chief Meteorology officer." My next ocean passage in *Sea Lure* was to cross the Tasman Sea, supposedly the most dangerous sea in the world due to its shallow depth and high winds, so I was anxious to be armed with the best meteorological weather forecast before setting out on this leg of the voyage. Fortunately for me, the chief was in his office that day, so we managed to have a chat. He was also a sailor and was quite aware of the problems faced by captains of yachts heading for Australia. Before we parted he gave me his card and said, "Call me when you are ready to leave for Australia and I will give you an up-to-date weather forecast." This information turned out to be invaluable about four weeks later.

We also took one of the sight-seeing tours of the city and harbour, partly by bus and partly by sight-seeing boat. We didn't find any outstanding eating places but I'm sure they were available had we done a little more looking.

On the third day about noon we took a taxi to the ferry dock, and using our passes boarded the ferry to Picton on the South Island. It is a 3.5 hour ferry ride from Wellington to Picton and a very pleasant one at that. The ferry is similar to the ferry vessels we have in British Columbia, and well equipped with dining room and snack bar. The weather was good, the winds not over 20 kts, and we arrived in Picton late in the afternoon. Picton is a small town with nothing particularly interesting to see, although the locals might dispute that statement, so we found motel accommodation for the night.

Our plan for the next 10 days was to see as much of the South Island as possible, leaving enough time to go to New Plymouth, on the way back to Auckland, to visit an old friend and also a ham radio operator on the DDD net, who operated the New Zealand end of the Canadian ham net. In order to do all this in so short a time, we decided to take the train from Picton to Invercargill, the southernmost town on the South Island, and then work our way back, stopping to see the most interesting places as we went. It is an all-day train ride between these two towns and the train moves along very well with only short stops in the main centres. The trains are also quite modern, well equipped with a dining car and comfortable seats, and of course our passes were also good on the train. Stops along the way included Kaikoura, Christchurch, Timaru, Oamaru, Dunedin and finally Invercargill. By this time it was after 6 p.m., but accommodation was not hard to find as it is a quiet little town, but very pleasant.

I believe we spent two nights in Invercargill and then took the bus to Te Anau, a resort area and the closest major centre to Milford Sound, an area we had decided to visit. When we arrived we went to the tourist information centre, which is the central booking office in most cities, and were informed that there was no accommodation left in Te Anau. It was a holiday weekend, and the tourists and New Zealanders flock to this area in large numbers. We accepted this information with "a grain of salt" and went looking on our own and inside of 20 minutes had found a comfortable room in a new motel in town. Milford Sound is about a two-hour bus ride from Te Anau, but it was necessary to book and pay for the bus and boat ride in Te Anau as it was done on a reservation basis only, to make sure the buses and boats could accommodate everyone. At dinner that night, we met a very friendly New Zealand couple from the North Island, who were also sight-seeing and going to Milford Sound the next morning. We travelled on the bus with them up and back, a total of about four hours, but they were booked on a different sight-seeing boat. However, after getting back to Te Anau that night we had dinner together and had a very agreeable time with them. The New Zealand people are more hospitable and genuinely friendlier than our Canadian prairie people, and this is quite an accomplishment. It seems that they are all from the farm or were living on farms one generation back, and they still have that small town/farm attitude. This couple was determined that we would visit them on the way back to Auckland, but this was not possible as time was limited and Lou had a return airline ticket back to Canada on a specific date.

Milford Sound is a very pretty area, similar to a Norwegian fjord, which runs about 15 or 20 miles and opens out on the ocean on the west side of the South Island. It has many spectacular waterfalls and sheer rock up to at least 1000 feet on both sides of the channel. The sight-seeing trip on the boat with about 200 people on board lasted about two hours, and lunch was served during this time. The weather can be nasty in this sound, but this particular day was sunny and warm and couldn't have been better. It was great picture-taking time, so we took quite a few. Our newfound friends were on the boat *Milford Haven* and I don't recall the name of our boat – it was a smaller one, as we had booked late and had to take what was left. This is really the most spectacular part of New Zealand from the point of view of breath-taking scenery. It was similar, in many respects, to the scenery in western Canada and Princess Louisa Inlet in British Columbia. The boat tour was carried out very professionally, with a description of each of the areas plus some of its history. Some of the ocean-going cruise liners go into Milford Sound for an hour or two before proceeding to Hobart, Tasmania or up the coast of New Zealand. After the two-hour bus ride back to Te Anau, over gravel roads part of the way, with stops at scenic places, we were ready for a hearty dinner and enjoyed it very much. This time we didn't have rack of lamb, but whatever it was it was well prepared.

The following day we carried on by bus to another resort area, about a two-hour bus ride, but in the opposite direction and this took us to Queenstown, a fully developed resort and recreation town of considerable size. It has a large lake system, and mountains in the background that are used for skiing in the winter months. It was very busy with tourists when we were there, and if they do as much ski business in the winter, then it is an all year around resort. We had some difficulty finding accommodation but a little perseverance paid off. The town is quite different from Te Anau, but is well maintained and a very pretty area with nice gardens, painted buildings and everything at a very high standard.

Our most interesting activity in Queenstown was a cruise on another boat, but this was a very special boat, the T.S.S. *Earnslaw*, also known as the "Lady of the Lake." It was a large steamboat built probably around the turn of the century, and the old steam engine was still functioning just fine. It was probably not the original steam engine, but it was steam nevertheless, and it was housed in a huge engine room. The vessel was over 100 feet long, very beamy, and took at least 200 passengers. The trip on the *Earnslaw* was very well organized, and they took us on about a two-hour cruise through a series of lake systems, along with a running commentary. We could tour the engine room and the bridge, which was above the third deck. Part way through the cruise we docked at a sheep station and watched a demonstration of sheep shearing, and their sheep dogs working a herd of sheep. It was a nice break in the cruise and was most interesting. The bar was open, food could be purchased, and ½ hour before the end of the cruise song sheets were passed to all passengers in the main lounge and a great singsong took place. It was a good way to end such a beautiful day.

While we were on holiday, I had to keep in mind that I needed a new crew of four to go across the Tasman Sea. I had one good possibility for a Watch Captain, an American by the name of Mike whom I had met in Fiji. He was sailing on another yacht and we had discussed the possibilities of going to Australia and he was interested. When I was away in Canada he had left word with Louis from *Drummer* that he was still interested and would probably go. Also a Canadian from Quebec City, by the name of Jacqueline, had contacted me at the Bay of Islands in David's tea room. She had been travelling a short distance by yacht and had some experience but it was very limited. They both knew my schedule and the place and date for the assembling of the crew. I was still two sailors short, and while we were at a street hot dog stand in Queenstown, I had a chat with one of the owners of the stand who indicated an interest in sailing to Australia as his home was a short distance out of Sydney. He was anxious to get back to his home area, as he had been in New Zealand for over a year. Stuart was this chap's name – he did not have any sailing experience, but he had some knowledge of engines and another great asset – a wonderful sense of humour. I gave him the details of my trip and how to find me in Auckland and we carried on with our very delicious hot dogs. I was quite impressed with Stuart's sincerity and wasn't surprised when he flew all the way to Auckland and showed up several days early for our departure. Before leaving Auckland, I had interviewed two Americans who were very experienced sailors and they agreed to go with me. But about a week before I was ready to depart they sent a telegram that they had changed their plans and would not go. I also interviewed another couple with plenty of boat experience and they were interested but Franz on *Cygnus* had also interviewed them, as his paid crew had now departed, and he was taking over the captain's job on his yacht. It turned out they went with *Cygnus* and I don't blame them, as it was a much nicer yacht. I did meet up with them in Sydney again when they arrived after us. This meant that I was still short a sailor, and every time we were around boats, which was often, I kept a sharp lookout for a suitable crewman.

After spending two or three nights in Queenstown, we set out for the North Island as time was getting short and we still wanted to visit New Plymouth. The train schedule did not suit us, so we went by bus to Christchurch. Unfortunately, we did not have enough time to stay over a day in that beautiful city, but pressed on via an overnight bus to Picton, where we caught the ferry the following day and ended up back in Wellington. There, we caught up on our sleep before travelling again. After confirming that our friends were at home, we caught the train in Auckland to New Plymouth.

Ian, whom I mentioned before, was a member of the Canadian DDD net. One night, many months previously, he had been talking to one of our Canadian female ham operators after the normal business of the day had been completed and, of course, at times like this many ham operators are listening in. Bob was still on the boat at that time and was making the daily calls to the DDD net. Ian's conversation got around to cooking chicken and the Canadian operator asked Ian if he had ever used "Shake and Bake." He said "no" and spoke as though he had never heard of it. We had been carrying packages of "Shake and Bake" on *Sea Lure* since leaving Canada, so I had Bob cut into the conversation to tell Ian that I would deliver a package to him in New Plymouth when we were touring New Zealand. This was part of the reason for going to New Plymouth, but also I had an old public school friend who had lived on the farm next to us in Dauphin, Manitoba, that I hadn't seen in years. He had moved to New Zealand some 30 - 40 years earlier, so I decided to visit him and his family.

After three or four hours on the train, we arrived in New Plymouth and got checked in to a motel. The first order of business was to call Ian at a small town just outside of New Plymouth and have him come over to the hotel. He arrived in several hours and I presented him with the "Shake and Bake" that we had been carrying in our suitcase since leaving *Sea Lure*. He was quite surprised, and I think amazed, that we would go to this much trouble to deliver an item such as this to him. I don't know if he ever used it in his cooking but he probably did, as he was a hobby chef. We also spent a very pleasant afternoon and evening with Ian and his friend, who were very hospitable and treated us very well. We also contacted the old school friend from Dauphin, who lived right in New Plymouth, and went over to his house for dinner and had a very nice evening with him and his wife. We were quickly running out of time, so the following day we caught the train in New Plymouth, which took us right to Auckland the same day. One of the outstanding sights in New Plymouth was Mount Egmont, a snow covered peak over 7550 feet high. It is visible for many miles and is a landmark in that part of New Zealand.

We arrived back in Auckland on a Sunday, and had to make our way back to the yacht in Half Moon Bay. We went by bus, but had to transfer to a second bus for the last half of the trip. After waiting for almost an hour for the second bus to come along we finally gave up and caught a taxi. In Auckland bus schedules are not followed very closely, especially on Sundays, as the pace of life is much more relaxed compared to North America.

Sea Lure was in good shape. I had hired Charlie's girlfriend to sand the hull of the boat – the underwater part, and she had completed this job while we were away, so it was all ready now for the two coats of anti-fouling paint.

CHAPTER 9

THE TASMAN SEA

Lou and I had an interesting six weeks in New Zealand, cruising with *Sea Lure* and, after leaving it in Half Moon Bay, travelling the North and South Island. I look back on that time with fond memories. Now she had only a few days left before returning to Canada.

A fresh water engine pump ordered from Canada from Simpson Power in Vancouver had arrived and was ready for installing on the engine. I still had a lot of work to do on the boat before setting sail for Australia, and I was also short one crew member. I decided to run an ad in the local newspaper for a crewman and got several replies. A New Zealander by the name of Dave Barker was selected to fill the last place on the crew. He had done a lot of fishing in New Zealand waters as a commercial fisherman, and had sailed on yachts several times. He turned out to be a very good sailor. I made him a Watch Captain on the new crew and Stuart, the Australian I had met in Queenstown, was his assistant. Mike Broda was the other Watch Captain and Jacqueline was his assistant. They turned out to be a very compatible crew as both Mike and Stuart were comedians at heart, and they both generated a great amount of fun and good humour on the boat. Their comments in the watchkeeper's log were priceless, and I will quote some of them later. The Tasman Sea can be very unforgiving, although it was very kind to us, so it was just as well to have a good sense of humour before departing, as there was considerable apprehension and a lot of stories about disasters on the Tasman.

I took Lou to the airport on 7 March 1985 for her return flight to Canada. I wouldn't see her again until 14 June after we anchored in Lautoka, Fiji where she met us after flying from Canada to Nandi, Fiji.

We now had only two weeks to paint the bottom of the boat twice, install the new fresh water pump, have the boat name painted on the bow on both sides by a sign painter, and do another two dozen jobs, in addition to getting my crew together. I also wanted to do overnight sail training to ensure the crew would be okay and to get them familiar with *Sea Lure*, in case we had to cope with a storm shortly after we left New Zealand. During the next week I accomplished a number of repair jobs, also I managed to inflict a deep cut on my index finger caused by an extra sharp fish-cleaning knife. One of the previous crew members had a fetish for sharpening knives, and he made sure all the butcher and similar knives had a razor sharp edge. I was not used to knives as sharp as this on the boat and I should have stopped him. I was cutting a piece of heavy hose for the engine when the knife slipped and cut down on my finger. Fortunately one of the workmen was installing the water pump so he drove me to the hospital. A doctor stopped the bleeding and put in three or four stitches. A bandaged finger was a bit of a handicap, but I had to continue with my projects. Fortunately, Mike and Stuart arrived four or five days before our departure from Auckland and moved on board. They did a lot of work, including painting the underside of the hull twice with anti-fouling paint, cleaning, waxing and buffing the upper part of the hull and cabins.

Sea Lure never looked better when it was lowered into the water at Bucklands Marina. Jacqueline arrived several days after the two men and varnished the bowsprit pulpit a number of times, which also saved me a lot of time. Without the help of the crew I would have been a week behind schedule. The only disadvantage with having this many on board was that the batteries were run down until they were almost flat. Two had to be removed and sent out for charging, so I would have enough battery power to start the engine after the boat was put back in the water, as the engine had not been running for over a month.

Finally on 20 March the mobile power lifter came along at the scheduled time and dropped *Sea Lure* back in the water. I tried the engine immediately and it started quite well. I soon went down to the engine room to see how everything was looking, and found water pouring in from an engine hose that had not been installed properly. This had been some of my handiwork. The hose clamp was put on too tight and it had crimped the metal under the hose. The water had filled the bilge in that short time and would have put the engine under water in another ten minutes, so I caught it just in time. I closed down the engine and shut off the intake valve. Stuart, our trustworthy mechanic, straightened out the pipe and reinstalled the hose, and it worked like a charm. We proceeded to the refueling dock and filled up the two 80-gallon fuel tanks plus the 5-gallon spare can. It was then I found out that the boat had only about two gallons of fuel left in the port tank. *Sea Lure* does not have fuel gauges and it is sometimes a guessing game as to how much is left in the tanks, although I have built up fuel consumption tables. The growth on the bottom had increased the fuel consumption considerably, and this was new information as far as I was concerned. Also, I find that when a boat has been out of the water for a month, a number of problems develop. Seals dry out, pulleys don't get lubrication and a number of other things happen that don't occur when the boat is used frequently. That is the reason I start the engine and run it for 20 minutes twice or three times a month during the winter season. It is important to have the engine temperature come up to normal operating temperature, otherwise a diesel engine will not clear out the sludge that collects around the injectors.

We finally moved to a slip and spent the night completing most last-minute items, but my last crewman, the New Zealand fisherman, had not arrived. The following day we continued the engine work, changed the salt water pump, as we carried a spare on board, and finished a few other items. Still the last crew member had not arrived. I planned to leave about 1600 hours and do an overnight sail out of the Auckland waterways to Great Barrier Island, which was about 55 miles away. From there I planned to sail to Whangarei, power up the 10-mile channel to the town and do the last-minute restocking of the boat, finish the last-minute changes to the sails and then depart for Australia, across the dreaded Tasman Sea. About 1545 Dave showed up with girlfriend in tow. I believe she was trying to talk him into staying in New Zealand, which was his home country, but fortunately for us she was unsuccessful. Finally at about 1630 hours we had the crew on board and were ready to depart. We followed the narrow marked channel out of Half Moon Bay and were making our way to Rengitoto Channel, the main wide channel that comes out of the downtown area of Auckland.

Everything seemed to be under control with Mike, a very experienced ocean sailor, on the helm. I was in the cabin doing some navigation work when I felt the bow of *Sea Lure* lift up. We were doing six kts under power and moving quite fast. I looked up at Mike and saw a look of terror on his face. I immediately ran to the helm and took the wheel, and at the same time I felt the stern of the boat lift up. We had gone over something, most probably a rock. I noticed we were close to a large buoy on our starboard side. I ordered the crew to look in the bilge to see if any water was coming in, and at the same time steered the boat in the direction I hoped was clear of rocks, which was towards mid-channel. In the meantime I had reduced power and the boat speed dropped to about two kts. The crew reported back that no water was coming in, so as soon as the boat was several hundred yards on the other side of the buoy I stopped the engine and Mike volunteered to dive off the boat and check the underside for damage. He was a strong swimmer and the sea conditions were good, so he put on his swimming trunks and dove into the water. He checked the underwater hull from the bow to the stern and reported only some paint off the keel about mid-ships but he could not see any damage. Undoubtedly we had just skied over a large rock. Fortunately *Sea Lure* has a full keel shaped like a large ski, with the draft increasing from the bow to the stern until it reaches 5 feet 3 inches at the stern. This is not much draft for a 40-foot boat and saved us from serious damage that day. Also, the boat is very sturdy with a keel about 10 inches thick, so it could carry this very heavy weight without doing more damage. I was responsible for the accident as I was the skipper, and the skipper is always responsible for everything that happens on his boat. In addition to that, I had not told Mike which side of the buoy to take and he did not ask. I had been having difficulty finding charts for the Auckland area as I suppose that hundreds of ocean sailors had been there before me, and had bought up all the stock. This was at the main supplier for the North Island in downtown Auckland, so as is frequently the case in the South Pacific, ocean sailors have to manage with what they have on board and then use their knowledge of waterways to muddle along. I did not have a chart out of Half Moon Bay, but this is no excuse for having gone on the wrong side of a major channel marker. It had been a difficult day getting away and my concentration on boat business was not as good as normal, as I had not been at sea for about 6 weeks and even a skipper gets rusty. Is that enough excuses?

Everything seemed to be under control now, and I had current charts from there to the Great Barrier Island for the overnight sail. It got dark shortly after this, and there is heavy boat and ship traffic in the Auckland area. It was necessary to change the salt water pump again, as it had been put on backwards and was not circulating the water properly. Mike and Stuart volunteered to change the pump, after I explained the problem, so we closed down the engine and they proceeded with the work. When they were about half finished, I noticed a big ship bearing down on us, about ¾ of a mile away. I've never seen two crewmen work so fast in my life. While I was preparing to get out some flares so we could warn the ship's crew of our location in case they hadn't seen us, I had a call from the engine room, "Start up the engine!" I started the engine immediately, and we got out of the path of the ship. Later I checked the work of the two fellows – they had completed it correctly and well, and we had no more trouble with the salt water pump for the rest of the voyage.

After all these incidents and problems in only the first three hours after coming on board, Dave was wondering what he was getting himself into. He had been a fisherman in the New Zealand area for several years or more, had considerable knowledge of the sea, and had also sailed on sailboats before, so he proceeded to check on me and other members of the crew, and I can't say I blame him. He did it in a friendly manner, but he did get me up in the middle of the night and asked me to take bearings on several distant lighthouses to confirm our position. I was quite happy to do this to put his mind at ease, and I determined that we were right on course and well clear of any danger that the islands and reefs not far away could have caused. The rest of the night was uneventful. At daybreak we were getting close to the Great Barrier Island, and at 0800 hours 22 March 1985 we anchored in Port Fitzroy Harbour. We stayed in that area for a couple of days. When running around in the dinghy we noticed another yacht anchored in the bay next to us, about three miles away, and upon further checking discovered to my pleasure that it was old friend Charlie Vaughan in *Bastante*. During our discussion in Half Moon Bay when we were both on the hardstand, he advised me that he was going out to this island, so I was watching for him. The following day we lifted anchor, moved over to the Bay where Charlie was located, and anchored close to *Bastante*. He had a couple of the crew on board and they were having a relaxing time. I had dinner with them that night and as Charlie had good luck in fishing in the area he gave me enough fish for a dinner for my crew.

Sunday 24 March we lifted the anchor and went in to the

closest port, filled up the water tanks, and then did some practice sailing clear of the harbour. The new crew had not done any sailing to speak of on *Sea Lure*, as we had powered all night out of Auckland, so it was time to familiarize them with the vessel with the engine off. After doing this for several hours we decided to have a photo session. Mike and Jacqueline were both professional photographers, and had some very good photo equipment along. In fact, Mike earned money by writing articles for a sailing magazine in the United States and he supplied photographs with his articles. We lowered the dinghy and they both got in with their equipment. The winds were just right, about 8 kts, so we hoisted all the sails and they proceeded to take over 50 pictures of *Sea Lure* under sail – many of them turned out very well. After about an hour the wind picked up a little and we pulled away from the dinghy with its 5 horsepower engine and they couldn't keep up. We finally furled the sails to reduce our speed to let them catch up, and then brought them on board and hoisted the dinghy up on the davits where I carried it when not on ocean passages.

The decision was made to sail for Whangerei and we set course at 1430 hours, which was rather late in the day to sail over 50 miles. I realized it would be late before we made the distance, but planned to anchor opposite Marsden Point in Urquhart Bay, the same place we had anchored on our way down from the Bay of Islands to Auckland. I had noted then that there were ship lead lights on both sides of the channel, so I reasoned I could use those lights to find our anchorage. It is noted in the watchkeeper's log that at 2200 hours we were among the Hens and Chickens group of islands and had just passed Taranga Island, with still 10 miles to go. It was after 2300 hours when we passed the first lead-in lights, the wind had picked up and it was getting blustery. We had furled the sails and were powering. It was important that we not get outside the lights, as it was shallow and we would probably go aground. It was rather a tricky approach but fortunately no other vessel was using the channel. After several hours of powering up the channel and with all crew watching that we did not shortcut any of the turning points, we finally found our planned anchorage and dropped the hook. By then, it was well after midnight, in fact it was 0200 hours and I was exhausted. On the positive side, I was fast getting my sea legs again and much-needed practice in navigation in the daylight and at night.

After a good sleep and a hearty breakfast, we lifted the anchor and powered up the channel for the ten scenic miles to Whangarei. It is a nice little town with a well-sheltered harbour right in the centre of town, and although I had been through it four times on the bus this was the first time by boat.

Shortly after docking Lou and Sylvia Beaurivage showed up at the boat, and we had a great get-together as I had not seen them since December 1984. They had stayed for a number of months on the hardstand at Opua in the Bay of Islands, where they had their boat engine overhauled. They also did a great amount of work on the rest of the boat, and now the boat was back in the water but still in the Bay of Islands area. They had purchased a car, so we drove down to a pub and had a beer for old times sake. The next time we were to see them was in Tonga on the 26th of July when we arrived from Fiji and anchored in front of the Paradise Hotel. *Drummer* was there well ahead of us. One of the great aspects of ocean sailing is that you keep meeting the same people, and after awhile it is like a large family with a great deal in common.

We now had two days to get ready for our passage out of Whangarei, up around the top of the North Island, and across the Tasman Sea to Sydney, Australia, and there was lots to do. I decided to buy the lines, blocks, pulleys, etc. to install a second reefing line in the main, as I expected very high winds on the Tasman Sea. This took up a better part of half a day with some of the crew helping, then there were the last-minute items to purchase – food, beverages, etc. But the most important thing was to determine when to depart. The weather was bad, and right in the harbour the second night the winds were gusting to 50 kts, also it was raining very hard. I was counting on the chief meteorology officer in Wellington to advise me before making that decision. He was the man I had talked to when we were passing through Wellington a month previously. The morning after the storm I called him and he looked at the weather forecast and said, "Go today. You will have at least four or five days of good sailing weather." So at 1130 hours on 28 March, after clearing customs, we departed for Australia.

By this time all projects were completed, the morale of the crew was high and they were anxious to get going. They had signed up for this passage to Australia, did not plan to continue with me on *Sea Lure,* and wanted get to Sydney as soon as possible. I felt the same way.

By 1430 hours we had powered the ten miles out the channel and set course well clear of Bream Head, and far enough out from shore that there was no danger of going aground in the night, even if the crew got off course. They were instructed to keep a sharp lookout for ships and small boat traffic, and get me up if any traffic came within a mile of *Sea Lure* and they didn't know what action to take. The two Watch Captains were experienced and responsible. Jacqueline was on watch with Mike and Stuart was on watch with Dave. This turned out to be a good arrangement. Mike taught Jacqueline how to steer a course by compass, and after several days of practice she became very good at it. The first night the watchkeepers reported hundreds of dolphins at midnight, but I missed the show as I was sleeping. The met man was correct – the weather was very good with winds in the 10 to 20 kts. range from the southeast. This was fine for reaching but our distance travelled was just slightly over a 100 miles per day as the winds were a little too light. Fishing was very good and we caught three nice tuna the first two days. We had fresh fish for dinner the second night out and kept the rest in the freezer. After catching several more fish we stopped fishing, as the freezer was full and we would only catch what we could eat.

At 2000 hours we had Poor Knights Islands off our starboard beam and at midnight Cape Brett was off our port beam 6.5 miles away. Cape Brett was a landmark for us, as it had been our destination all the way from Fiji, and the coordinates were programmed into the Sat Nav. We had passed very close to it when going from Whangaroa to Auckland, and it is the main navigation point when entering the Bay of Islands. It was almost like an old friend. I missed it this time, as I was asleep. In fact it was the same time the dolphins came to visit, so they may have come out of the Bay. At 1200 hours the next day we were opposite Cape Karikari and at 1840 hours off Cape North, when we set course for Sydney, Australia. The course was 255 Compass with 1243 miles to go based on the *Sea Lure* distance log.

So far the crew was getting along great, just like previous passages, and *Sea Lure* was performing in an exemplary fashion, which was also normal. Even the skipper was settling down and getting back into the ocean sailing routine. This was to be a very pleasant passage and it was mainly due to the humour generated by Stuart and Mike. As they were on opposite watches it meant there were always great jokes and fun 24 hours a day. They did keep their voices down so the opposite watch and I could get sleep when required. I still did not go on watch, as it was a full-time job to maintain the engine and other mechanical equipment, do the navigation, keep the official log, and supervise the overall operation. I did spell off the crew if one was sick or really tired and this did happen from time to time.

At 0624 hours the following morning the Three Kings Islands came in sight. They were some miles off our starboard bow, but they are high and visible from quite a distance. At 1800 hours we were among the whales according to the watchkeeper's log, but I do not recall the incident, or they may have been at some distance and the crew did not give me a call. That evening the ship's clock was retarded one hour so we would be on the same time as Sydney. This does keep daylight and darkness at the normal time of the day and we then had our meals at the regular time. Our stomachs had to make the adjustment, but this did not seem to be a problem for any of the crew.

We had a few line squalls that day and on 2 April we had our first storm. We had been under way for five days and the weather forecaster had been right on the money. The winds were from the northeast and we had gusts to 46 kts. We started our storm watch routine of changing the helmsman every 20 minutes and I went on watch, so we had five crewmen to handle the helm and there was always a second crewman in the cockpit. We had a following sea and it built up to quite a height, but *Sea Lure* performed well in these conditions and was easy to steer. This is the advantage of the full keel and the extra weight. The watchkeepers recorded a tough night, and at noon the following day the Sat Nav indicated we had been blown off course 20 miles to the north. I'm not quite sure what caused this unless it was a steering error resulting from the storm. We were now making good speed and our average day's run over this period was 124 miles. By that evening the storm was over, and everything got back to normal on the boat. The main had developed a seven-foot tear in the seam because it had been left up too long in high winds at night, so we took it down and did some sewing. *Sea Lure* will sail as fast with only the genoa and mizzen. Everyone had a turn at sewing the main, 27 feet in all with two rows double-stitched. When the sewing was complete, we hoisted the main again, as the winds had now dropped to 10 - 15 kts from the east and southeast. The boat speed did not change, as our daily average distance was still the same. By now we had passed the mid-point to Sydney, Australia and so far the Tasman Sea had been kind to us, but there was still another storm in the program before we docked in Sydney.

On 5 April we were about 160 miles directly south of Lord Howe Island, so could not see it. I had purchased a detailed map of this island in case we got into serious trouble and had to head for a refuge for boat repairs etc. Fortunately this did not happen, and we were almost in as good shape as when we had left Whangarei. That night when Stuart and Dave were on watch they got lazy and stopped looking ahead of the boat. Dave undoubtedly knew how to steer the boat while sitting down, which is considered bad practice. They didn't see another yacht approaching from the west, but eventually saw its lights when it was abeam, only about 200 yards away. There could have been a head-on collision if the helmsman on the other yacht had not seen us in the dark. They were probably on autopilot or self-steering with no lookout. This underscores the importance of the Watch Captain and helmsman following the boat rules. This was probably our closest call on the entire voyage; although there were many times we were on a collision course with another vessel and had to alter course to avoid a collision. Needless to say, I was not pleased about this dereliction of duty and the Watch Captain heard about it.

The same day shortly after lunch the winds came up again to storm force and I recorded gusts to 52 kts. The winds were from the northeast and the ocean built up until the waves were 24 feet estimated, and my estimates are usually on the low side. *Sea Lure* was still easy to steer even in these conditions, and the stern always rose up sufficiently so we had very little water in the cockpit. Stuart was on the helm when one of these huge waves came along, and he left the helm and ran into the cabin and closed the door. He thought the wave would swamp the boat. We yelled to him to get back on the helm and not to worry so much. I don't think *Sea Lure* even missed him! It was a rough night – it was blowing and raining. The following morning the winds subsided, and it was a beautiful day for sailing. This was 6 April and we were progressing towards Sydney at a good speed. That morning we caught another fish and it was on the menu for dinner.

The following day, 7 April, was the skipper's birthday. The official log records the event but notes that "age is unknown." It was another great day of sailing and we caught two more fish. Jacqueline very kindly baked a birthday cake for the skipper, but unfortunately that miserable stove never did work right and one end of the cake was burnt. The stove has since been replaced but for the entire trip we had to contend with a very temperamental oven. However, most of the cake was okay and we devoured it with gusto at the end of the dinner. All in all, it was a very good day for my 61st year and we also managed to sail 128 miles, making it complete.

This was day 10 since our departure from Whangerei, and Sydney was getting close. One of the problems I had to consider now was that I had been unable to purchase a chart in New Zealand for the entrance through the Heads going into Sydney Harbour. The best I could do was borrow a chart from a yachtee in Half Moon Bay and have it photocopied. They had just the letter size photocopier so we had to do the chart in about eight sections, then put it on the floor and staple the pieces together. It did not turn out very well, but it was better than no chart. Also, I was able to purchase an old chart from an Australian yachtee that showed a plan view of the coastline in the area of the Heads, but it wasn't much help. With the Sat Nav and the radio direction finder, I knew I could find the opening in the shoreline, and then after that we had to manage with our patchwork chart.

On 8 April the winds dropped a little, so to maintain boat speed we used the engine for some hours. The crew sighted a whale, or it may have been an Australian submarine, as we saw one operating in the area later. Only one ship was sighted and it soon disappeared. The winds had dropped to about six kts, so we ended up powering the rest of the way. That night we drifted to port about 15 miles due to the ocean current that flows south along the east coast of Australia. At 0600 we altered course 25 degrees to starboard onto a heading of 280C and at 1057 hours Sydney was sighted. We were out in the direction of the Sydney airport, and my radio direction finder picked up the aircraft radio beacon. This gave us a fix and confirmed the position the Sat Nav was giving, so we powered in directly to the Heads. I called the Sydney radio on the VHF and asked for instructions for customs clearance. They told us to anchor in Watsons Bay. A customs vessel would come alongside and the personnel would give us a preliminary clearance to enter Australia – this happened within 1.5 hours. We lifted the anchor and then powered to the Cruising Yacht Club in Rushcutters Bay with directions from the customs officials, as our chart was sufficient to get us there. At 1700 hours we were tied up at the yacht club where space had been reserved for us in advance. The time on the passage from Whangarei, New Zealand to Sydney was 12 days 3 hours. The distance was 1442 nautical miles which worked out to about 119 miles per day, considerably over our average.

The Tasman Sea had treated us very well indeed, even though we had winds to 52 kts, and *Sea Lure* as usual had performed so well in the huge following sea. The humour contributed by Mike and Stuart, and the good work by the entire crew probably made it the most fun passage and not too long. The following humorous comments from the watchkeeper's log were contributed mostly by Mike and Stuart: "Sneaking across the Tasman," "Whatsfur breakfast," "Not french toast," "I'm sick of tuna," "What about rabbit," "The ocean is a desert," "Sydney express," "I want a refund!" "Rocking down to Sydney town," "Seeing the world at 5 mph with Sea Lure tours," "Booking with Ray Archer," and "Tuna disguised as salmon."

CHAPTER 10

THE LAND OF OZ

The Cruising Yacht Club is the second largest and most prestigious club after the Royal Sydney Yacht Club in Australia. It sponsors the Sydney to Hobart Yacht race that starts each year on New Year's Day; a very famous yacht race in which Canadian yachts have taken part from time to time. The conditions are often very bad and in some years, a few of the boats do not complete the race and have been known to break up as a result of the high winds and waves.

They had just completed a new addition to the club, with very nice bar areas, dining rooms, games rooms, etc., all at a very high standard. Docking there was free for the first week and after that, if we rafted next to another yacht, it was very reasonable. We couldn't use shore power, as the two systems are not compatible and I did not have a converter. This was not a problem as we did enough cruising and sailing in the Sydney harbour to keep the batteries charged.

We had a crew party in the Yacht Club that night, and we also had dinner in the club – a change of fare after eating on the yacht for 12 days. It was a great party with lots of good humour and kidding. Mike stayed on the boat for most of the five weeks I remained in Australia. Stuart left the boat the following day, as his folks lived close to Sydney and he hadn't seen them for several years. Dave and Jacqueline stayed on board for several days, then they left. None of the crew had planned to go beyond Sydney, so I needed a new crew for the next passage to New Caledonia on the way back to Canada.

One of the first orders of business was to write a card to my meteorology friend back in Wellington, New Zealand to let him know that we had arrived all right, what kind of weather we had encountered, and to thank him for his very accurate forecasting. I managed to get this away in the first few days. I also had to report to customs for my final clearance, but didn't get around to it until a day later and was questioned by the customs official on the delay. Australia has the most antiquated system for customs clearance of any of the countries we visited on the voyage. The initial clearance in Watsons Bay is miles from downtown, and not a convenient place for anyone. Their customs office should be in the harbour, which is the case in most countries, but it is a half-hour ride on a bus or train from the harbour area. With a vessel such as mine I had to post a bond. Finally, I had to call my bank manager back in Vancouver at my expense and dictate a telegram to him over the phone. He sent the telegram to customs in Sydney, also at my expense. The problem they don't consider is the control of the crew members leaving a boat and staying in their country. This is a much more important issue since they complain about illegal immigrants. All the crew had to have visas in addition to our passports, and many other obstacles were placed in our way. One of the Canadian yachtees was so infuriated with the country in general and the many roadblocks placed in his way, that he stated that Australia is a third-rate country. I'm inclined to agree with him.

Sydney is a very large city by Canadian standards – it is like Toronto and Montreal combined. Traffic is very congested in the downtown area, but the transportation systems are quite good. The subway system reminds me of the subway in London, England. It is fast and covers the main city and suburb areas very well. The buses ran frequently and seemed to be mostly on time. I carried an American Express gold card and as they provide a service of holding mail for travellers, I normally gave the American Express address in the countries I visited. Soon after arriving in a country I would make a trip to their office, pick up the mail and draw some money. In Sydney, the American Express office was downtown so I would catch a bus close to Rushcutters Bay and it would take me downtown in about 25 minutes. Needless to say, I made quite a few trips to their office during the five weeks, and they did provide me with good service mailwise. I did find, though, that the Visa credit card company provided better service when it came to obtaining money than American Express, and their annual charge is considerably less.

The yachtees, as usual, were friendly and we would get together on our yachts, or more often before dinner in the bar area of the Yacht Club, and the parties would go on for many hours. For meals we had a choice of the main dining room or the sandwich bar right in the same area. The Australians are generally friendly but they are quite different from the New Zealanders.

Sailing in the Sydney Harbour area can be pleasant with good winds, but on weekends the water is congested with boats of all types and it can get positively dangerous. One Sunday I took out a group of friends on *Sea Lure*, including Robb, the Australian who crewed for me as far as New Caledonia, along with one of his friends and his wife. They owned a large sailboat. The weather and the visibility were poor along with lots of wind. We had a fine day of sailing and went out into the ocean for several hours through the Heads. The weather deteriorated, and I made the mistake of turning over the operation of the boat to the two supposedly experienced Australians. They got *Sea Lure* going over 6 kts under sail and were not keeping a proper lookout ahead. A large power cruiser pulled right in front of us, which he should not have done as we had the right of way. However, right of way or not, it is incumbent on both skippers to try to avoid a collision. The cruiser was not more than 100 feet in front of us, and we would have definitely rammed him had I not run forward and motioned to the cruiser skipper to go reverse. He did so in just the nick of time, as we sailed across his bow at full speed and only missed him by feet. Needless to say, I took over control of the vessel for the remainder of the afternoon, and the two Australians were relegated to passengers. The rest of the day went smoothly, but the visibility was down to about 50 yards before we went in to dock, and there were still boats in all directions. It reminded me of the sail-past at our yacht club in Vancouver when things get really mixed up. I'm sure a number of boats are damaged in the Sydney Harbour each weekend when the visibility is poor. Otherwise it was a delightful day, as the guests brought a great spread of food for lunch, after which we went into the yacht club for refreshments.

Several weeks after I arrived in Sydney, our youngest daughter, Coleen, made the 16-hour flight from Vancouver and visited me. She was in the travel business at that time and getting a ticket at a discount was no problem for her. I met her at the airport, which was about 20 miles from *Sea Lure*, and we made our way by bus and subway to Rushcutters Bay. I hadn't seen her since January and it was quite a get-together. She was in Sydney for about 10 days and stayed on the boat. We went sight-seeing a number of times, and on an extended tour of the Sydney Opera House. It is a unique structure and rated one of the best in the world. The history of its construction and the immense size of the building are most interesting. It took an hour for the guided tour, for which there was a charge of about $5 per person, but it was well worth it. The Japanese Philharmonic Orchestra was practicing for a concert at the same time, and the number they were playing was "Waltzing Matilda." How appropriate! We also took the ferry across the harbour to visit the Sydney Zoo – a very large, outstanding zoo. It has almost all the wild animals imaginable, which are all contained in permanent buildings made of concrete blocks or brick and mortar. The animals are very well cared for and have lots of space so it is quite humane. We spent many hours at the zoo and of course saw the koalas. Coleen met a number of Australian people about her own age and was invited out to parties with them. They took her swimming, surfing, dancing at clubs, etc., so she enjoyed her short stay very much.

I met a member of the Cruising Yacht Club who had a large sailboat moored in the same area. He was one of the nicest Australians I have met. During the Second World War he was aircrew stationed in England and served with a Canadian Bomber Squadron. I believe he was a navigator pilot. He got to know Canadians very well, and had a great liking and affinity towards them. He soon found out that I was a retired Wing Commander from the Royal Canadian Air Force, which he found fascinating, and insisted on calling me "Wing Co" rather than by my first name. During the war a Wing Commander was a very high rank in the eyes of all twenty-some year old Flying Officers. He commanded the Wing of bombers and very often led the squadrons on the most dangerous and difficult bombing missions. Wing Commanders enjoyed a great amount of prestige, no doubt earning it the hard way, as many of them did not survive.

This Australian and I became very good friends. He was a pilot and owned an insurance company in which he was now semi-active. He was an avid photographer, and did aerial photography on a contract basis for engineering companies. At that time his contract was to research the traffic volume in one area of Sydney, and in the late afternoon he took pictures of the traffic in certain streets with his professional camera. He had owned an aircraft with three of his friends but they had sold it, so he now rented an aircraft for these picture-taking sessions. He knew that I had been a pilot and had flown in many of the Canadian Air Force jet aircraft before retirement in 1975, so he invited me to go with him on one of his picture-taking flights. He picked me up from *Sea Lure* on the appointed day, and we drove out to the airport in his car. He rented a Cessna 180 with a special bracket outside the window on the pilot's side so he could mount his camera for the photographing of the traffic flow. After takeoff, it was obvious that he was a very competent pilot so he took me on a sight-seeing flight of the greater Sydney area plus all the small towns on the outer limits of Sydney. I was quite surprised at the size of the city, and the fact that we had to be cleared by air traffic control before we passed from one part of the city to another. There is so much air traffic over the city it is necessary to have positive control of all aircraft in order to maintain air safety. We spent about an hour sight-seeing, and then it was time for the photographs of the applicable arteries of the city. My friend opened the window on the pilot's side and mounted his camera on the bracket. After he got the aircraft into the right location, I did the flying and he took the pictures. After that we went back to land and by then our flight had lasted about 1.5 hours. It was a very pleasant flight and one that I seldom experienced during our trips.

The same chap took Coleen and me and several of his other friends on a Sunday cruise in the Sydney Harbour on his yacht. After stocking his boat with a fantastic lunch and plenty to drink, we went out sailing for several hours and then anchored in his favourite spot in Manly Cove, which is in North Harbour about 1.5 miles north of the Heads. It is a good anchorage used by only a few boats. It was such a beautiful day with just enough winds for sailing, quite unlike the day we had gone sailing in the same harbour in *Sea Lure*. My friend was just as professional on his yacht as he was in the aircraft, and it was a real pleasure to sail with him. In the afternoon after lunch we sailed for several more hours. It was quite a day, and Coleen enjoyed herself immensely. He had permanent moorage in the Cruising Yacht Club, as that was his home port. He obviously had done very well in his insurance business, which he started in 1945 after returning from the war. This was 41 years later and he was now reaping the rewards of his many years of hard work. He and his wife came on board *Sea Lure* several times for drinks and we saw each other frequently right up to the last few days before I left Australia for New Caledonia.

Pat and the late Sebbie Collins from Botany Bay, a town just south of Sydney, were friends that we met in Vancouver. Their daughter and son-in-law live in North Vancouver not far from our house and that of our mutual friends Holly Martin and the late Bill Martin. Pat and Bill were great Rotarians and became good friends. They had sailed with me on *Sea Lure* in Vancouver so I had promised to call Pat when I reached Sydney on my voyage. This I did after several weeks at Rushcutters Bay, and they invited me to go to their place and spend a few days. It was a one-hour ride on the subway to get to their area. He has a very nice home on the water in the Botany Bay area, having lived there for a long time. They have a small cabin cruiser tied up at a dock at the end of the property. Pat is the past president of the Saint George Yacht Club and is still very active in the sail racing program. He races on small sailboats with a crew of three. Even though he is in his late 80's, he is still racing, but not as competitively as usual. We had a very nice dinner that night.

The following day was Anzac Day; the day the Australians celebrate all the wars that they have fought in. They are great fighters and got involved in most large wars in the past century, and have a proud record. In addition to the parades and ceremonies honouring the men and women lost in the wars, there are activities such as sail races, etc., and in the afternoon gambling games are considered legal for that day only. At least that was the law in 1985. We went to the Yacht Club for the day and had a great time. Pat, his oldest son and two crewmen were in the sailboat race. The winds were about 20 to 25 kts and they were leading in the race when the mast broke and they capsized. This is apparently a normal kind of mishap in this type of racing and the Australians just take it in their stride. The racing lasted about four hours. In the meantime, Pat's other son, Brian, entertained me in the club and we did watch the racing part of the time, but the boats were out of sight for long stretches.

After lunch the gambling was going great downstairs with many people taking part. In addition, the club also had a room with slot machines, which were well patronized this day. When the sail race was over Pat and his other son came up to the club, and we had more celebrating. Then after all that, Pat took me home for dinner. After dinner, Pat showed slides of their many trips in Australia. I had considerable trouble keeping my eyes open after such an active day. Besides, I wasn't used to such celebrating. All in all, it was a very happy time, and the following day Pat drove me to the train station and I took the subway and bus back to

Rushcutters Bay and *Sea Lure*. The boat was fine as Mike was still living on board – he had a large party with his friends during my absence but the boat was none the worse for wear. The other yachtees on the dock filled me in on the details.

In New Zealand you seldom hear of sharks, but they are a problem in Australian waters. Shark nets are put up in swimming areas and shark attacks are common, usually with fatal results. There are lots of sharks right in the Sydney Harbour, and I have read of long distance swimmers swimming across the Sydney Harbour in a cage dragged along by a boat, so the sharks cannot attack them. There are many poisonous snakes and other dangerous reptiles in Australia. I can see why the English chose it as a penal colony area when their jails in England were overflowing with convicts a long time ago.

Unfortunately, I did not have the opportunity to travel out of the city very far, so did not see other parts of Australia. I did meet yachtees from some of the other cities along the coast, such as Melbourne, and they were party types. I was invited several times to one yacht for champagne breakfast, but I cannot tolerate champagne so early in the morning so I did not accept.

Around this time an Australian ocean-going yacht came into the harbour and tied up alongside of *Sea Lure*. I was already rafted against another yacht, so they were third out. During the first night they had a large party on board with just the crew. I was trying to sleep in the aft cabin, but the noise was too much so I got up and was standing in the cockpit behind the helm listening to the loud noises next door. Suddenly one of the crewmen from the Australian boat bolted across his deck and through *Sea Lure*'s cockpit, nearly knocking me down. The skipper of the Australian yacht was threatening to kill the escaping crewman. This is sort of typical of the Australian seamen when they have had too much to drink. The next day they were all very sheepish and the skipper came over to apologize to me.

Carol and Doddie, who had crewed for me from Tonga to Fiji and one of them to New Zealand, live in Sydney. They came down to the boat where we had a get-together. They also held a dinner party for two other ocean-going skippers and me, plus some of their other friends. The other two skippers were single-handing around the world each in his own boat – they were extremely competent sailors. One was from France and the other from Spain or Italy. We had a very pleasant time and after dinner made a taped recording for Bob Dormer and sent it to his home in Barrington Passage, Nova Scotia.

Several weeks after our arrival in Sydney, some of our yachtee friends started to arrive from New Zealand. Charlie Prendergast on his catamaran arrived first and tied up in the same yacht club for a few days, but then anchored out in the bay. He and his crew were quite short of money by this time, and Charlie decided to set up a painting contracting company to earn some cash. He bought an old car and with some of the crew proceeded to get some painting contracts. This seemed to work out very well, and I would see him from time to time at the Yacht Club. I presume that when they had made enough money, he sold the car and then proceeded on his round-the-world voyage. His next destination was the Indonesia area and as pirates were still known to cruise the water, he was concerned about finding the best route to take. He was such a resourceful fellow that I'm sure he found a way and within a year completed his circumnavigation of the world. He was a good friend and we had many happy times together, although our spread in age was quite large. Charlie and his girlfriend attended our farewell party at the Cruising Yacht Club the night before our departure for New Caledonia, but I have not heard from him since. Unfortunately some of the addresses, etc. disappeared after we went through very severe weather conditions on the next passage and were almost rolled over by a monstrous wave.

About two weeks before our departure Franz McVay on the Swan 65 *Cygnus* arrived from New Zealand. I had seen Franz in Auckland while walking down the street, and knew they were planning to go to Australia. Also, I had interviewed the crew people in Half Moon Bay who were interested in going to Australia on a yacht, and they finally went with Franz. They had a rather difficult time crossing the Tasman Sea and had to heave-to for two days during a severe storm. For *Cygnus* to have to heave-to was quite extraordinary, as he had a large crew that would normally keep the boat sailing, but perhaps the wind was on the nose, which would make it impossible to continue sailing when the winds exceeded 70 kts per hour. Franz's paid crew left him in New Zealand, and Franz was skippering the boat himself. He had some very bad luck shortly after arriving at the Cruising Yacht Club. He was anchored out not far from the club because there was no space for his large boat at the dock, and an Australian yachtee ran into the side of *Cygnus* and did extensive damage to the hull. I went out for dinner with Franz and his girlfriend and some other people, and just that day Franz had bought around-the-world airline tickets, as he was so fed up with all his boating problems. Several days later he left on the flight, which was to take six weeks or more, and he left the couple I had interviewed in New Zealand on board *Cygnus*. They had free accommodation while the hull was being repaired. This ended a long and happy association with Franz and his crew of *Cygnus*, as we had been following each other around since August 1984.

After three weeks in Sydney, I had to start thinking about gathering together a new crew. As I mentioned before, my previous crew all dropped off in Sydney as they had planned. Louis, a retired airline pilot, had approached me in Vancouver before I departed on the voyage, about crewing on the return trip. At that time I had thought it would be from Tahiti but my plans had changed. Louis agreed to sail from Australia. He was able to arrange a pass on one of the airlines so it was not too expensive for him. He arrived about a week before I planned to leave for New Caledonia, and brought a new main heat exchanger for the boat engine. The old heat exchanger had corroded and was letting salt water into the fresh water radiator. This was discovered when checking the antifreeze level. Instead of it going down a little as is normal, the level was coming up, so I had another problem. Corrosion in all parts of the boat is common for ocean sailors, and it seems to work faster in the warmer temperatures experienced in the South Pacific. This problem had first appeared in New Zealand and I had disconnected all the hoses, drained the block and taken the heat exchanger off and down to a radiator shop. By testing it in the tank they were able to determine which lines in the cooler were leaking so they then plugged the leaky ones. This worked as far as Australia, but again the fluid level in the main radiator started to go up as more lines had sprung a leak, so it was time to install a new heat exchanger. The part, which is quite large and heavy, was available in Vancouver at Simpson Power so Louis brought it in his baggage. Apparently customs in Sydney gave him a hard time as he was bringing in a part they thought I should have bought in their country. Unfortunately, the Australian parts for the same engine are not compatible with the Canadian parts even when the part numbers are the same. Eventually Louis convinced them that the part was for *Sea Lure*, a Canadian boat, and that he was not smuggling. I installed the new heat exchanger and it worked just fine from then on and is still working to this day. We did have trouble with the transmission fluid cooler later during the voyage.

I put a notice on the Yacht Club bulletin board for crew and had a call from an American couple. James Bond, that is his real name, and Patty had been in Australia for some time while he had coached the Australian lacrosse team. The game of lacrosse was invented by the North American Indians and is played in Canada. I was quite surprised that the Australians even had a team. Patty had just graduated from university and had travelled to Australia to join James. They had a little previous experience on sailboats, and this suited me just fine. As long as they had the right attitude, I could train them to do the required duties on *Sea Lure*.

Robb, the Australian who almost rammed the cruiser with *Sea Lure*, indicated an interest in joining the crew as he had had considerable experience on ocean passages. In fact when I met him at the Cruising Yacht Club he had just come in off the ocean on a yacht that had come around the south coast from Perth. He had since gone back to Perth, his home town, but I had his telephone number, so I gave him a call to see if he was still interested. He said he would let me know in a day or two, and a telegram arrived two days later indicating he would go on the next passage to New Caledonia, and if all went well, he would be interested in going farther. This gave me a full crew with sufficient experience, with a little training, to do the job. Robb arrived a few days before our departure date, so I took the full crew out on *Sea Lure* for a day of sail training in Sydney Harbour to familiarize them with sail hoisting, furling, tacking and other peculiarities of the boat. Louis had been on board for a week and knew his way around the boat, so he helped with the domestic operation, i.e., how to light the stove, oven etc. They all performed well during the training day. I was satisfied that I had a good crew, but was I in for a surprise!

During the next few days, we finished stocking the boat with food, beverages, etc. for a two-week passage, took on fuel, which turned out to be full of dirt, and the last day we filled the water tanks, etc. Charlie, the skipper of the English catamaran, was able to get me two bottles of propane and deliver it with his car. The night before departure, our Australian friends decided to have a going-away party for us, and a number of our yachting friends from previous countries showed up. We had a good party in the bar area of the Yacht Club and bade farewell to the many friends who came to see us off.

The weather the previous five weeks had been wet much of the time. *Sea Lure* was damp and in danger of growing mould. Storms from the south and southeast were coming through Sydney at regular intervals, and the winds were very high during many of these storms. It was necessary to watch the weather maps in the newspaper and on television to determine when to depart. I could have called the airport for a weather forecast, but didn't bother and I was confident that enough information was available to make a judgement.

CHAPTER 11

THE BIG STORM

Everything looked good for Wednesday 15 May for departure, and at 1115 hours we left the dock. This was a struggle as an Australian yacht was rafted on the outside of us and the skipper was late showing up, so we decided to leave and have the crew on the dockside boat pull his boat in. While we were getting the lines organized someone threw a line that flipped my expensive sunglasses into the ocean. I noted the spot where the glasses went into the water and as good luck would have it, a diver was working just a slip or two away. I hired him to retrieve my glasses and he picked them up off the bottom on the first dive. This was the second time these glasses had gone into the ocean and had been retrieved. The previous time was with the crew from New Zealand, when the glasses flipped off my nose and Stuart, who was with me, saw them go. He just dove into the water and caught them as they were going down. For this performance above and beyond the call of duty, a bottle of Beefeater gin.

Finally, we got away from the dock and headed for Watsons Bay where I had made prior arrangements with Australian customs to come alongside and clear us out of the country. This was one of the reasons for undocking on time. Shortly after we arrived the customs vessel showed up, so we did not put down an anchor. We just drifted with the customs boat rafted alongside. After about 20 minutes, all the paper work was completed and the crew paid their departure tax of $15 each. I was exempt because I owned the boat. They gave me our departure papers, reboarded their vessel and departed.

At 1230 we went through the Heads for the last time, and set course for New Caledonia. The weather was pleasant, the winds were 10 to 15 kts from the northeast right on the nose, so we were powering. We also had the current running along the east coast of Australia to contend with, so we needed the help from the engine to get us clear of it without undue delay. Consequently we powered for 18 hours, but this was good for the engine, as it hadn't had much work for the past five weeks. Diesel engines always run better when they are used frequently. Even with all this help plus the wind, it took a long time to get the Sydney lights out of sight. This seemed to be a worry for the new crew, as this was the method they were using to determine our progress. I intentionally left the engine running longer than normal, just to make sure the Sydney lights were over the horizon the following night.

Our progress the first several days was slightly less than 100 miles per day, since the sea current was definitely slowing us down. Patty and James were both seasick the first day or two – this is normal for crew their first time on the ocean. They have to get used to the motion and I think there is always apprehension as to whether they are doing the right thing. Also, the boat and skipper are really unknown quantities at this stage, so this created more uncertainty. They got over their sickness after several days and from then on did not suffer.

The following day, I took some sights to practice celestial navigation, and when my calculations and plotting arrived to within one mile of the Sat Nav position, I put away the sextant for the rest of that passage. The ham radio was working, with the DDD net from Canada and New Zealand and Tony's net from the New Zealand - Australia area coming in loud and clear. We did not have a licensed ham operator on board, so we did not transmit, but just listened out at the appropriate times. I would have transmitted if we had an emergency, but this did not happen for the entire voyage. Fortunately, we did not have to break the rules. It was unfortunate that we did not have an operator on board, as it would have been nice to have chats with the people back home or with the friends we had just left in the previous country, as this was always a good morale booster. I had taken the ham radio course back in Vancouver before departing on the voyage, but did not write and pass all the exams to qualify for a license. I was, however, quite familiar with the operation of the radio, having watched Bob transmit for hours. He also gave me instruction.

On May 17 and 18 the winds had backed around to north and northeast with speeds of 15 - 20 kts and as a result we were getting good sailing. On Sunday 19 May we all had a shower and cleaned up the boat. The skipper prepared the meal as usual, and James donated the wine to go with the meal. He had brought on board quite a stock of good quality wine, which we enjoyed very much. By 0100 hours the following morning, the winds had picked up to 35 kts and a storm was threatening. This was another of the storms that had passed through Sydney before we left, but this time it was going to give us a rough ride. The operation of the boat had settled down to a steady routine and no one was sick now. Robb, the experienced ocean crewman, was starting to show some minor signs of instability, but at the time I did not read them correctly. By the following afternoon at 1250 hours the ocean had built up, as high winds had been blowing for about 12 hours.

Patty was on the helm and James and I were in the cockpit. We each had a safety harness on, and the cabin doors were closed with the boards in place under the doors. We had finished our lunch and the crew of the other watch had just gone to bed when a monster wave hit us. Nobody saw it coming, and it hit broadside and put us up to about 60 degrees of heel. This must have been the seventh wave. At this angle, *Sea Lure* hesitated, trying to decide which way to go, either over for a knockdown or back to an even keel. Fortunately, we still had a heavy load of fuel and water, over 7000 lbs. of ballast, and as well the boat has a low centre of gravity. This, plus its beamy design, saved us from a knockdown. While we were over on our side, the crest of the wave went straight through the cockpit and unbuttoned the cover, but luckily only about a bucket of water ended up in the cockpit. The rest went straight through like a bolt of lightning. Patty had been off course about 20 or 30 degrees, and we yelled to her to get back on course. This she did immediately, so the second very big wave following the one that nearly knocked us down hit the stern of the boat with a bang and the water came right over. This wave did not cause us any trouble.

Sea Lure had performed beautifully again in a really tough spot, and possibly saved our lives. I am not sure that the doors to the cabins would have withstood the water pressure on them in a knockdown situation. If they had broken and the boat foundered, we would have had tremendous difficulty surviving, as launching the life raft in these conditions would have been almost impossible. Louis was sleeping in the starboard bunk in the aft cabin, with the piece of plywood beside him to keep him from falling out. When he woke up he was airborne, and fortunately crashed on the soft settee and was not hurt. Robb was okay in the small cubbyhole berth in the main cabin, but his confidence was shaken badly. After this close call, with weather deteriorating further and waves getting higher, he came to the conclusion that we were not going to survive. He had been on the ocean many times before and in storms, though never with winds in excess of 65 kts, but he underestimated the determination of *Sea Lure* and its crew. I had been in high winds on *Greybeard* in very bad conditions when the sails started to come apart, but as the mast and all the stays, etc. were handling the strain on *Sea Lure*, I was very confident that we would not only survive, but that we could keep sailing on course towards New Caledonia. It was just a matter of me keeping my cool, and the crew continuing to perform their duties. Robb was on watch with Patty that night and they managed to backwind the genoa. By the time I got up, Robb was up on the bow trying to control the genoa but we had lost boat speed, so I started the engine to bring the boat back on course as we didn't want to jibe in these conditions. This worked out all right, everything returned to normal, and I went back to bed. That was the last time the engine started in the next 24 hours. Not that the engine was needed especially, but it was handy to charge batteries and keep the freezer temperature down, and more importantly, it was a morale consideration for the crew.

In the meantime Robb became more unhinged as time passed. He was swearing at his crewmates and showing other signs of a mental breakdown. We really didn't need this, when we had hurricane wind conditions to contend with for the next 24 hours. The winds were getting higher and higher and the anometer indicates winds to only 60 kts. Beyond that it just bumps the stop, and it was doing so regularly. In fact, it bumped three times in quick succession, so some of those wind gusts were in excess of 70 kts. Hurricane force winds start at about these speeds. In the southern hemisphere these high winds are known as cyclones, but they are one and the same. The lower wind speed of a hurricane is about 70 nautical miles per hour and the upper limits run up to 200 or more nautical miles per hour.

We had made some preparation for the storm, and had a checklist of things to do before storm conditions arrived. We lashed the main and the mizzen to the boom so they could not get loose. The spare halyard on the main mast was taken forward and fastened securely to the anchor winch and the large forward cleat. This was to give extra support for the mast in the event the forestay let go. This seems to be a problem on a lot of ocean-going yachts, and skippers have had them go at the most inopportune times. The shrouds will normally hold the mast up if not too much pressure is exerted on them. But if one goes when the mainsail is up, there is danger that the mast will come down. I had carefully examined the top of the mast in Sydney, and had replaced the bolt that holds the forestay to the mast, so felt reasonably secure, but one never knows when metal fatigue has set in. After more than one hundred days of almost constant wear on the ocean, almost anything can happen. During the storm the vessel occasionally vibrated or shuddered, and it was a most foreboding feeling. We found out later that the bolt was not left loose enough so the mast and forestay could move or work when the boat was going over these monstrous waves. Lack of experience was my problem, however, everything held together and it was corrected later.

The crew had had plenty of rest and were well fed before the storm, and the food prepared during the storm was assembled in a handy secure place, so it could be used later. Hatches were secured, and all crew on duty wore safety harness and floater coats. All loose items were stowed. We listened out on the radios for the weather, and got a report that a yacht had foundered about 200 miles west of us, and part of the crew was lost. This did not exactly help the morale of my crew, but did make them more careful and more attentive to their job. I changed the watch system so nobody was on the helm for more than 20 minutes at a time, as this seemed to be the maximum a person could concentrate and keep the vessel on course with few steering errors. We were steering by instrument during the day and the night, as the boat steered relatively easily when it was on course for New Caledonia. This put the wind off our starboard quarter as it was from the southeast, and the boat was going over the huge swells quite well. Also there was a minimum of spray coming into the cockpit, although the helmsman wasn't exactly dry after the 20 minutes on the helm. The next person to take the helm was also in the cockpit as morale support and to help out if an emergency occurred. This seemed to work very well, as most of my crew were quite inexperienced and needed all the help they could get.

The one crew member who had a lot of ocean experience lost his nerve and became a real problem, in fact, the worst crew problem on the entire trip. He had never been in a storm as bad as the one we were heading into, and had never experienced a yacht knockdown. The close call we had set him right off and his actions were such that I had to remove him as a Watch Captain and take his place on the watch. Fortunately he had a good stomach and could help me with the cooking, as the other crewmen were too woozy to do any cooking. The meals were not fancy, as it was a matter of emptying cans of stew or beans in a large pot, stirring in canned vegetables, etc., heating it up, placing it in a bowl in the sink and then passing it out to the crew in the cockpit. Food is important at all times on a yacht, but it is even more important during a storm, so the crew can continue to perform. Fortunately I had a safety belt attached to the stove that could be hooked up and used to lean back against, so both hands would be free to do the cooking on the gimballed stove. In some cases it was necessary to hold the pot on the stove so hot food would not hit the cook or spill on the deck. It was a major juggling act, but anything for survival in a storm. Humans rise to the occasion and accomplish things they never dreamed of during normal times. I had a good stomach and had experienced major storms before. During the next two days, I was on duty in the cockpit every 40 minutes around the clock, and the navigation and engine work still had to be done. 30 minutes sleep was the most I could manage on the seat in the main cabin after completing the navigation. I never did get to my bunk during the 72 hours of the storm.

During the first day when it was time to start the engine to charge batteries and reduce the temperature in the freezer, the engine would not start. It was my job to troubleshoot the problem and correct it. To ensure we had lots of battery power, we started up the Yamaha charger, hooked it up to the batteries and charged for some hours. The charger is fastened to the bulkhead opposite one side of the freezer, and the heat generated from this motor speeded up the thawing of the food in the freezer. The thawed meat then proceeded to spoil, and before we arrived in New Caledonia some terrible odours were coming out of the freezer. The charging of the batteries did not correct the engine problem, as it still would not start. I then decided that it must be the glow plug switch. A lot of water had been flying around the cockpit and some of it would undoubtedly get into the switch, as it is located near the bottom of the cockpit. To replace this switch it was necessary to crawl over the engine and wedge myself in the corner of the engine room behind the exhaust pipe. It was very important that I not get hurt in the engine room or anywhere else on the boat as the operation depended very much on me. I managed to take out the glow plug switch with Louis' help and hooked up a new switch. I then tried to hold the switch by hand from the back of the panel, while Louis screwed the nut on the outside of the switch from the cockpit. He tightened it with a wrench, but I was unable to hold it firm so the switch rotated and touched the instrument next to it. This immediately caused a short in the electrical system, and the insulation on the wire running to one of the terminals on the switch began to burn and flame. I realized immediately that an engine room fire under these storm conditions would be fatal, so I reached in with my bare hand and tore the flaming wire off the terminal. Fortunately, I used enough force to part the wire from the terminal on the first try, although I did burn my hand. There were more important things to do, so I did not feel the pain from the burn until much later.

It was now necessary to find new wire and connectors located in the boat stores and rewire the switch, as it had not been damaged. This took about an hour and finally, after it was completed, we tried installing the switch for a second time. We were very careful to turn the switch so it would not touch the instrument next door, and when this was finished, I got out of the engine room safely, pushed the glow plug switch for 15 seconds and turned the key. The engine started with a roar, and the crew's morale went up about 50 percent! I must admit I heaved a sigh of relief. We could have sailed into New Caledonia without an engine, but it would have been tricky threading our way through the reefs, and we were going to get ourselves into enough trouble even with the engine running. We left it running for a couple of hours to charge batteries some more, but the food in the freezer was too far gone to be saved. However, when the mess was frozen the smell was reduced somewhat.

From 0024 hours on Friday 24 May to 2230 hours on Monday 27 May, the yacht's main log did not have any entries. I was too tired or too busy to complete the log, however, we did make an effort to maintain the watchkeeper's log. This too ceased at 0900 hours on 26 May and there were no more entries for the rest of the passage into Nouméa, but I did not blame the crew. We were just too exhausted and could only complete the essential tasks.

By the third day the winds subsided, and we started to clean up the boat. It was a shambles. I had hoped to pass up Nouméa and go straight on to Fiji but this was impossible. We had a number of boat repairs to carry out, and had to throw out what was left of our food and procure some more. Besides, I had to replace the unsatisfactory crewman with another sailor, as it was a bit much for me to do a watch plus all the other duties on the boat.

The last entry in the watchkeeper's log said "43 miles to go to Nouméa" and it was to be a difficult 43 miles. The wind came up again and was gusting to 40 knots, but this time was from the northeast and right on the nose so we furled the sails and powered.

New Caledonia is surrounded with a large reef, particularly on the south and southwest side. To get to Nouméa we had to go through the reef and then another 10 to 20 miles to the town. There were more reefs to be avoided on the way in, which normally would not have been a problem, except that I could not buy detailed charts in Sydney. A lot of yachts sail from Sydney and other parts of Australia to Nouméa. In fact, a race is run from Sydney every year or every other year, but they still don't sell proper charts, even at the best suppliers. As a result, I did not have a chart to navigate the Boulari Pass through the reef, as this appeared to be the most suitable passage and within 20 miles of Nouméa. I did have the sailing directions from Canada and the instructions were as follows, as I wrote them on the chart. All true courses have been converted to compass course. Quote: "When Tabu reef light is ½ mile off and bearing is 284C alter to 314C. Go ¾ mile and pass between lights and alter to 344C. Go 8¾ miles until north extremity of light on Maitre Island bears 253C and Island Amédée is 1½ miles off. Alter to 306C for Nouméa." Unquote.

I was still exhausted when I calculated the distance to go to the Nouméa harbour and the number of hours of daylight left, using the nautical almanac, and made an error of one hour. After threading our way safely through the Boulari Pass, where there was one yacht high and dry and, we found out later, another yacht had been hauled off the reef earlier that day, we were feeling pretty good. I had Louis take the helm, as he was an expert helmsman after all his years flying with the airline. I gave the instructions and did the eyeballing on distance off etc. We went through the pass with no problem, but then I realized that the sun would be setting soon and that we still had 15 miles to go. We put on full power and had the boat going almost 8 knots, but by the time we had travelled seven miles we ran out of daylight, and the charts I had were completely inadequate.

Prior to going through the pass at Amédée I had called the

Nouméa radio on the VHF and advised them that we were proceeding through the pass. There were very few VHF radios in Nouméa and those had been procured quite recently. The one I had called was in the control tower at the airport and fortunately for us, Jean Lafleur, a large boat owner, was down at his boat that afternoon. He was listening out on his VHF and monitored all the conversations over the next five hours between the Nouméa control tower personnel and us. Many yachts had been in trouble and Nouméa had lost yachtee business because of the difficulties with the reef, etc., so Jean and a few other locals were making an effort to help yachtees with their problems. This was one of the reasons Jean had monitored our conversations with the control tower. Also, he was fluent in English, which was a blessing for us, although Louis was completely fluent in French and therefore was able to talk to the radio operators in the control tower at the airport. New Caledonia is, or was, a dependency of France and all commerce is transacted in French. In order for me to do business in Nouméa, it was necessary to take a translator along, and Louis was most obliging at times like this.

After going through the pass and setting course for Nouméa, I allowed for drift, which I seldom did unless it was obvious by the action of the boat. This eventually took us 1.5 miles to the starboard of our course for the town. As daylight was fast disappearing, I applied more power to increase our speed, hoping to get to the town before dark, but to no avail. Darkness closed in on us, and with the steering error everything became confusing. This was partly due as well to our lack of sleep. There were several lighthouses with flashing lights but our charts did not indicate the light signals and the lights did not seem to be in the right place. This was because we were so far off course, and it soon became evident that we were lost among the reefs. This can be a very hazardous situation especially as our depth sounder is an oddball type that will only work if a light is shining on it. We tried using a flashlight to get it to work but this was unproductive, and eventually we gave up. I reduced speed and finally stopped. We then had great discussions as to our location, but none of the explanations satisfied me. After several hours, Louis contacted the radio operator in the control tower to try to determine our location.

Shortly after this, James went up on the bow, as he had become a very good lookout, and he watched for a surf that would indicate a reef. He also watched for land. I then proceeded at slow speed, and after about half an hour James gave me the word that he could see land not far ahead. We then started orbiting while Louis was still conversing on the radio, and he told the radio operator on shore what he could see. Some high towers with aircraft clearance lights now appeared right ahead of us, and the radio operator determined our location. He stated that we were in a very dangerous area with reefs close by, and to stay put and not to move. Jean Lafleur had been monitoring all the conversations, and then came on the radio in English. I took the microphone and he advised me that I was in considerable danger, but to stay where we were, and he would come out in his 50' power cruiser and lead us in to the dock. We arranged to flash our lights at the appropriate time and Jean came to our rescue. We then followed him into the harbour and he showed us where to dock. We were a long way off our intended course, and thanks to the radio operator and Jean we were rescued from imminent danger. If they had not helped us, I probably would have dropped the anchor and with 250 feet of chain would have reached the bottom. We could have anchored for the night and found our way the next morning in daylight, but it was much better to be tied up to a dock and know that we were all safe.

Jean Lafleur and his brothers were prominent business people in Nouméa and owned a number of large companies. They were obviously wealthy and Jean was a great person. He not only rescued us that night, but drove us around the city in his car to pick up parts and charts and get other items repaired that had been broken in the storm. I gave Jean two large bottles of liquor as a thank-you for all his kindness and he reluctantly accepted one, but suggested that I give the other to the men in the tower at the airport. I agreed to this so he drove me to the airport and I presented the bottle to them after making a small speech, which he translated into French. They had bought the VHF radio only several months before, so were in a position to guide and help yachtees as well as pilots. They appreciated the bottle, and I'm sure helped other yachtees who called them on the radio.

I had been reluctant to go into Nouméa, as I had been warned in Australia that there was trouble in that country. The rebels, who wanted to separate from France, were causing lots of trouble and when we were listening to the radio several days before our arrival we heard of a boat being blown up in the harbour. The city was under martial law and several thousand French troops were stationed there. Right next to us in the harbour was a French warship, and aircraft and helicopters were flying around all day. At night everyone had to be off the streets by 2100 hours. A thousand French troops were employed to guard the Governor's residence. We violated the curfew once and, although we were not bothered by the French troops, there was nothing open and the streets were clear of people, whereas during the day the streets were thronged. We found the people to be friendly and helpful as long as the language barrier was bridged.

James had met a young fellow in Sydney, Australia who came from Nouméa. He was now married and living back in New Caledonia, so James looked him up. He came from a large family and his father and mother were living in their home in Nouméa. We were all invited over to his father's house for an entire day. I think it was a Sunday or a holiday as no one was working that day. We had many drinks and a large dinner early in the afternoon, and then they insisted that we also stay for another meal later in the day. They were most hospitable and made us feel very much at home. During the dinner conversation (they all spoke English) it was mentioned that a yachtee had been rescued by a French ship in a storm and that the ship was at the main dock in Nouméa. There had been a write-up in the newspaper the day before and lo and behold, it was my friend Les, the skipper of *Sea Song*.

A number of weeks after I left New Zealand, Les had found a couple to sail with him to Fiji. Melody, his girlfriend, had left him by this time as she was not anxious to make a long ocean passage in *Sea Song*, and perhaps she had other reasons. Les had departed from the Bay of Islands about the same time I left Sydney. He was making satisfactory progress when a very large storm hit him. *Sea Lure* was tied to the dock in Nouméa at the time of this storm and I had noticed that the winds were gusting to 50 knots that night. The winds on the ocean would have been 70 knots plus, and *Sea Song* started to take in some water. Les had a full range of radios on board, but with only two other sailors he was undermanned to cope with these conditions. This was a subject we had discussed at great length when we were together in New Zealand: a large crew vs a small crew. Most yachtees go with a small crew, but Les said he thought of me a number of times during the storm with my large crew, and wished he had made the same decision.

152

The water had knocked out some of his radios, but his ham radio was still working. His Sat Nav had stopped working, probably because of the water problem, and he was soon lost in the storm. He did, however, talk to a ham operator in New Zealand, or perhaps it was Search and Rescue, and advised them of his predicament. The New Zealand Air Force sent out a search and rescue aircraft, and the crew did a search in the general area of the vessel and found her. A French ship was in the area and the search & rescue officers asked the captain of the ship to locate her and provide assistance. This he did, and when the ship came alongside of *Sea Song*, the two people on Les' crew decided to go aboard and leave Les behind. I suppose they had had enough of ocean sailing in storm conditions and wanted to get off. Les decided that he could not cope by himself, especially in those conditions, so he decided to abandon ship. In this situation it would not have been possible to tow *Sea Song* due to the difference in speed of the two vessels. So *Sea Song* was set adrift, but fortunately the entire crew had been rescued.

Our kind hosts in Nouméa drove me down to the harbour where I met Les again. The French ship was a very large one, and Les was a guest of the captain. We had a great reunion and he told me of his adventures in the storm, how he had nearly lost his life and had to set *Sea Song* adrift. Les said he had gone through a horrible experience, and although he did not elaborate, undoubtedly a great amount of fear and anxiety would have been evident for many hours after the vessel took in water, some of the radios went dead and the Sat Nav stopped working. There must have been some monstrous waves that night, as it was very bad at the dock in Nouméa. Just evacuating *Sea Song* in such conditions must have been a very tricky operation, and the crew of the French ship deserve a great amount of credit. His plans were indefinite at that time, but after returning to Canada in 1986, I talked to Melody on the telephone and she related the next chapter of the saga of *Sea Song*. Shortly after I saw Les in Nouméa, he had chartered an aircraft and went looking for his yacht, as he reasoned that she would still be afloat. The automatic bilge pump would continue to pump the water out of the boat as long as the battery power was sufficient to keep the pump operating and when he abandoned her, the batteries were fully charged. Les searched for several days but without success. In the meantime, he had passed word to the New

Zealand Air Force that he was looking for *Sea Song*. The Wing Commander, the commander of the aircraft the night that Les and his crew were rescued, decided that he would go looking for *Sea Song* a second time, and apparently he did find her. He had gone down to low level to read the name on the stern and sure enough, it was *Sea Song*. The New Zealand Air Force would undoubtedly have a better chance of locating the vessel as they had located her in the first instance, and knew the latitude and longitude of her position when she was abandoned. Les may have not had this information, as he was lost at the time, although I'm sure the captain of the French ship could have given him the facts if he had thought to ask. Also, the sails would have been furled so *Sea Song* would be drifting. The Air Force officers would be able to calculate the drift direction and speed over the succeeding days, and would come up with an estimated position of the yacht. They would start searching from this position and by doing a square search come across the vessel within several hours. From there on the story got a little sketchy, but from the last I heard, Les and *Sea Song* had not found one another.

Sea Song was a 40-foot ketch not unlike *Sea Lure* in size and design, was valued at more than one hundred thousand dollars and had been insured for this amount – but I understand Les had let the insurance expire prior to leaving New Zealand. This was probably because of the very high premium charged by the insurance company – several thousand dollars a year. Most of us did not have insurance because of the cost and the lack of companies prepared to take the risk. If Les did not find *Sea Song*, she sank or more likely was claimed by someone who found her drifting with no one on board and took her in tow, or put a crew on board to sail her to shore. The law of the sea is that anyone finding a vessel such as this is entitled to keep her with no remuneration to the owner. I cannot complete the story of *Sea Song* at this point, as I have been unable to locate anyone who has heard the final details. Les was a lawyer from California and had a practice in one of the large cities, so I'm sure he would not have any trouble recovering the value of the yacht through his practice. But I'm sure there was more than a monetary consideration for Les, as *Sea Song* had been part of his life for several years.

According to the *South Pacific Handbook* by David Stanley, New Caledonia has been inhabited for over 3,000 years, as shown by lapita (pottery) sites on the Isle of Pines, carbon-dated at earlier than 1000 B.C. Captain Cook discovered New Caledonia in 1774, landing on the northeast coast at Balade. Caledonia was the Roman name for Scotland and the mountain range stretching the full length of the island reminded Cook of the Scottish Highlands. Both he and La Pérouse explored the area extensively. After more navigators (d'Entrecasteaux and Huon de Kermadec), traders looking for sandalwood and beche de mer arrived. Then came the Roman Catholic missionaries; a French bishop arrived there in 1843, even before the French flag crew. The natives drove them out four years later, but the French Navy returned in 1853 to claim the whole of the main island for France. At that time it came under the jurisdiction of Tahiti. New Caledonia became a separate French colony in 1860. Early relations between natives and colonizers were traumatic, the French arming a native constabulary which assiduously suppressed or wiped out all insurrections, though most were justifiable. In the latter part of the 19th century, the islands' beautiful climate drew thousands of French colonists to nickel and chrome mining (nickel had been discovered in 1863), and to the copra industry. The resulting demand for land forced sizable numbers of Melanesians onto French-created reservations, which soon brought their clan systems, old traditions and hand crafts to an end. Cattle grazing by beef-hungry Europeans disrupted the Melanesian taro terraces and many now lie abandoned. There were serious native uprisings in the 19th century, the last quelled in 1917, and subsequently the French confiscated much native land. By 1939 New Caledonia had become the world's second largest exporter of nickel and seventh largest producer of chrome. The Japanese were the main importers right up to the outbreak of the Pacific war. In June 1940, after the fall of France, the Conseil Général of New Caledonia voted unanimously to support the Free French government and the pro-Vichy governor was forced to leave for Indo-China. New Caledonia became a French Overseas Territory in 1946, a status which continues to this day.

After three or four days, *Sea Lure* was getting back in shape. The freezer had been cleaned out and the bottom layer of foam replaced to get rid of the smell of rotting food. A leak in the deck drain was repaired, several blocks repaired, and a multitude of other things needed attention. Robb, the Australian, flew back to Perth the first day we arrived, so I started looking for a replacement sailor. Several came down to the boat, and I decided to take Frederique, a young chap from Paris who had been living in Nouméa for several years. He met all the requirements, although he did not have much experience on boats, but was a scuba diver. The only drawback was that he could not speak English and I cannot speak French. But Louis was still on board, and James and Patty could get by with high school French, so I decided to take him on after asking all the questions from my checklist. One question was, how much money did he have on him? I think he said several hundred dollars or equivalent, and I'm sure he did at that time, but little did I know that another crew member would sell a number of his possessions to Frederique over the course of the next passage. When we arrived in Fiji, Frederique had very little money left. He tried to be helpful, but tested my patience to the utmost during our passage to Fiji. The language difference was the root of most of our problems.

Almost a week had gone by, and it was time to get in our stock of food for the passage to Fiji. We made up the menu and the shopping list in the usual way, gave Patty and James sufficient money, and off they went to shop. They did a reasonable job of it. The menu, however, seemed to be slightly changed to suit their appetites and the quantities were reduced, I think so Patty and James could conserve their money. However, we did have enough food to see us through to Lautoka, Fiji along with the fresh fish we continued to catch.

On 3 June 1985 we filled the water tanks, stowed the food, said good-bye to our friends from Nouméa, and prepared to leave first thing the following morning. We didn't need fuel, as we still had enough dirty fuel picked up in Australia. We continued to have engine problems because of this fuel. I can't recall if it was in New Caledonia or Fiji that I finally opened the small covers on the top of the fuel tanks and with a hand pump drew out about five gallons of dirt and sludge before we finally started to get clean fuel. This is a constant hazard in the South Pacific.

Our friend Jean Lafleur contacted us again to find out when we would be departing. He promised to be a few miles out to give us assistance, if necessary, to find our way out through the reefs and islands when heading for Fiji. It was no trouble this time, as I was able to buy a good detailed chart of the area. Even though it was in French, it was easy to read. At 0915 hours we left the dock in

Nouméa and Jean had left his dock just a few minutes before us. On our way out, we came rather close to Maitre Island and could see Jean standing by, perhaps half a mile away, but he did not call on the radio and I did not require help. It was 1700 hours that day before we sailed and powered through all the channels, probably a distance of 30 miles, before we were clear to set course for Fiji. I imagine Jean left his VHF on all that time to answer any call we might have made, but we were in daylight now, with a good chart and good weather so there was no difficulty and the navigation was not even challenging. The crew was working out just fine including the new crew member and we were on our way on a very pleasant sail for Lautoka on the west side of Fiji, about 20 miles past the Nandi international airport. I will always be indebted to Jean for the friendship and the help he gave us. When I returned from the trip in June 1986, I wrote Jean a letter and invited him to come to Canada and stay with us in Vancouver.

The passage to Fiji was slow as the winds were often on the nose and varied from northeast to north-northeast to east and this was the direction we wanted to go. The weather was nice and warm, the wind rarely over 20 kts, and we were ready for a slow leisurely passage after the one we had just been through. Our worst day was 81 miles and our best 109, so it took us 11 days to make 988 miles. It was the slowest passage since the start, but I just wasn't interested in speed. It was time to get in the holiday mood, as *Sea Lure* had three months of relaxed sailing ahead, with only a day once in a while that was challenging to keep us on our toes.

On the second day out, on 5 June, Frederique plugged the forward head. I go stark raving mad when anyone plugs a head on the boat. I have cleaned all the plugged heads I am going to clean in this lifetime and I refuse to clean anymore. Whoever plugs it, cleans it! I give the instructions and open it up, but from then on it is the responsibility of the person who did it. I did try to control my temper in this instance, but poor Frederique spent about two hours with rubber gloves unplugging this head before it would pass inspection and was operational again. That evening, with Louis as interpreter, I went through the complete instructions with him on how to flush the head, and then he had to explain everything back to me so I would be sure that he understood. From then on there were no more plugged heads and now, twelve years later, *Sea Lure* has never had a plugged head.

Frederique was on the watch that worked more hours of darkness than the other watch, and normally he should have slept for at least four hours in the daytime. The aft cabin was quiet and dark and ideal for daytime sleeping, but he either refused to sleep or couldn't sleep. I don't know which, but he would go to sleep at the helm when on duty. Weather conditions were such that *Sea Lure* would look after itself and there wasn't much traffic, so I wasn't too concerned. We were dragging our fishing gear off the stern all the time, with the three shock cords attached to let us know if a fish took the lure.

One beautiful night while we were sailing with the engine on slow speed and with light winds, Frederique went to sleep at the helm. He could actually stand behind the wheel, propped up against the front of the aft cabin, and be sound asleep. The boat slowed down as there was no wind in the sails and the fishing line started moving faster than the boat. It got in under the boat and became wrapped in the propeller. As the wrap got tighter and tighter, the shock cords were pulled longer and longer, and finally the fishing line broke. The shock cord came flying forward with great force and hit Frederique in the back of the head, which woke him up. I guess he thought someone was out to get him, but I considered it poetic justice. The crew all had a good laugh the following day at Frederique's expense, and Louis explained to him what had happened. I'm not sure this was a deterrent to sleeping at the helm, but I didn't hear of it again.

On Friday 7 June the Sat Nav receiver started to act up. It would fail its automatic test when the computer was being programmed, and some of the fixes didn't seem to be right. It was time to get the sextant out and practice my sights, sight reductions and plotting to make sure I hadn't forgotten anything. The first two or three seemed to work out all right, so I went back to checking the Sat Nav. It seems it didn't like the storm any better than we did, but it appeared to gradually improve and started to give correct information, although it still failed its receiver test. Navigation didn't seem to be a problem, so I turned my attention to more important things like cooking the steak dinner on Sunday 9 June 1985. According to both log book entries, the steak dinner was good, so I will accept that with no argument.

I hate to pick on Frederique because eventually I actually got to like the guy. Back in Paris, he had undoubtedly learned to cook.

In fact, I suspect that he was a chef in one of the better restaurants at one time, even though he was still in his twenties. He was anxious to show his abilities as a cook, and convinced me that he should be allowed to bake a cake. I warned him that the oven on the stove did not work properly, but to go ahead and do his cooking. He had ingredients all over the galley before he was finished, and used about half of the quantities of most ingredients that had been procured for the 12 days, but finally he had his cake ready. I'm sure it would have been excellent but that no-good oven burned part of the cake. However, we all ate it with great relish and complemented Frederique on the fine job. He actually had many talents, but it took him awhile to adapt to shipboard life.

In the meantime, the engine developed an alternator problem and was not charging the batteries properly, but I carried a spare alternator and it was not a big job to change them. The seas were relatively calm for the entire passage, so it was quite pleasant working in the engine room after the episode in the storm. Also the Sat Nav was giving accurate information again so it wasn't necessary to take more sights with the sextant. On 14 June at 2000 hours, we sighted Fiji. The mountains are quite high in that area and the aircraft clearance lights were visible from a long distance in clear conditions. We still had to carry out a repair on the water system, go through the reef to the south of the islands, and then power to Lautoka. This took us another 9.5 hours. One of the metal connections for the water hose that runs to the freezer had corroded. I could not buy a suitable connection in Australia, and it finally gave away about 0230 on the morning we were arriving in Fiji. I had to modify and install an entirely new connection system from plumbing spares carried on the boat. This took about three hours.

I wanted to delay until daylight before going through the reef this time. There appeared to be lots of room to spare, but I had learned the hard way not to take chances, particularly in the dark. The old rule that you never, repeat never, do a landfall at night is one of the best rules for yachtees, and I would never violate this rule again. Several miles from Navula Passage I have a note on my chart "anchor." This means attach the anchor to the anchor chain in preparation for a landfall. Always, after leaving a country, when there was no possibility of requiring the anchor, several of the crew loosened the anchor chain, hoisted the anchor up from under the bowsprit, brought it on to the deck and removed the big bolt shackle that attaches the anchor to the chain. The anchor was then stowed in the bilge and the end of the anchor chain dropped into the chain locker with a colored wire attached so it would be easy to find later for attaching it to the anchor. This ensured that there was no anchor on the bow of the boat to break loose in a storm. It was quite a struggle to get the 40-lb anchor onto the deck and then carry it back to the cockpit. I did it many times, but it was well worth the effort and peace of mind to know that it could not cause trouble when conditions were bad. A number of yachts have had serious trouble when an anchor on the chain was loose on the bow of the boat, and doing considerable damage each time it bashed the bow as the vessel went through the big waves.

We took the anchor out of the bilge, took it forward to the bow, and one of the crew passed the chain up through the hole from the chain locker. We then fastened the chain to the anchor with the shackle, tightened the bolt with the big crescent wrench, and placed the anchor back under the bowsprit. Then we tightened the chain with the anchor winch, thus confirming that the winch was still working properly. When this was completed, we turned the wheel on the winch to lock the chain in place. I do not use a safety rope or chain on the anchor as I have always found that the locking wheel is sufficient. If we had to use the anchor for emergencies or for normal anchoring, it was now in place and ready to go.

Directly across the bay from Navula Passage, about five miles distant, are lead-in lights installed on the mountains. By lining up the lead-in lights on a course of 077T or 045C on *Sea Lure*, a safe route was indicated through the reef. There are very large reefs on both sides of the pass but it is about two miles wide, so it is really quite safe. Near daybreak, we made our way through Navula passage and by this time we could see the reef and also still see the lead-in lights so everything went smoothly. It was a beautiful day with very little wind, so we powered up the ship channel past Turtle Rock, the International Airport at Nandi and finally to Lautoka, a distance of 25 miles. Lautoka is the largest city on the west side of Fiji, with a population of approximately 28,000. It has a nice port, sheltered by mountains and an island close by. Anchoring close to the water's edge and just in front of the reef is very good, as there was just enough water for *Sea Lure* at low tide. With two anchors down, there was plenty of space. Under excellent weather conditions for the next week, there was no danger of going aground, although we could see the reef just off the stern in the clear water when we swung into shore.

We arrived in Lautoka at 1130 hours and as no ships were in dock, we used the main dock to find customs, etc. It was a Saturday and the dock was pretty well closed, but we did find someone who advised us to get back on *Sea Lure* and to anchor just beyond the main dock. They would advise customs that we were requiring clearance, and of course we flew the special yellow quarantine flag indicating that we had just arrived in the country, and required the doctor to come on board to check out the crew. After a wait of several hours the doctor showed up and after a short visit gave us clearance. Then after another wait the customs people came on board and cleared us, except for Frederique. He had spent all his money buying spear guns etc. from James, and he didn't have any money left. Had I known about the business transactions on board, I would have had James return the money and reclaim his equipment, but this did not become obvious to me until some time later. The result was that customs held me responsible for Frederique. As I had brought him into the country, I would also have to take him out of the country and must look after his welfare while in Fiji. This became a real nuisance, as Frederique had planned to get off the boat in Fiji and sail over to Vanuatu to join his fiancee, who lived with her parents. But he did not have enough money to satisfy the Fiji immigration people. Several days later we telephoned Frederique's mother in Paris, France to send him money, which she agreed to do. But a week later when the money still had not arrived, Frederique was still stuck with us. We were delayed going to the Yasawa area, a long line of islands on the west side of Fiji and reported to be one of the best parts of the country.

Lou flew from Canada and had arrived at the Nandi International Airport several days earlier, as we always seemed to be late arriving. As prearranged, she was staying at the Dominion International Hotel, close to the airport. When I was able to get to the telephone I called, or one of the Fijian officials called on my behalf, and the message she received was, "The *Sea Lure* is in Lautoka and get down here as fast as possible." This wasn't quite the message I intended to send. With the information coming from the captain of a yacht, the mix-up in emphasis and the different customs in a foreign country, the message came out as an order, but it had the desired results. She dropped everything, caught a taxi and arrived at the dock some 15 miles away in about half an hour. We were still anchored off the dock waiting for customs to show up, but the doctor had come and gone so it was decided that she could come on board. One of the crew took the dinghy in as soon as we removed it from the engine room, blew it up with the pump and put the outboard engine on. I had not seen Lou since March, so it was quite a reunion. The crew, who had not met her before, were quite impressed.

The customs clearances were at last all completed, and I see in the Official Log of *Sea Lure*, "Approach thru reef on lead-in light -- Lautoka Wharf – Customs – anchored in Lautoka Harbour – doctor on board – immigration and customs – $40 for overtime plus a bottle of rum." The customs in Fiji were not about to turn down a bottle of good rum, particularly when they had to come out on their day off, and I presume the $40 also went to the customs officials as overtime pay. Some yachtees would sit around on their boat until the following Monday, and then clear customs and immigration, but we were always anxious to get to shore. This kind of delay would have been intolerable for the crew and myself. We were to remain here at anchor for a week with the crew on board, so we put down the second anchor in case the wind increased and, as mentioned before, we were only feet from the reef, so could not afford any anchor-dragging.

Lou and I stayed at the hotel in Nandi for the next three or four days and travelled back and forth by taxi or bus. The bus was quite primitive and the ride not very smooth. The drivers always had the music blasting away but they were very accommodating and would make a special trip to the passengers' destination if it wasn't too far off their route. Passengers would bring bags of grain and occasionally a live chicken, and the locals did not object. The hotel facilities at the Nandi Airport were better than downtown Lautoka and the price was within reason, so we were quite happy there and went out for gourmet dinners every night at the main dining room in the hotel, where they put on a Fijian show most nights. It was nice to get away from the vessel after all those weeks on board, and I'm sure the crew were happy to have the boat to themselves.

Lautoka, the second largest city in Fiji after Suva, is a tourist area, as well as having one of the largest sugar mills in the South

Pacific. A guided tour of the mill is available. Unfortunately we did not go for one reason or another and I'm sorry we missed it, as I'm sure it would have been interesting. One day when the wind was from the wrong direction the boat was covered with white ash from the sugar cane mill. It did sweep off the deck all right and fortunately blew over on us only the one day.

The city has a number of good eating places with reasonable prices, and there are a lot of shops and market places to buy and barter for watches, electronic equipment, etc. One chap was trying to sell us something right on the street and a Fijian came up to us and said "Don't deal with this fellow, he is dishonest." Obviously he was trying to protect us from some unscrupulous salesman. They value their tourist trade and want to keep the tourists happy.

The weather was beautiful, *Sea Lure* was riding at anchor with no problems, and it would have been a very pleasant time if we could have gotten Frederique organized. Three more days had gone by and still no money had arrived from Paris. We found out later that France had restrictions on the transfer of money out of the country, also it has to be approved by a government department, and obviously they do not move very fast. We had planned to sail in the Yasawa Islands that run about 100 miles north and east of Lautoka, a very beautiful area, but we could not leave until we had Frederique's troubles solved. On about the sixth day Frederique suggested that he call his future father-in-law in Vanuatu, which is not far form Lautoka, probably three or four hundred miles. He agreed to send him enough money to fly over to that island. On the strength of this promise, immigration agreed to let us sail in the Yasawa islands for two weeks with the under-standing that after we came back, if Frederique was still there I must take him back on the boat and out of the country. This was agreeable to me as it freed us up to do the holidaying in the Yasawas that had originally been planned.

The Yasawa Islands are high volcanic islands with magnificent white sandy beaches, cliffs, bays and lots of reefs stretching northward. It is a very scenic area for sailing and cruising, but few yachts go to this area because of the dangerous reefs and the lack of charts. Fortunately we met a Frenchman, the owner of a 50-foot yacht, who had been lost in the Yasawas but did not damage his boat. He was able to buy a set of home-made charts and sold them to me for $16 Fijian dollars. He was very concerned about our safety, and spent about two hours briefing me on the routes to take and the places to anchor. He had gone to four places, so we decided to take a similar route and anchor in the same places. This was a fortunate decision as some areas are extremely dangerous. It was necessary to power through reefs for several miles, twisting and turning while James gave me directions from the bow of the vessel. He could see the reefs as the water is very clear. He became very skilled at judging the depth of the water over the reefs, and with hand directions we safely navigated our way through some very dangerous channels. Without the home-made charts we certainly would have been in trouble.

CHAPTER 12

THE YASAWAS

Before starting out for the Yasawas it was necessary to get a cruising permit from the Department of Agriculture. There was no charge for the permit, but before issuing it, the staff gave us an extensive briefing on the do's and don'ts of cruising in this area. The inhabitants of the Yasawas are all pure Fijians. East Indians are not permitted to live there and we met only one person that was not Fijian. They are a very proud people and it is important that their customs not be violated. I was instructed that each time after anchoring in front of a village that I must go ashore alone, find the village chief and present him with kava root. He then performs a small ceremony as a thank-you and the crew is then welcome to his village and his people are most hospitable and helpful. If this is not done, I understand they can be quite hostile and may board the vessel and steal equipment. We did not violate their rules so did not have any trouble. We bought the kava root at the market in Lautoka for $25, divided it into four bundles and presented it to each of the four chiefs in the villages where we anchored.

On 25 June, after restocking the boat with food for two weeks for five people, we were ready to go. Lou was going with us, but we were leaving Frederique behind as he had found friends to stay with. We powered out of Lautoka and headed for our first stop in the Yasawas – the island of Waya. It was about 35 miles away, so we arrived shortly after lunch and anchored in the bay between Wayasewa and Waya Islands. It was a beautiful anchoring area and well sheltered – the beaches were excellent and we had them all to ourselves.

James and Patty had met a young couple in Lautoka down at the dock and had become quite friendly with them. Their names were Sau and Kathy and they lived in the village on Waya Island. He was the pastor for one of the many faiths and his wife, I think, was from Australia. She was permitted to live on the island as she was married to a Fijian. They were very friendly people, so Patty and James looked them up. We invited them to *Sea Lure* for dinner the second night. I have forgotten how I handled the kava routine, but must have given it to Sau to give to the Chief. Since the two couples had met before, we were certainly welcome in their village. We had a very pleasant dinner on board. Our food was a change for them, although the food we eat is not all that much different. At the end of the meal, Sau said, "We would like you all to come to our place for dinner tomorrow night, but I would like to borrow your dinghy for three or four hours in the afternoon so I can spear some fish and other sea food that we will have for dinner." We were most agreeable to this arrangement, so the following noon he came down to the boat.

Lou and I decided to go with Sau in the dinghy to watch him spear the fish, run the engine and take care of the fish, etc. after he caught them. There are lots of sharks in this area so the locals and everyone must be careful. In fact, one of the natives in the village had only one arm, and we were told that a shark took the other one and I do believe the story. Sau, who was born and raised in this area, was very skilled at spearing seafood, as it is one of their main sources of food. In three hours he had caught enough for dinner for 10 people and had about four kinds.

Late that afternoon we went to their thatched hut for dinner. A house was being built for them, but it was not yet finished, so they were still living in the typical Fijian thatched hut. It was very well built, neat and had all the essentials for living. The food was cooked over a fire in front of the hut, which was equipped to handle pots hung over the flames, and pans for cooking the fish right on the fire. Sau's mother was present and also several of his brothers and friends. They helped with the preparation of the food and the serving, so this left Sau and Kathy free to visit with us. They were really very well organized. The drinks before dinner were kava. Although it is the custom to drink it bottoms up from a coconut shell, Sau did not insist, as there were foreign ladies present. Kathy was pregnant with their first child, who was born about a month later, so Sau would not permit her to drink kava and I think he was wise.

After the drinks we enjoyed a very delicious meal with many dishes of food, including vegetables that they grow. I believe they even served a dessert that Sau's mother had baked to celebrate the occasion. After several hours of interesting conversation (Sau or Kathy translated where it was necessary) and good food, we came to the picture-taking time. One of the pictures appears here in the book. It was one of the most pleasant evenings of the entire voyage. Being invited to share a meal with these wonderful people in their own environment was such a privilege and memorable experience for us all. We said our good-byes that night before walking the mile back to the dinghy and proceeding to *Sea Lure*, as we were leaving the following morning. Fortunately we were to meet this family again in Lautoka several weeks later.

The bay in this area was one of the best for swimming and we all swam as often as possible, but normally close to the beach. The following morning James decided he was going for a swim off the boat. I was much against it as I had seen a shark tail fin sticking up in the water close to the boat. However, after some discussion it was agreed that James would swim at his own risk and that I would not be responsible. Fortunately, he did not come to any harm, but after we lifted the two anchors and were powering out of the bay we saw three large shark tail fins. They were cruising for food and probably had seen James, but it shows how careful one has to be in these southern waters when it comes to sharks.

We were on our way by 0800 hours, and had a long way to go that day to our second anchorage. We stayed three or four days in each of the four anchorages over the two weeks, but the distance was a little greater this day. When we lifted the second anchor that morning, I didn't tell the crew to bring the anchor back and stow it and the 200 feet of gold braid anchor line, so it was simply laid on the deck. As I could not see it from the helm, I completely forgot about it. During the day while we were sailing, a gust of wind hit the boat and keeled us over to about 30 degrees. Later we were looking for the anchor and it was nowhere to be found. Either Louis or James had untied the end of the rode from the cleat on the bow and it had all gone overboard. About $400 worth of equipment, including a Danforth 40 anchor and the two hundred feet of gold braid nylon rope. Needless to say, I was quite annoyed, but as the skipper is always responsible, I could not lay blame on the others. It just goes to show that utmost care must be taken at all times, but since this turned out to be the largest loss of equipment for the entire voyage, I suppose it could have been worse. I lost the dinghy and motor twice, once in Fiji and once in New Zealand, and got it back both times. We still had two anchors on board, another Danforth 40 and a Bruce 40, but only about five feet of chain, so we had to use the spare lines on board to improvise a new anchor rode and start using the Bruce anchor again. This did work all right, and when we got back to Lautoka, I bought 20 feet of chain and a heavy ¾ inch line about 100 feet long, which served as our second anchoring system for the remainder of the voyage. At 1600 hours, after some difficulty, we found a good anchorage at Sawa-i-Lau Island. The difficulty was caused by the inadequate charts, but a Blue Lagoon cruise vessel with a large number of passengers on board went into the area ahead of us and anchored. We followed him in, and anchored about ½ mile away in what I thought was a better place. Not long after that the skipper of the cruise vessel lifted anchor and came over right beside us, dropped his anchor and sent one of the crew ashore with the tender to tie a stern line to a tree so his vessel would not swing into us. This worked very well, as we became friendly with the skipper, who was a Fijian, and we also had music from the live band, but it did play well into the night when we were trying to sleep.

Blue Lagoon Cruises operate out of Lautoka with three large vessels. The largest vessel cruises the Yasawa Islands for a week at a time while the other two go for three or four days. They appeared to be well patronized at that time and the skippers seemed to be very professional. The skipper we met told us of going aground several months before in the same area. Apparently he and his helmsman were not getting along very well, and the helmsman did not respond to an order as quickly as he should have, which was probably deliberate, so they ended up going high and dry on a reef. They had to be pulled off the reef and the vessel sustained some damage. The skipper was suspended from work for several weeks and I expect the helmsman was fired, although this was not clear.

After taking the kava ashore and presenting it to the chief of the village, we were then welcome to this island, but James and Patty went ashore in the dinghy after I came back, and when they returned James had a black eye! I never did hear the full story, but James had a confrontation with one of the local young men, I believe egged on by Patty, and he got the worst of the deal. This incident did not seem to dampen our welcome to the area, so we spent the next three nights at this anchorage. The beaches were beautiful for swimming and sunbathing. There were only one or two other yachts anchored a long distance away, and the cruise boat left the following morning. The weather was still perfect, and it was all very pleasant and relaxing. It was a skipper's holiday, as

SYDNEY, AUSTRALIA – THE HEADS

SYDNEY OPERA HOUSE

AUSTRALIAN SUBMARINE – SYDNEY HARBOUR

FRENCH WARSHIP – NEW CALEDONIA

OUR DINNER –
FREDERIQUE
AND SKIPPER

DINNER WITH THE PASTOR – FIJI – THE YASAWAS

THE YASAWAS –
VILLAGE
    CHILDREN

ROCK IN VILLAGE –
YASAWAIRARA
    BAY,
YASAWAS

SKIPPER, JAMES
AND PATTY

TONGA -
THE BLOWHOLE

LOADING A HORSE IN TONGA

SUNRISE ON THE SOUTH PACIFIC
C. Sheffield

TONGA – DAUGHTER DENISE DEWAN AND SKIPPER

NUKU ISLAND, TONGA – OUR FAVOURITE

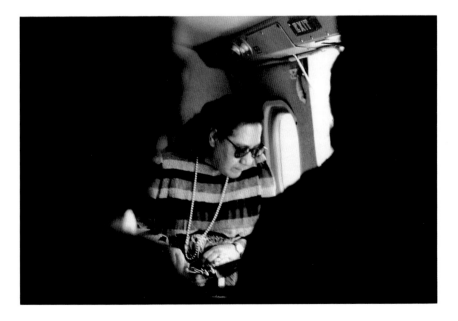

THE QUEEN OF TONGA

TONGA – BARTERING MOTOR OIL FOR FISH

DRUMMER WITH LOUIS AND SYLVIA

LOU – CANADIAN TWIN OTTER AIRCRAFT

JERRY WESTON, AMERICAN CREW MEMBER

PETER HAVING A DIP

DEPARTING HONOLULU – HOMEWARD BOUND

CRUISE BOAT – MANELE BAY, LANAI, HAWAII

U.S. COAST GUARD VESSEL
SEARCHING FOR DRUGS

TONY AND SKIPPER – NEW BEARDS

WE HAVE ARRIVED

there were very few things that I had to look after. Even the sharks gave us a holiday.

Navigation in this area is quite difficult, as there are no beacons, buoys or lighthouses. The only navigational aids are sticks here and there, and I suppose they mark the channels and reefs. The cruise boat skippers know what they mean, but it became a real guessing game for us. The home-made charts that I purchased from the Frenchman saved our day more than once, and a little luck helped too. Also James had become very expert in giving me directions when reefs were close, and giving the right directions to power to keep us out of trouble. I now understood why most yachtees do not sail in this area, but they are missing the best sailing scenery and swimming areas in Fiji for the lack of a little nerve.

The following two days, 29 and 30 June, we stayed at this same anchorage and continued to enjoy the area. Patty and James didn't get into any more trouble and it was all very enjoyable. On 1 July we lifted anchor and departed for the Blue Lagoon, where the movie of the same name was made a number of years ago with Brooke Shields as the star. It took us from 0900 hours to 1500 hours to sail to this area as the winds were blowing 15 to 20 knots. We anchored inside the reef in front of the village, and because of the high winds we dropped two anchors, which were properly set. I went ashore in the dinghy and went looking for the chief who was in a conference. I was invited in to sit down on the floor cross-legged and wait until the meeting was over, which took about half an hour. Then the chief carried out the little ceremony which is like a blessing, accepted the kava, had a look at my cruising permit, and then told me that we were all welcome to the village and if we would like to see the caves on the other side of the bay the charge would be $5. I paid him the money, thanked him very much and went back in the dinghy to *Sea Lure*.

For the next three days we stayed anchored in this area, visited the caves, and had a generally good time. As I recall we were the only boat in this anchorage – there may have been several yachts some distance away, but it was like having our own private anchorage. There were several lagoons, and the water is a number of shades of blue when the sunlight shines on it. The water depths are minimal. Some of these scenes are spectacular and are rarely seen in our part of the world. The cave was quite interesting and we took the dinghy over to it – about a mile from our anchorage. We climbed a stairway to enter the cave well above the water level, and inside could look up and down to get the full view. We also went swimming inside the cave, which was like a warm bath. The only thing that detracted from the visit here over the next several days was the wind. It kept blowing around 15 or 20 knots for the entire stay, which made it very bumpy for sleeping.

On 4 July, we lifted the two anchors and sailed up to the northwest corner of Yasawa Island to Yasawairara Bay, our last anchorage in the Yasawas. This is the end of the Yasawa Islands and about 100 miles from Lautoka. It took us a number of hours to sail to this bay, as the distance must have been about 40 miles. On our way we met another yacht coming back from the same bay. This was fortunate, as after threading our way through the reef for about 2 miles with James' guidance, we anchored in front of a big rock on the shore, right in the middle of the village. With the bow anchor down, there was room for only one yacht to swing in the small area and there was a reef between the boat and shore. I had been briefed very thoroughly about this area by the Frenchman, and knew the situation before arriving. We were the only yacht there for the next three days, as the yachtees sailing that area would not attempt to go in before we came out of the bay.

I went through the same routine with the kava again, but this time the Chief was not home. His son was filling in, so I presented him with the kava. He was very hospitable, and invited us to his house to buy jewelry, necklaces, etc. that the family made, as this was undoubtedly one of the ways they made a living. The beaches were long, sandy and deserted, so we went for long walks and also did some more swimming. A young boy and his sister came out to *Sea Lure* in their small home-made outrigger canoe, and my wife invited them on board to show them the yacht and then gave them each a gift. They were so well behaved, and were fascinated with the boat. They spoke English quite well as it is taught in school. This was the first time they had been on an ocean-going yacht, and were really amazed. A picture of them is included in the book. They were two of the nicest children we had ever met!

The second evening the chief's son invited James to go cray fishing, and as they needed the dinghy I decided to go with them to see what it was all about. A friend also came along, so there were four of us in the little boat with spear guns, underwater lights, etc., so we had a full load. We had to power about two miles to get to the cray fishing area and by this time it was after dark. I decided to stay with the boat while the other three went fishing, but before they departed the chief's son said a very long prayer. It must have taken about 10 minutes and several times he mentioned the sharks. They have a great deal of respect for the sharks for obvious reasons, and a little divine protection was in order. The chief's son took the light and spear gun, and his friend also had a spear gun. James carried the bag for the crayfish. For the next hour and a half while they were searching for crayfish, I could see the underwater light as they did a circular route about half a mile out. Apparently a shark followed for the entire time, but did not attack. After catching a number of crayfish, they were on their way back when the chief's son caught a fish and deliberately cut it so there would be some blood in the water. This was to scare James, and it had the desired effect, but fortunately the shark did not attack! I guess by now he was quite sure that the shark was not in a feeding mood and so took the chance. These natives have to learn to live with sharks as they get most of their food from the ocean, and they tell me that they can tell before a shark is going to attack by its actions in the water. Two or three of them attack the shark before it attacks them, and they kill it with their spear guns. I guess the old military strategy that the best defence is offence also applies when it comes to sharks. I was happy to see them all come back unharmed, and carrying a bag full of crayfish. We then made our way back in the dark to *Sea Lure*. It was getting windy by then, but the waves were not too big, so the little boat got us back with very little trouble. The chief's son and his friend had a drink before dinner with us, and of course the crayfish were cooked for dinner. They were delicious, similar to our east coast lobster.

After three days at this anchorage, it was time to make our way back to Lautoka as the two weeks were almost up, and it would take us two days to sail the hundred miles with one overnight stop. So, on Sunday 7 July, we lifted anchor and said good-bye to our last village in the Yasawas. We had good sailing from 0830 hours until 1600 hours, and since we were only about half way back, we found a bay to anchor for the night. This time, because we were not going ashore, I did not have to go in with the kava. In fact, there was no kava left! After a good sleep and with a minimum of ocean action, we were off again for our final sail to

Lautoka. The navigation was still very tricky, and in one area it is necessary to eyeball the distance about a mile off the first reef to miss the other reef which is about 1.5 miles off. Here the depth of water doesn't exceed 15 feet. It took us over an hour, but with a little bit of luck and good concentration, we stayed off the reefs and anchored in Lautoka at 1630 hours, in the same place we had anchored previously. It was thoughtful of the other yachtees not to take our place. I expect it was a little too close to the reef for most of them, but that was fine with us. By this time we had seen so many reefs and passed over or around them that we felt quite at home.

After going ashore, the first thing to do was to find out if Frederique was still there, or if the money had arrived and he had taken his flight to Vanuatu. I didn't bring up his name and customs did not mention him again, so I can just assume that he had left. Otherwise, he would have been looking for a bunk on the boat, so I'm sure everything worked out for him. It was an experience to have him on our crew, but I'm not sure I would want to go through it again. I must admit he was a colourful fellow and did add some more interest to the passage.

After several days in Lautoka, James and Patty decided that they wanted to go on a long hiking trip, so we arranged to meet in Suva which is approximately 100 miles from Lautoka by land. This left Louis, Lou and me to sail around to Suva – an overnight sail. The distance from Lautoka through Navula Passage again, along the south coast of Viti Levu Island, through the passage between Viti Levu and Mbengga Islands and finally into Suva, was approximately 140 miles. We set sail from Lautoka at 0630 hours on 11 July and from there through Navula Pass. It was excellent sailing with good winds and beautiful sunshine, but when we went through the pass the winds picked up considerably. In fact they went over 30 kts before we realized it, and we tore the main sail again, as we didn't reef or furl it soon enough. The tear was again in the seam, but it was rather difficult to get down with the winds and the reduced crew. Finally, we furled it and left it furled for the rest of the passage. The reef along the south coast extends out over one mile in some places, so we had to stay well away to keep us out of danger. Louis and I set up a watch system, i.e. he took one watch and I took the other and Lou assisted and did most of the cooking.

There are many very nice harbours and resort places on this

south coast, and I would have liked to stop at several of them, but time was a factor. I still planned to spend a month in Tonga, my favourite country, then go on to Western Samoa, American Samoa, Fanning Island and finally Hawaii, arriving well before Christmas, and was planning to spend the rest of the winter in Hawaii. Our progress was rather slow with the engine on most of the time, however, we did some sailing with the genoa rolled out when we had sufficient wind. By 0400 the following morning, we were getting close to Mbengga Pass, which was between Viti Levu and Mbengga Island, for which it is named. Again, I did not have proper charts, but the ones I had were the best I could buy so we had to manage. I wanted to go through the pass in the early morning, and at 0340 hours we had a Sat Nav fix that put us about 5 miles from the entrance to the pass. From the charts there appeared to be some reefs, rocks and a stick to guide us. We reduced speed and I kept a sharp lookout forward, but didn't see anything, not even the stick. Thankfully we did get through the pass safely and didn't hit anything. We still had about 25 miles to go, and finally about 1300 hours, we went through the reef into Suva again. This was becoming old hat, as I had been through this pass twice before the previous year. The range markers were still in place, so it was easy and safe. At 1330 we were at customs again for a quick clearance. Even through we had not been outside the country since leaving Lautoka, we were still required to check in so they could keep track of us, and we always obliged. But this time we did not have to go through the medical and agricultural routine. We did have to report that Patty and James had left the boat, were proceeding to Suva on foot, and would join the boat again in Suva. Customs didn't like this particularly, but we had not been a problem to them the previous year, and this seemed to help. They were more inclined to bend the rules from time to time, but not very much. We then went to my favourite anchorage in front of the Royal Suva Yacht Club.

Lou and Louis, who had not been in Suva before, obviously wanted to see the sights, so we went downtown for dinner several times over the next week and had a very enjoyable time.

The freezer and the winch motor on the boat had both stopped working. After several attempts I found that I could not fix them, so removed the compressor and the winch motor from the boat and took them to a large engineering company close to the yacht club.

After several days they fixed the motor at a reasonable price and overhauled the compressor. I brought the boat into the dock at high tide and the refrigeration mechanic installed the compressor, purged the system a number of times to get the moisture out, then recharged the compressor and system with Freon. Unfortunately, the young fellow didn't know much about boat compressors and after we paid a bill of over $500 Fijian dollars, the freezer worked for one day after we left for Tonga, then quit again! Obviously, the problem had not been located.

Louis decided to leave the crew in Suva, as he had had enough, and I wasn't sorry to see him leave for a number of reasons. This meant that we were then short a crewman. I had noticed an ad posted on the bulletin board at the yacht club, so I called up a young German fellow by the name of Uve who was looking for a ride to Tonga. He came down to the club, and after an interview I decided to take him on the crew. He didn't tell me that he was suffering from a staph infection (boils) and this was to cause me considerable difficulty several weeks later.

CHAPTER 13

TONGA AGAIN

After doing the provisioning – this time it was only for a week – and filling up the water and fuel tanks, we were ready to go on 20 July. James and Patty had arrived at the boat after a very enjoyable hike from Lautoka, and they were all ready for another passage, although I have to admit that relations were getting rather strained at times. After so long in such a confined space, even the slightest little thing tends to aggravate a person, and of course this worked both ways. However, we were to put up with each other for two more passages, but fortunately they were short ones. It was important that we set out for Tonga soon, as our oldest daughter Denise would be arriving by air in Nuku'alofa, Tonga's capital, in about two weeks.

At 1100 on 20 July we had completed all the crew transfers between vessels through immigration and had our clearance certificate for departure. We pulled up anchor, and were on our way. We had to go well south to clear the reefs and the ship that was still high and dry on the reef. We also passed the cable-laying ship that was laying the new telephone cable from Australia to North America. It is a large ship with a modified bow for paying out the cable. Although I haven't seen it in operation, I presume it goes astern across the ocean letting out the cable as it goes. This cable makes possible the very good telephone reception we get between the mainland and the South Pacific. After going about eight miles south of Suva, we turned port and set course for Tonga. The weather continued to be very nice and the winds were favourable, so we had good sailing. The Sat Nav was still having some problems, as it was failing the receiver test when first programmed. I did not trust it completely, although it was giving fixes, so I decided not to push my luck and proceeded to Tonga via the southern route, through and around the islands that lie east of Suva. I had five people on board, but Lou was not working on a watch, so I had to do a watch in addition to the normal duties. Consequently, there wasn't as much time for navigation. This was good training for the passage of about 28 days, with a stop in Fanning Island, which was in store for me, when I had to stand watch for the entire period. Sunday, the following day, we altered course from 080C to 120C at 0100 hours so we would pass south of Ngau Island and the reef that lies south of it. As we sailed south of Moala and Totoya Islands and north of Matuku Island, this put us in the right place to pass Ongea Ndriki Islands to the south. We came very close to Matuku Island, and I recall altering course in the middle of the night when we were only a couple of miles away from it. I also note on my chart that in 1779 Captain Cook had anchored just a few miles south of where we passed. Also, we were near the place where Captain Bligh was set adrift in the lifeboat after the mutiny aboard his ship, the *Bounty*.

23 and 24 July were good sailing days, but near the end of the 24th the wind had moved around to the east right on the nose. Because the sailing was so ideal, I decided to make long tacks in the direction of Tonga, and we did this for two days. Finally the weather deteriorated, and the morale of the crew was sagging a little. It was getting rough, and we were not making much headway towards our destination, so I decided to use the engine to speed it up. We had only about 110 miles to go, with the winds still on the nose. It was rough, but we powered straight ahead for the next 24 hours and eventually arrived in Tonga. I had a choice of doing this or continuing to tack for two or three days, so I chose the former.

We had plenty of fuel, and with our powerful engine could make about 80 miles per day. Also, our freezer had stopped working the second day out, so we had cooked up all the meat, hoping it would keep with no refrigeration. By then we were opening cans for meals, so the rations were not up to their usual standard. The conditions were rough, and we took considerable salt water spray into the cockpit, but again the boat performed very well and took us into Tonga without any further delay. On 26 July, at 0442 hours we were two miles north of Late Island in light fog, which cleared shortly after. I was surprised to find we were so far south. The night before I had briefed the crew that Late Island should be visible in the morning, but when I got up to go on watch and found we were very close to the island I was quite surprised. Perhaps the Sat Nav was not giving good fixes or the helmsman had not steered a good course – I suspect a little bit of both! This gave us a very good fix with 40 miles to go to Neiafu, Tonga. At 0900 hours we sighted the peaks of the islands in Tonga and at 1300 hours were docked in Neiafu. It was 8 October the previous year when I left Neiafu for Fiji, making it less than a year since I was there. Things had not changed very much.

As usual, there was a long wait for the customs officials. They were probably having a party on a yacht that did not offer them a bottle. While we were waiting, one of the local boats with about 30 people on board came alongside. There really wasn't any room for their boat at the dock, but I moved up as far as I could go and let the stern out so they were able to get about half of their bow to the dock and raft against *Sea Lure*. The passenger vessel that came in from Nuku'alofa once or twice a week was on the main dock and the stern was sticking out about 20 feet, so the local vessel had a hard time getting enough space.

The skipper was a friendly fellow, as most of the Tongans are, and soon I saw a horse being led down to the dock in front of the boat. Having owned horses all my life, I was indeed interested in what was happening. The skipper and about four of the strongest men from the boat went on shore, and proceeded to tie ropes to the horse's feet in such a way that the horse could not stand when the ropes were pulled tight, and he fell to the ground. We had done this frequently when trying to shoe unruly horses, but I was surprised to see it right on the dock in front of the boat. After the horse was well tied up and stopped struggling, the men standing around the horse, and there must have been 6 or 8 by now, gently picked it up, lifted it over the bowrail of their boat and placed it on the deck! I was fascinated with this exercise, and took pictures of each operation. One appears in the book. Before departing, the skipper came over and gave us some yams as a thank-you and welcome to Tonga. As their boat was pulling away, I was ready to take a final picture when the horse started struggling again and got his head up just as I took the picture. The skipper then promptly sat on the horse's head so it could not struggle any more. The large group on his boat was obviously from one of the neighboring islands, so I expect the skipper was also the chief of the village and had decided to buy a horse and take it back to his island. We had noticed that some islands in Tonga and Fiji had one horse, so I guess it was the latest fad.

Shortly after the local boat departed, the customs people came back to their office and I offered them only half a bottle of gin as my stock was getting low. I reminded them that I had given them two bottles last time I arrived and they said, "We remember," so they cleared us with no trouble. Then we powered over in front of the Paradise Hotel and dropped the anchor. Lo and behold, there was *Drummer* and her owners, Louis and Sylvia Beaurivage. This called for a reunion and an updating of experiences.

I had last seen the Beaurivages in New Zealand at Whangarei, a day or two before we departed for Australia. They had stayed in New Zealand for another month and then had gone directly to Tonga, as they had passed up Tonga the previous year. They apparently had a wild sail, hitting some of the storms that were common in those waters in May and June 1985. Conditions were so bad they closed up and went below, and the yacht sailed itself for some time. They had two knockdowns during this time, but they survived and fortunately didn't cross course with another vessel during the storm. They made it to Tonga in record time, but it sounded hair-raising and dangerous. Their Sat Nav had been repaired in New Zealand, so it was working now and navigation was not a problem. *Drummer* had been all cleaned up with a paint job, engine overhauled and many other repairs, and was looking very nice. Everything was so inexpensive in New Zealand, it was the place to get boat work done or anything that had to do with boats. I'm sorry I didn't take greater advantage of this situation.

That night we all went out for dinner and had a great get-together. There were also some Americans in Tonga. In fact the couple who brought our ladder from Auckland to the Bay of Islands some months before were anchored close by and we met them again.

This was a busy year for Neiafu, as far as yachtees were concerned. Before we departed a month later, I counted over 40 ocean-going yachts anchored in front of the Paradise Hotel. This was double the number of the previous year. Louis decided to splurge a little, so instead of anchoring he tied *Drummer* to a buoy for which he paid a rental fee. Several nights later a strong wind came up in the middle of the night and *Drummer* started to drift. She went part way across the harbour and up against another yacht before Louis could get up and start the engine. He was still towing the buoy, so he dropped his anchor, and the next morning he investigated to find out why the buoy had not held. To his astonishment he found that the buoy had just a short piece of chain hanging under it. Someone had stolen the remainder of the chain that fastened the buoy to the cement or large piece of metal that rests on the bottom. We all had a good laugh at Louis' expense and he took it all in the spirit in which it was intended.

As we had promised to meet Denise in Tonga at the airport in Nuku'alofa on a specific date, we debated on whether to sail down, an overnight sail of about 100 miles, or to fly down and back. She was about five months pregnant with her second child, so we decided it would be safer for her to fly rather than be bounced around on a rolling boat. I made reservations on the Twin Otter aircraft operated by the Tongan airline. This aircraft, which was made in Toronto, Canada, had been purchased by the King of Tonga. It flew three times a week to Nuku'alofa. The schedule was not very reliable and the mechanic travelled in the aircraft so he could repair unservicabilities at the next stop. They did not have a backup aircraft, so some days they did not fly at all. They took our reservations all right as they collected quite a large sum of money.

We still had about twelve days before Denise would arrive, so on 31 July we sailed to Port Maurelle, a short distance away, and anchored for the night. We still had our local chart from the previous year, so we could still sail by numbers and this was No. 7. We spent a very pleasant night anchored there and as the next day was Lou's birthday, we decided to sail to my favourite island from the previous year, Nuku No.8. Since it was only 1.5 miles away, we anchored in the usual spot off the northeast corner of the island. I had no difficulty anchoring there before, and the winds were light. It is also a very sheltered area, so one anchor was sufficient, just beyond the reef where the bottom was secure for holding an anchor. The island was just as beautiful as ever. We went in with the dinghy almost every day for sunbathing. The only creatures on the island were half a dozen roosters, but they didn't give us much trouble.

On Lou's birthday, 1 August 1985, we were sitting on the side of *Sea Lure* looking down into the water and for about twenty minutes there was not a breath of wind and the ocean was like a giant aquarium. We could see hundreds of coloured fish swimming in formation – probably about twenty different species all at one time. It was a once in a lifetime experience and we were most fortunate to have been in the right place at the right time. We checked many times later but there was always too much wind to leave the surface crystal clear. What a fantastic sight! On another occasion we were sunning ourselves on the beach when one of the local Tongans from the village stopped with his boat to have a chat. He had caught two fish, about 3 or 4 pounds each, and he wanted to trade the fish for a quart of outboard engine oil, which was apparently in short supply. I just happened to have a spare quart on *Sea Lure* so we did business. He got his motor oil and we had fresh fish for supper! We visited a number of other anchorages in the Vava'u group of islands, but no other place compared with Nuku, however we were prejudiced as we had so many good times there.

We stayed in this anchorage until 5 August. That morning I was doing some work in the engine room when a local boat owner came alongside. He said, "I think you are drifting." Sure enough, the wind had come up and the boat had dragged anchor, and by now we were half a mile from the place we had been anchored for five days. Of course I hadn't bothered checking the anchor during this time, but no harm was done. We thanked him and I winched up the anchor, as it was now dangling in 200 feet of water. Just as well it didn't drag at night, but I probably would have woken up, as any change in the vessel's motion or noise would usually wake me. We had planned to leave that day, so we just carried on and were anchored in front of the Paradise Hotel by noon. We had just one more day before flying to Nuku'alofa on 7 August as Denise was arriving on the 8th.

Dick and Sharon were an American couple whom we had met in New Zealand when they had their boat on the hardstand at Half Moon Bay at the same time as *Sea Lure*. We had talked to them several times but were only nodding acquaintances. I discovered that Dick had been a refrigeration repairman back in the U.S. and still carried equipment for testing compressors. He also had a tank of Freon so I hired him to repair the freezer on *Sea Lure*. It didn't take him long to discover a leak in one of the pipes running to the freezer, which he repaired. Then he recharged the system with Freon and it worked well. In fact, it did not give any more trouble for the rest of the voyage. The leak had been causing the trouble in Fiji but the young fellow was not experienced enough to track it down. At a much reduced price, Dick corrected the problem. Some ocean-going sailors carry test equipment and Freon on the boat for such emergencies.

On 7 August we caught a bus to the airport and then boarded the Twin Otter aircraft. The field was very primitive for flying and the ceiling was low. There was no control tower as very few aircraft landed at this airport. The pilot had difficulty locating the field, but when he did he flew the downwind leg very close to the runway and then did a fighter aircraft approach so he would not lose sight of the field, then landed. The Twin Otter aircraft was suitable for this type of operations. I had previously flown in one when they were being tested in Toronto in 1970 and I was familiar with the short takeoff and landing for which this aircraft is famous.

We took off on schedule and there were one or two stops along the way before we arrived in Nuku'alofa. At one of the stops all passengers were requested to leave the aircraft, as a very important person would be coming on board. A few minutes later several limousines arrived and the Queen of Tonga, with one of her grandsons and bodyguard boarded the aircraft – then the passengers were permitted to return to their seats. It was indeed an honour to fly with the Queen of Tonga, but it was a very uneventful flight to Nuku'alofa. Just before the Queen departed from the aircraft I was able to take her picture, which appears here in the book.

The next day Denise arrived and we met her at the airport. She had flown from Ottawa to Vancouver, where she dropped off her oldest son Philip with our younger daughter, then to Honolulu, on to Nandi, Fiji where she stayed overnight, and from there to Nuku'alofa. It was a very long trip even by air. She was in good spirits and it was great to see her after such a long time. We stayed over an extra day at the Dateline Hotel so we could all tour the island of Tonga Tapei, the King's residence and the town. On 9 August, we returned to Neiafu by the same airline and then back to *Sea Lure,* which was still riding peacefully at anchor. Louis and Sylvia had been keeping an eye on her but they did not have to take any action. In the meantime, Patty and James had moved to shore and were staying with friends, so for the next eight days we had the boat to ourselves.

The Tongan feasts were still popular entertainment and a way of having a good meal off the boat at a reasonable price. There were two or three organizations operating the feasts, so this year we went with Isaiah's organization. He was a very nice person and we got to know him quite well. We did attend several of his feasts and took a large number of people with us each time. He gave us a discount if we had more than six people. His entire village took part in the preparation of the food, the dancing, singing, and the general operations of the feast. He had a large van that he used to pick up food, transport customers to and from the feast and a number of other jobs. In fact, he offered to drive us to the airport several times and he told me that the major income for the village was from the feasts. He worked very hard, but must have been doing quite well, as I noticed that one of the men from the village drove him most days. These feasts were very well run and we all had a lot of fun at them.

A German fellow owned a restaurant on an island about a mile from the town of Neiafu, and every Sunday he held an outdoor BBQ. It was a very popular event and a number of yachtees would take their boats, anchor close to the restaurant, and then go ashore in the dinghy. Also a number of tourists staying in Neiafu or at the Paradise Hotel would be taken over to the barbecue in special boats. So, the first Sunday after Denise arrived we decided to attend. We anchored in front of his place along with about eight other yachts and went in with the dinghy, although Denise insisted on swimming in, as it was not a long distance. The German and Tongan food was outstanding, and beverages were also available, so we had a very pleasant several hours. Then we went back to the boat, lifted the anchor and sailed back to our favourite island, Nuku. We stayed there until the following afternoon, then powered over to Port Maurelle and spent the night at anchor.

The following day was Tuesday and Isaiah was having his feast that night. Since Denise had not been to a Tongan feast, we decided to sail over to No. 10 bay (it does not have a name) and anchor in front of the area where it was always held. Dick and Sharon were already anchored, so we got together with them. Unfortunately Lou was sick that day, so we did not go to the feast, but Denise went with Dick and Sharon. Isaiah very kindly sent food out to us on the boat after the feast was over. They all apparently had a very good time and we were sorry to miss it. The next day Lou was still sick, so we sailed back to the anchorage in front of the Paradise Hotel. Luckily her sickness was not serious, and she was all right in several days.

Lou and Denise were both scheduled to go back to Canada on 17 August, and it was difficult to get their reservations confirmed on the airline out of Neiafu to Nuku'alofa. From there on was no problem, as they were going to Nandi, Fiji, Honolulu and Vancouver, but not on the same flight. Denise had to leave on an earlier flight, but they went together as far as Nandi.

We had had a very relaxing time and a good visit, although too short. Lou had been on the boat for six weeks and had made the passage from Fiji to Tonga and that was enough for her. Crashing through a heavy sea for 24 hours with the wind on the nose was not her idea of fun, but it isn't everyone that is cut out for offshore sailing. After several attempts, I finally got the bookings confirmed for the morning of the 17th, and Isaiah drove us out to the airport. The flight was delayed for several hours due to unserviceabilities, but it finally arrived. The cloud layer was quite low (about 800 feet) and the pilot had difficulty finding the airport. When he finally came through the clouds he flew parallel to the main runway, then did a fighter approach near the end of the runway, so he would not lose sight of it, and then landed. This would still leave Lou and Denise enough time to make connections in Nuku'alofa so it worked out all right. I was sorry to see them leave, but now I had to devote all my attention to getting the boat in shape, properly crewed and stocked with food, as I had been in Tonga for almost a month. It was time to depart if I was to arrive in Honolulu before Christmas.

Uve had left the crew, as he had signed on for only the passage to Tonga. He planned to settle down in Tonga and I believe he bought a small vegetable farm. James and Patty remained on the crew but we needed two more crewmen. When we were down in Nuku'alofa, I had met an American who had indicated that he would be interested in sailing with me as far as Honolulu. Although he had no sailing experience, he had a dream of doing an ocean voyage. He was now in his 70's and a heavy smoker, so did not want to delay much longer. He tried to arrange passage on another yacht, but at the last minute, the skipper changed his mind so he was dropped off the crew. His name was Jerry, and he had had a career with the Eastman Kodak Company at quite a senior level and after retirement moved to Hawaii. When the cost of living had risen and after his wife had passed away, he needed to move to a country in the South Pacific, and eventually came to Nuku'alofa. He had several pensions so he would not be a drag on the country.

I also met a young Tongan fellow who had sailed on another

yacht and agreed to go, but his father was not too much in favour. About a week before our departure I called Jerry, and he confirmed that he would come to Neiafu on the Tonga boat several days before our departure, and he would check on the Tongan fellow. On the appointed day, I went down to meet the inter-island boat and Jerry was on it, but the Tongan fellow had backed out. Just as well, as I would have been responsible for him, and probably would have had to pay his airfare back to Tonga from Honolulu. But this meant that I was still short a crewman. I met a young Australian at the Paradise Hotel who indicated an interest in going as far as Pago Pago, and although I was wary of Australians by now, I finally agreed to take him on the crew. He claimed to have had plenty of sailing experience, but this turned out not to be the case. He also had a friend from Tasmania and the deal was that I had to take them both, which gave me a crew of six. This was all right, as I had sailed with six before. The second chap, Craig, who was a very good sailor, turned out to be a very big asset to the crew and stayed with us all the way to Honolulu. So I now had plenty of crew, in fact too many.

It was now time to check the boat over for wear and tear and get it ready for another ocean passage. I had not been to the top of the mast for several months, and liked to check the condition at the top before starting out. Louis volunteered to go up and that was fine with me. I was getting a little old for these high wire acts, so we hauled Louis to the top of the mast on a bosun's chair, along with the extra halyard and safety harness as a precaution. He found that the forestay had three broken strands of wire. These were three out of 19 strands, but according to some sailors this weakened the forestay by 30% to 50% depending on who you talked to, so I decided that it must be replaced as soon as possible. The forestay holds up the main mast and takes a great deal of strain when the genoa is out. As this is the main power sail for *Sea Lure* and generates about 70% of our speed, it was essential that it be strong and safe. The next big question was how to order the new parts and where should they be delivered.

Pago Pago, in American Samoa, had good air service from the mainland and to all parts of the South Pacific. As most airlines stopped there, I decided that was the best port in which to replace the forestay. In the meantime we would nurse it along, reduce the strain on it as much as possible by not rolling the genoa out all the way except in very light breezes, and hopefully it should get us to Pago Pago. The next step was to order the parts correctly so the supplier could identify them. With hood furling gear on the forestay, it is not a simple matter to change the equipment when a long list of items is required. Fortunately, I had the manufacturer's handbook on board with the part numbers of all the items, and the directions for changing the gear. The next thing was how to communicate this information to my wife in Vancouver, so she could arrange for the ordering and delivery of the parts. I tried on the telephone for several hours, but the lines were down or unserviceable beyond Nuku'alofa. They would, however, accept a telegram. After many years in the logistics organization in the Canadian Air Force, I knew that great detail and correct part numbers were necessary to acquire the right parts. The 200-word telegram was expensive, but it did the trick. Lou took the telegram to the company in Vancouver that was originally Pacific Spar. They were able to supply the forestay from their stock, after making it up to the specifications I had sent. Some of the parts for the roller furling gear had to be ordered from the USA and sent separately. There were some delays, but it did work out satisfactorily in the end.

CHAPTER 14

A ROUGH RIDE TO THE SAMOAS

The next passage to Western Samoa would only be about four days, so the food shopping project was quite small. James and Patty had returned to the boat, so they looked after the shopping and we all chipped in an equal amount for the cost of the food. On 21 August everything was completed, and we were ready to depart the following morning. The next morning we said our farewells to the good friends in Neiafu, part of the yachting family, lifted the anchor and moved over to the main dock to clear customs, etc. before departure.

Although Uve had left *Sea Lure* he had left behind staph infection, i.e. boils, and I had caught it! By now, I had one large boil on my arm, and indications that another one or two were on the way. I recall we had some difficulty with the sails, etc. at the dock that morning in quite high winds, and in the struggle to get everything under control I bashed my arm and ended up with a big patch of blood on the deck. These boils were very nasty. They required dressing changes every day, and about six days later I had to go to the hospital in Pago for special medication to get them under control. I suppose this is one of the hazards of having a large and varied crew and not knowing all their problems.

Clearing customs and getting our clearance certificate was completed, and we cleared the islands and set course for Apia, Western Samoa at 1110 hours. The winds were good, 20 to 30 kts, but we were not making good speed, as the genoa was rolled out only half way to keep the strain off the damaged forestay. Also, we had the spare halyard tied firmly to the cleat on the bow to give the forestay some added support. I chose not to tell the crew about the three broken wires in the forestay, but James and Patty somehow found out about it, which was to cause a problem with Patty later.

The first thing we had to do, after the routine on the boat settled own, was to retard our date a full day or 24 hours – this was done at midnight by having 23 August twice, so now we were on the same day as the people in Western Samoa. The winds were quite high over the next four days and the sea choppy. Wind direction was east and, as we were travelling almost due north, made for good sailing. James and Craig were put on a watch together and as it turned out, they were the most experienced sailors and should have been Watch Captains. Craig did not emphasize the previous experience he had on sailboats, whereas the Australian talked a good line despite his lack of experience, so he ended up as a Watch Captain for the first day. This was a mistake on my part, as he was not experienced and did not exercise good judgment. However, despite this problem *Sea Lure* looked after us. Daytime was no problem as I was up and could give directions, but one night the winds went up to 40 kts and apparently it got a little confusing on deck. Right after this I changed the watch and this straightened out the difficulties.

Jerry Weston was a most dedicated sailor, and tried very hard despite his lack of boating experience. Steering a course with a compass was completely foreign to him, and it became a challenge to explain to him how to steer. At first, when Jerry was off course he would ask me, "Which way do I turn?" and it became obvious that I needed to find a very simple rule he could follow so that compass steering would be easy for him. I had not run into this problem before with any sailors, and had been steering boats or aircraft for so many years (since 1943) that I did it automatically. I also could not remember how the flying instructor taught me on my first flight with the RCAF during World War II. After thinking about this problem for some time I finally said to Jerry, "Turn towards the compass needle." The needle is always pointing to magnetic north so the boat has to be turned until the correct heading comes up on the compass. If you are off course to the right or to the left, you turn towards the needle. This seemed to satisfy Jerry and from then on he had no trouble keeping the yacht on course. In fact, he eventually became an excellent helmsman.

As we had an extra crewman, Patty started out doing the cooking, but she still took a turn at the helm from time to time. One afternoon she was on the helm and I heard her say, "I hope this forestay hangs together." She knew it was my policy to say nothing about the trouble with the forestay, so I called her into the cabin and proceeded to get after her for talking about it. She began to give me a hard time, so I ordered her out of the cabin. She was almost out of the cabin when she came back and made some very discourteous remark, and shook her fist about two inches from my nose. I held my temper and she then left the cabin immediately and went back on the helm. The subject of the forestay did not come up for the rest of the passage, and she apologized to me later for such obnoxious behaviour. The wind remained high for the entire trip and at 2000 hours on 24 August was up to 40 kts. Our boat speed picked up and on one day we covered 149 miles, which was unusually good for *Sea Lure*.

On Sunday 25 August we were getting close to Western Samoa – it was still rough and very windy. At 0600 hours the watch-keeper's log records gusts to 50 kts and winds at steady 35 kts. It had been a tough night and I had not slept well. At 0900 we sighted land, and were heading for the passage between Savai'i and Upolu Island. Apolima Island is right in the middle of the passage. I could not remember on which side of the island I had passed a year previous when going from Western Samoa to Fiji. The Sat Nav told me to keep the island on the starboard side, the sailing directions were not too clear, and the charts were poor as usual. I finally decided to keep this island on my port side, after being more or less talked into this decision by a member of the crew, and this almost resulted in disaster. After passing Apolima Island, the water started to get shallow, so I asked James to go up on the bow and watch for reefs and we proceeded at slow speed. The reef was getting closer as we progressed, and James was all for picking our way through the reef as we had done before in Fiji. All the other crew were sleeping at this point, and the weather was not good with a light rain and poor visibility. Suddenly, I saw the large marker buoy off our port bow about half a mile away. We were obviously in the wrong place and could have gone aground on a reef in a few minutes. I told James we had to get out of there as fast as possible. While he kept a sharp watch on the distance from the reef, I made a 180-degree turn and we went back about a quarter of a mile until we were clear of the reef, then headed on the other side of the buoy. It marked the edge of the reef and if we had proceeded much further, we would have been high and dry and would have probably lost *Sea Lure*. The shore was about a mile away and we would have had difficulty getting six people there safely in those conditions. Another close call, but we got lucky.

It was still quite a long distance from the pass into Apia with many reefs around, so it took us until 1110 hours to finally get into the harbour and anchor. As this was Sunday and customs do not work, I decided that we would all stay on board and go into the dock early on Monday morning to clear customs. This worked out rather well as we were all tired and needed a good sleep. Besides, the linkage on the gearshift had broken down so we had a three-hour job to repair the linkage and hook it up again.

The next morning we lifted the anchor right after breakfast and powered over to the customs dock. They cleared us rather promptly this time, but we had a miserable time getting out from the dock area as usual; the tide flows swiftly in this confined space and most yachtees have difficulty here. This time I tried to turn around with lots of power, but the bow wouldn't come around fast enough. Craig had the presence of mind and experience to leap onto the dock and push the bow around, after we had hit the dock with some force. I think *Sea Lure* still carries the scar on the starboard side. Finally we were anchored again in front of the town in our favourite spot in front of Aggie Grey's Hotel and this time the crew could go ashore.

I decided to move into the hotel again for three or four days, as I had enjoyed it the year before, except that something made me sick for a day or two. Sure enough, on about the third day I was sick again. Three large meals were supplied along with the room and I expect that something in the food or water was not good. I took several days to recuperate. In fact, the day we left for Pago, I was still not feeling so great.

Patty and James decided that they would leave the boat, take the ferry to Pago and then fly to Honolulu. After many months they were finally leaving the ship. They had been good crew despite small problems, but it was time for a change for them and for me. Instead of a going-away party, I took them to Aggie Grey's Hotel for a nice dinner. It was very pleasant and a most happy time. The next day they moved to a place on shore. It took them the better part of a day to move everything in the little dinghy and clean up the forward stateroom, which they had occupied for about four months. About five or six weeks later we were to meet, by chance, in Honolulu at a restaurant in the harbour.

We spent a week in Apia this time and it was all very pleasant. We visited the usual places of interest, and went out for dinner several times. The crew enjoyed it very much as they had not been there before. The Western Samoan people are such happy and congenial people.

This time the Canadian flag on *Sea Lure* was not hoisted each morning to band music, as Bob was not there. It was flown most days, but raised and lowered when someone thought of it.

Aggie Grey was in a wheel chair as she had a stroke during the past year, but she was still around the hotel doing the P.R. Most of the guests went up to speak to her. She was the last living legend of the South Pacific.

The forestay had held together, and I was anxious to get to Pago Pago to see if the parts and new forestay had arrived, and get the work done as soon as possible. I had confirmed by telephone to Vancouver that the forestay and the parts from Vancouver had been shipped, but I didn't have any word on the parts that were to be shipped from the U.S.

On 1 September I moved from the hotel back to *Sea Lure* and at 1530 we lifted the anchor and left for Pago. The clearances with customs had been arranged the previous day. The weather was not that pleasant; the wind was from the east right on the nose, so we had the engine running. By midnight it was raining, and towards morning the wind was 30 knots and it was choppy. Quite often it is choppy and miserable between Apia and Pago, at least it was both times we made the short crossing. At 0400 the crew altered course to keep clear of a freighter. By 1000 hours we were looking for the harbour entrance to Pago and after a little difficulty we found it, though the beacon I was looking for was not readily visible. At 1130 hours we arrived in Pago.

This was a Monday, but customs were not open as it was a holiday, so we anchored and waited until the following day to clear customs. Quite a large number of yachts were anchored in the Pago harbour, but very few were heading for Hawaii. As we were going into the harbour I noticed a nice-looking yacht with furling gear on the bow and decided to talk to the skipper at the first opportunity. We had to make plans to change the forestay and decided, after studying the furling gear handbook, that we were short of expertise to do the job. If we could find a sailor who had experience in this type of work, and if he could be hired, the crew would work as his assistants. When he was going by in his dinghy I hailed him and he came over. We were really in luck, as he was sailing around the world from England with his family, and had a lot of yachting experience. He had also changed the forestay on his own boat as well as on a friend's boat, and agreed to supervise the job on our yacht at a reasonable price. How lucky could we get! He turned out to be very skilled, very pleasant and a first rate person in all respects. That day we made our plans to do the job, providing the parts had arrived and I could make a reservation with the Pago Harbour authorities to get space at the dock one day that week. The Englishman also examined the furling gear and had a look at the handbook. He considered that it would be a straightforward job if we had all the replacement parts.

The next morning bright and early we went into the dock to clear customs. Two or three boats got in ahead of us, so we rafted third or fourth out, much to the consternation of the skipper on the inside. I did put on an extra bow line right to the dock to reduce the strain on his lines. It didn't take us very long to find customs and get cleared, as I knew their routine, having been in Pago once before. Then we went back out and anchored again. The next order of business was to go into the dock and catch a bus to the airport, which was about six miles from downtown Pago, and check with a shipping company to see if the boat parts had arrived. The shipment from Vancouver had arrived, but the shipment from the U.S. mainland had not. I decided that I could wait until Thursday for the arrival of the rest of the parts, but if they had not arrived by then we must go ahead with the job, as the English chap would not be available later to supervise. Reserving a spot at the dock was not easy as it was the main customs dock and was frequently in use with incoming yachts. After getting the runaround for several hours, I got a permit from one of the senior port officials to come in on Thursday and remain only 24 hours, providing any incoming yachts could raft against us. This was quite acceptable and we were fortunate to get the space. The following day I made another trip to the airport, but the parts from the USA had still not arrived.

The weather in Pago was as bad as ever. It rained every day for at least part of the day, and the winds were high in the harbour, although the temperatures were quite warm. John Wood, from Keri Keri, New Zealand came over to *Sea Lure* for a visit. I hadn't noticed his boat anchored in the harbour – hadn't seen him for almost a year, but he had told me that he planned to do some ocean sailing. I believe he had gone to Tahiti, and was now sailing his way back to New Zealand. We had a good visit and discussed our mutual crew problems plus a lot of other things, but he was leaving the following day so I didn't get the opportunity to see him again.

My crew was getting smaller; the Australian chap left in Pago,

191

so we were down to three. Jerry, Craig and I needed at least one more to handle the two watches for the 2500 miles to Hawaii. Even with one more, I would have to go on watch for the entire time, but I was game to do it and knew that I could handle two jobs. An American skipper, who had lost his boat on a reef or by some other misfortune, had agreed to go on the crew, but we had trouble getting together. Besides, Jerry thought he would not be suitable so I didn't press it. In the meantime, a German who lived in the U.S. became friendly with the crew. He had been trying for a month to find a yacht that would take him to Fiji and then to New Zealand, but so far he was unsuccessful. I hoped that if he got an offer he couldn't refuse, he would come with us, but the time was not right yet. We had a forestay to change, which might cause some unforeseen problems!

5 September we moved to the dock bright and early after breakfast, before any other yachts docked in my space. The Englishman had come on board as we pulled up the anchor, and as soon as we got tied up he went to the top of the mast to unhook and lower the forestay. In the meantime we slackened the backstays and disconnected the forestay at the bowsprit. With the help of Craig and Jerry we were able to lower the forestay to the dock beside the boat. When the Englishman took it all apart he discovered that one of the bearings in the furling mechanism at the bottom had broken and disappeared, probably in the storm, and the furling gear was rolling on the one remaining bearing. This was our first and only major problem that day, so all work came to a halt while the Englishman and I took the other bearing as a sample, and caught a bus to a company that specialized in bearings. They were over on the other side of the harbour, a twenty-minute bus ride, but to our great delight they kept this particular type of bearing in stock and for $20 U.S., we were back in business. This caused a two-hour delay, but right after lunch we proceeded with the change of all the equipment, and by using some of the parts that were still intact we were able to complete the job without the parts that had not yet arrived. It did take us all afternoon to finish the job and hoist the forestay again, tighten the backstay, and complete all the miscellaneous jobs. We then tested the furling mechanism by rolling the genoa out and back in and it worked quite well. A minor adjustment at the top carried out by the Englishman, and it was rolling perfectly. It was such a relief to

get this big job done with minor difficulties. I paid the Englishman $100 U.S. for the day's work and took Jerry and Craig out for dinner at the best restaurant in town. It was a delightful meal, and now we could make our plans for the extra crewman, date of departure, take the boat to the refueling dock, get the food, etc.

As we were leaving the restaurant we spotted the Englishman and his family. He had decided to take them out for a nice dinner, and what he earned that day would cover the bill quite nicely. It had been a good day. Pago Pago had been the right choice of places, due to the number of companies operating there, and the good transportation from the mainland. In most other places we would not have found that bearing and would have had to order it, with a delay of at least a week.

About this time we met and became quite friendly with an American from Alaska, who had just sold a landing barge to the government in Pago. I call it a landing barge, but this description may not be quite correct. It was designed to carry vehicles or some other heavy load, had a square bow and a large watertight loading ramp that could drop down on a beach, etc. It had two powerful engines on the stern just above the water level, and a bridge and living quarters on the next deck. He and an assistant, along with an engineer, had just ferried this vessel all the way from Alaska to American Samoa via Hawaii. It was not quite clear if he had owned the vessel previously or not, but he was responsible for delivering it to Pago and had just arrived a few days before we did. The vessel had been sold to the government in Pago, was in very good condition, and probably was worth more than one million dollars. He had just handed it over to the government officials, but took me for a tour of it as he still had a set of keys. He also gave me part of the first aid kit and a few other small things that he said the Samoans would not use.

We had good times together and he was on *Sea Lure* several times. In fact, when he helped us move the boat from the main dock to the anchorage, we went in a little too close to shore and went aground for the first time. He suggested that two or three of the crew stand on the bowsprit and the weight lifted the keel off the mud and we backed off with no problem. This works when a vessel has a full keel and draws the most water right at the stern. Over the next week we saw a lot of him as he had about a week to spare before flying back to Alaska and he got along well with my crew.

He originally came from the State of Washington, so we had a lot of things in common, although he was considerably younger.

The 13th of September, 1985 was a Friday. A great deal of superstition exists with sailors in that it is an unlucky day to sail, so I decided that the day before, Thursday, 12 September, would be a better day. At least I shouldn't get any static from my crew.

I was still trying to find one or two crew to sail to Hawaii, but at that time of the year there were very few in Pago. One local bartender agreed to go, but at the last minute he changed his mind, and the skipper that had lost his yacht was nowhere to be found. The day we went to the refueling dock to fill up the diesel tanks we saw him at a distance after we left the dock. I guess he thought we were leaving for Hawaii, as he didn't show up again. Finally I made an offer to Peter, the sailor who had been trying to get to Fiji. If he would crew for me to Hawaii, I would pay for his food plus $400 U.S. After we arrived in Hawaii and after he had a holiday there, as he had never been in Hawaii before, I would pay his airfare to Fiji and give him a letter of recommendation that would help him get on a boat to New Zealand from Fiji. He agreed to this very good offer, and although it cost me $700 plus his food for a month, it was a good deal for both of us, as he was an excellent sailor, in fact, one of the best on the entire voyage. Peter was a graduate of one of the top U.S. universities, I think it was Cornell, and his father was a professor at Harvard – people of very high intelligence. After several weeks on board, Peter could read my mind – in fact it was uncanny – and he would go ahead with projects, etc. that I was just thinking about. He would, of course, always confirm first that this was what I wanted done. I had never had a member of my staff with such abilities, so it was incredibly easy to work with Peter. I suppose our thinking processes were very similar, and we seldom disagreed on anything.

The weather was still terrible in Pago, raining and blowing most of every day, but we proceeded to get ready to leave and get out of this dreadful place. We replaced a battery on the boat, filled up the water tanks, bought the food and beverages and had them delivered to the boat. Finally, after clearing customs and getting our clearance certificate by 1530 hours on 12 September, we left the Pago harbour. It was blowing and raining, but as soon as we were 10 miles on our way the weather cleared up, and it was beautiful for the next 21 days.

CHAPTER 15

BACK TO HAWAII

The passage from American Samoa to Hawaii can be very difficult. Most yachts have more than their share of trouble on this route. It is generally against the trade winds and some yachts have taken more than 40 days to make this passage. In fact, when Dick and Sharon came the same route several months later, it took them about 42 days, as the winds were most unfavourable. However, the pilot charts indicated that September is the month of the year with the best possibility of favourable winds, and 1985 proved to be a normal year.

Our most direct course was 032 T, and the winds were southeast and east 12 of the 15 days that we sailed on that passage. The wind speed was 10 to 20 knots, which is normal for the trade winds. The other three days the wind was in the northeast, so we had to sail off the wind about 25 degrees. This took us port of our intended track, but once the winds changed we very easily returned to our best course.

We were short a crewman, but I enjoyed being on the helm for six of every 24 hours. It was such beautiful sailing most of the time that it was a real pleasure. Even though I had to do the navigation, engine work and cook my share of the meals, which was five or six a week, it all seemed to work out fine. Jerry was on watch with me, with Craig and Peter on the other watch. We changed the watch system to six hours on and six hours off with the same watch each day. I cannot function properly with changing watches, so this put everyone into a routine that continued all the way to Hawaii. I'm sure it contributed to better morale and a more enjoyable time. We still had our happy hour each day and the usual routine on Sunday.

Craig and Peter took their shower in the ocean every day; a procedure we hadn't used before. It was Peter's idea and I guess he learned it from other yachtees. About the third day out of Pago Peter came to me and said, "Do you mind if Craig and I drag behind *Sea Lure* to wash off rather than take a shower every three or four days?" I would normally have said no to such an idea, as I just don't want anybody in the water while I am operating the yacht, particularly since I didn't have insurance. However, he was such an outstanding crewman that I said, "Peter, show me how you are going to do it." He then took my heaviest docking line, about 20 feet long, and tied a loop in one end with several large knots spaced up the line right up to the stern of the boat, and fastened it to the large dinghy davit on the port side. Then he went over the stern, using the knots in the line to let himself down the five or six feet to the water, and then went hand over hand until he reached the loop at the end. Here he dragged for 10 or 15 minutes at the speed of the boat – this day it was six knots. When he had enough he pulled himself up the rope hand over hand using the knots, and finally over the railing onto the deck. He did all this quite effortlessly. Obviously he was very strong, and a powerful swimmer. While all this was going on, the life ring was dragging about 25 feet behind him, and the idea was that if he miscued and lost the drag rope he would catch the life ring as it went by. There were lots of sharks in these waters, but that was a chance they were both prepared to take, and I went along with it.

Craig went through the same procedure and he did it fully as well as Peter. From then on, for the rest of the voyage to Honolulu, the boys had a wash off every day in the ocean when they were not on watch. One dragged while the other kept a lookout for any danger that might appear, or if his partner lost the main rope or missed the life ring. The ocean was reasonably calm most of the time, so it would have not been a great effort to slack sheets, start the engine and go back for the crewman, but this did not happen.

A picture of Peter dragging behind the boat appears in the book. I would not have let most of my crew do this maneuver, but these two fellows could handle it with ease and I didn't worry about them after the first day or two. This also saved the water in the shower tank, so Jerry and I could waste water during our fresh water shower.

On 14 September we changed the genoa as it had been torn slightly. This sail was new when I left Vancouver and had served us well, but was now showing signs of wear. With a four-man crew it is quite easy to lower the genoa onto the deck, and then push it through the forward hatch into the forward stateroom. It is not quite as simple to hoist the sail, but with all these hands it is comparatively easy if the winds are not too high. If this happens, it is then necessary to wait until the wind subsides. The second genoa, that came with the boat when I bought it, was still in good shape. Although the dacron was of a lighter weight, we just had to be a little more careful with it in high winds, i.e. roll it in part way when the winds went over 20 knots. I had bought and installed another winch on the port side and it was used for reefing the genoa only. The sail could then be set or rolled in to any extent, and the line from the drum was wrapped around the winch to hold it in position. This worked very well and left the other winch for the genoa sheet only.

On 24 September at 1408 hours we crossed the equator for the second time. Our longitude was 161 degrees 54 minutes West – this was less than a mile from the place on the ocean where we crossed the equator on 22 August 1984. This time, Jerry suitably inscribed the opposite side of the board used the previous time and we took pictures and celebrated the occasion in a fitting fashion. The Sat Nav was still working just fine and it never ceased to amaze me how, when crossing the equator, the latitude would suddenly switch from North to South, or vice-versa this time. Of course the longitude switched from West to East when we crossed the International Date Line. The electronic age makes life so much easier and the calculations much more accurate as long as the machine is functioning.

The coordinates for Fanning Island are latitude 3°, 51' North, longitude 159°, 22' West so we didn't have far to go before we reached this island again. This passage was quite uneventful with very little ship traffic. Neither log indicates a ship sighting, so I presume there was nothing. This is common in this part of the world, as there is little commerce and few shipping lanes.

It took us 15 days to get to Fanning Island, where we had stopped on our way to the South Pacific the previous year, compared with 11 days 4 hours going down. This was still good progress compared with what it could have been. Our best day was 141 miles and our slowest day 86 miles. We had sailed 1597 miles, considerably more than on the way down, and our average per day of 106.5 was close to our overall average. Not bad for a slow boat on the way back to Vancouver!

On 27 September we sighted Fanning Island at 1430 hours. Two hours later we had threaded our way through the reef, and were anchored in English Bay again, in front of the village. The customs man, who was also the radio operator, and his family were getting ready to move to another island – he had been transferred. He remembered us from the previous year, so decided not to put us through the customs clearance procedure. This saved him and us several hours of time, so I was looking forward to several days of crew rest before we pressed on for Honolulu 1000 miles straight north, but *Sea Lure* had other plans for us.

After we had dropped the anchor in front of the village, while going astern to set the anchor, I noticed that it was difficult to shift the transmission from reverse to neutral. This was strange, so after we were properly anchored with two anchors (one off the bow and the other off the stern), I decided to have a look at the transmission fluid. I was shocked to find there was only foam on the dipstick and no transmission fluid showing. This meant that the fluid cooler had corroded and let salt water into the transmission, where it had mixed with the fluid and resulted in foam. The transmission could not function in these conditions, and could be seriously damaged if the problem was not corrected immediately. If this had to happen, Fanning Island was about the best place, short of Honolulu. We had replaced the oil cooler the previous year in Honolulu on the way down, but did not have the foresight to also change the transmission fluid cooler. It had corroded after all these months, and finally gave up. The first thing to do was to change the cooler to prevent more salt water from running in. Unfortunately I did not carry a new spare cooler, but still had the used oil cooler that was taken off the year before. It was similar in size, but one end connection was a different size. With about two hours of work, Peter and I found enough adapters on the boat to finally get it hooked up. Although it was not the right type of cooler, I was hoping it would get us to Honolulu.

The next job was to get the foam out of the gearbox. I had only about two litres of transmission fluid on board and should have been carrying at least six, so I went ashore in the dinghy and found the Englishman who ran the store. This was the same chap that had been on board for dinner with his wife the previous year, and I was sure he would provide help if possible. I needed to buy about two gallons of transmission fluid, but he didn't have any to spare. After considerable discussion he finally agreed to lend me two gallons, as long as I would return it after flushing the gearbox. This was the best we could do, so we had to manage. I saved my transmission fluid for the final fill-up, and used his fluid for the flushing. This was a long tedious procedure. Each time we filled the gearbox with fluid after the first time, I started up the engine and put it into forward gear and back to neutral several times. I was hoping this would aid the flushing of the gears and it seemed to work out this way. At first it was very difficult to change gears, but each time it improved. We pumped out the foam and fluid with the hand pump the first few times, but then switched to the electric pump and this speeded up the process. The batteries were well charged so we could afford to use up some current. All the following day we spent filling the gearbox, running the engine and shifting gears, and then pumping the fluid out. Each time the quantity of foam was reduced and the fluid looked cleaner. On the seventh pump-out, near the end of the day, the quantity of foam was negligible so we stopped the procedure, and filled the gearbox with clean Dexron 11 transmission fluid. The gear was shifting forward and reverse almost normally now, and since it was the best we could do we would try for Honolulu. If the transmission failed, we could sail to the entrance of the Ala Wai yacht basin, drop an anchor, and ask another yacht crew to tow us in.

In Pago Pago when we provisioned for food, we had kept the quantities of everything to a minimum for four people for a month. The two young fellows had hearty appetites, and we should have bought more food. There was a store on Fanning Island where I bought a few things, but money was getting short and I had to save some money for our arrival in Honolulu, when I could get more. Fortunately we were catching fish and had fresh fish for dinner each week, or we would have definitely run out of food. Also the propane tanks had not been topped up, and we were working on our last tank. I knew it would be close on the food and propane, particularly if we were longer than planned on the passage and this normally was the case.

At 0800 hours on 29 September we lifted the two anchors and powered out of English Bay and the route through the reef to clear the island. Incidentally, late the previous night I had returned the two cans of used transmission fluid to the Englishman. He wasn't home, so I left the cans at his door with some money and I'm sure he got it all right. At 0956 hours we set course for Honolulu and closed down the engine. The gears were working all right but the gearbox was getting extremely hot, so the fluid cooler was doing a poor job. With the right cooler the gearbox would be warm, not hot. For the rest of the passage, when we needed the engine to drive the boat, we would power for one hour and close down for three hours to let the gearbox cool off. Fortunately, gearboxes of this type will take a great deal of heat before packing up, so this worked in our favour. Only once do I recall did we sit for three hours and not move at all while the gearbox cooled off (this was in the doldrums). The rest of the time there was plenty of wind from the right direction, or we could use the motor. Charging batteries and keeping the temperature down in the freezer was not a problem as I could run the engine and leave the gear in neutral, but even this was necessary only once or twice.

The wind was from the east at 10 to 15 knots and, as we were going almost directly north, the beam reach was our best point of sail. The second day we made 123 miles – our best day. The winds continued from the southeast and east and we had two or three days from the northeast, but we were always able to sail on or close to our desired course. Wind speeds were 10 to 20 knots on the average, but occasionally dropped to four or five knots for short periods and went up to 30 or 35 knots, also for short periods. There were no storms on this entire passage, and on 29 September the main log recorded "Still beautiful weather." It had been like this without a break since we left Pago.

4 October marked the end of the beautiful weather, which had lasted for 21 days, including our two-day stop in Fanning Island. The conditions did not deteriorate that much, just a little rain and clouds, but the winds picked up to 20 kts from the northeast and we sailed faster. That day we made 102 miles; back to our overall average.

We still had six days to go, and I was getting concerned about the quantity of food and propane left. We had a box of pancake flour that had been on board for a long time, perhaps several months, so we decided early one morning it was time to use it up. I had a pancake breakfast, but for some reason Jerry did not have any. Perhaps he knew something I didn't. Some time later, Peter and Craig got up, and I mentioned they could have pancakes and syrup for breakfast. They have younger eyes and before mixing up a batch they spotted small worms in the pancake flour. I hadn't noticed the worms and so had a little more protein with my breakfast, but at least they were well cooked. We all had a good laugh at my expense! I was all for throwing the flour out, but the boys objected, and they ended up putting the flour through a screen they found in the galley and throwing the worms overboard. The next morning we had pancakes and syrup sans worms, and utilized that food to the fullest.

Jerry wanted to do some exotic cooking, I've forgotten exactly what. We did have the ingredients on board, but his cooking was going to take lots of propane, as it had to be baked in the oven. I got him to delay his project until the night before we arrived in Honolulu, when if he used up all the propane it would not matter. In the meantime, we worked out the food supply and determined that we would be one or two dinners short. So I said to the crew, "We just have to catch another fish." For the next 24 hours we really concentrated on fishing, hoping not to make any mistakes, and sure enough we caught another tuna, about 10 lbs. This time we stopped the boat as soon as we heard the shock cords rattling, and used the net to hoist the tuna up onto the deck. This was a most welcome catch and we had two dinners of fresh fish. After dinner on 10 October, I advised Jerry that it would be all right for him to do his baking. Honolulu was getting close and I expected we would be in the next morning. The winds were from the east-northeast at 20 to 25 knots and we were making good time. *Sea Lure* was performing well so, short of a disaster, we would make it the following day before noon. Even if Jerry used up all the propane we could still manage. Sure enough, about the time Jerry finished his baking the propane supply gave out. That meant no tea or coffee during the night and no toast and coffee, etc. for breakfast. We still had soft drinks on board and some bread so we didn't exactly go hungry, but it was a little inconvenient. It didn't take us long to devour the baking that Jerry had done.

At 0512 hours we sighted land – the island of Oahu. The visibility was good that morning and the mountain peaks were in sight. Shortly after this a large power boat came towards us. The crew had been briefed on our evasion maneuvers in the event it was drug smugglers coming out to seize *Sea Lure* and knock off the crew. We had not made any radio transmissions, as it was my policy, when getting close to Hawaii, to go to radio silence so another vessel could not home in on us when we were transmitting. At that time, i.e. 1984 – 85, Hawaii had the worst reputation for drug smuggling of all the countries we visited. I was on the helm at the time so did not alter course, but had the engine running in case we had to try to get away from the other boat. With the sheets slacked and the engine at full power, which would give us over eight knots, we could keep clear of another boat at least for a few minutes, while we called the coast guard in Honolulu to give them our lat and long, plus a description of the attacking boat. At the same time, by getting down low behind the helm of *Sea Lure*, I would not be an easy target for a rifleman on the approaching vessel. All these things went through my mind, but fortunately the plan did not have to be implemented. The other boat came quite close to us, but it became obvious they were a fishing charter boat, out early that morning to fish. They were not particularly interested in us at all. Just as well.

As we approached Waikiki from the south, about four or five miles out, a maze of tall buildings appeared, and it was a little confusing as to which tall building to head for to find the entrance to the Ala Wai Yacht Basin. Eventually, we could see a tall building with coloured ceramic tile, and although I could not remember for sure, I thought this would get us close to the entrance. Jerry, as usual, was trying to show his knowledge of the Waikiki water front, although he had never seen it before from the ocean, and finally I had to tell him to "shut up" as he was interfering with my thinking process. About 20 minutes later Peter came back to the cockpit and asked me where I thought the entrance to the harbour was located. By then, I could see the tops of a large number of masts and knew my course was correct, so I said to Peter, "Straight ahead, see the sailboat masts?" This satisfied him and he passed the information to the rest of the crew. We had no trouble finding the entrance to the harbour, and although it is against the customs rule, I stopped at the refueling barge on the starboard side on the way in, and bought a tank of propane and some sandwiches. The attendants on the dock made some comments about us clearing customs, as they could tell from our appearance that we had been at sea for a long time. I assured them that everything was all right, and we went from the refueling dock straight to the customs dock to phone for them. In the meantime, we got the stove going and boiled water and had some coffee, sandwiches, etc.

It was 1130 hours by the time we tied up at the customs dock, and the official showed up about two hours later. We were cleared with no problem, and then moved over to the Hawaii Yacht Club. One of the club members and his son had stopped at *Sea Lure* while we were waiting for customs, and advised us that there was space at the Yacht Club and to see the manager to make arrangements. This was typical of the hospitality of the Hawaii Yacht Club members, a very fine group of sailors. By mid-afternoon we were tied up in front of the club in one of their choice moorage spots. The very congenial manager prepared all the papers, etc. and made us most welcome. We were again permitted to stay there for a week at a very reasonable fee, and could use all their facilities which included showers, dining area where they had an orchestra playing during and after dinner most evenings, the bar, etc. By 1700 hours we were all showered and shaved, had changed clothes and were attending their large happy hour on Friday night along with about 100 of their club members.

We were in very good spirits after such a long but most successful time at sea, and a voyage of over 2500 miles. Each passage seemed to be unique because the crew changed most times, and *Sea Lure* and the weather kept throwing new problems my way with which I had to cope. The input of the crew was most helpful on many occasions, as they had varied backgrounds of experience, and some of it was often applicable to the problem at hand. This was the first time on the voyage that I had taken a full shift on watch for the entire passage, and it had worked out very well. I was tired at times and had lost over 20 lbs., but found I could cope all right with the extra duties. Jerry was a great help as we were on watch together, and the hours he was on the helm I was able to complete most of my other vessel duties except cooking.

Jerry became an excellent helmsman, and he learned not to backwind the genoa! The first two times he did this I handled the sheets while we did a 360° turn or jibed to get back on course. The third time he did it, I said, "To hell with it, you can do the work!" Jerry was sweating a little by the time he let out the one sheet and pulled in the other after we had made the jibe. That was the last time he backwinded the genoa. For a 71-year-old sailor he was agile, with a quick mind and great determination. It was a pleasure to sail with Jerry, and I hope he is still living happily in Tonga.

This was the last passage of my voyage for 1985. I had previously decided that the North Pacific Ocean is too rough and too unforgiving to sail after October, that the yacht would spend the winter in Hawaii, and that I would be on it as much as possible. Jerry left the boat a day or two later, as he had previously lived in Hawaii, and had friends he could stay with who lived some distance away. Peter and Craig stayed on board with me for several weeks, as they had not been to Hawaii before. They toured around most of the day and slept on the boat. Peter advised me of the date he would like to leave for Fiji, and I was able to purchase a one way ticket on one of the main airlines for about $300, as had been agreed. I also wrote a glowing letter of recommendation that he could give to a prospective skipper who was sailing to New Zealand and needed a crewman. It was the time of year that a large number of yachts would congregate in Suva to make the dash to the Bay of Islands in New Zealand before the hurricane season. I knew from experience that some of the yachts would need more crew, as this was the place I had picked up two more crewmen before leaving for New Zealand the previous year. I had no doubt at all that Peter would find a boat, and that the skipper would be extremely happy with him. He was one of a kind in my experience, and exactly the type of sailor every skipper hopes to get on his crew. He was very capable, but I realize I felt this way partly because our thinking processes were similar and, as a result, we differed on very few things. Craig was also a very good sailor and a congenial fellow as well as being a good cook. It was one of those times when the right crew was on board, the weather was almost perfect, and the boat problems were minimal with exception of the gearbox trouble, which we coped with admirably. Whereas most ocean sailors consider the passage from American Samoa to Hawaii pure misery, we couldn't have been luckier.

After a few days of rest, the next problem was to find a dock for *Sea Lure* that wasn't too expensive, where I could tie up the boat for several months and fly back to Canada. There were mooring buoys available at considerably less money, but I decided against this, as theft was common. The winds can get very high at this time of year, and there was always the possibility of a hurricane. I wanted a dock where I could tie up the boat, preferably with locked gates to the marina where there is at least some control. If there were live-on-boards this would be so much better. The manager of the Yacht Club put me on to a large marina-boat repair facility out close to the airport so I called them up. They did have space for me at a cost I could afford, so I went out to see the company. The marina being close to the airport, the jets took off right over it, but having lived on RCAF airbases for many years during my career, I could put up with the noise. Besides, I would be living on board only about two weeks total, so it would not be a hardship. When we ran out of time at the Hawaii Yacht Club, Peter and Craig went with me as they were still living on board, and we took *Sea Lure* to its new home. By then it was the latter part of October, and the boat was to remain at the marina until the end of January the following year.

The slip we were assigned to did not have enough space, as *Sea Lure* is quite beamy. One of the other skippers offered to move his boat to my slip and give us his, as he had plenty of space. It was very kind of him and we moved the same day, before my vessel and the boat next to it suffered any damage. This same chap, an American, also agreed to keep an eye on *Sea Lure* while I was away. This turned out to be a very good arrangement. The boat was absolutely safe and only needed a hosing off when I returned three months later.

While the two boys were still on board, I decided to go to the top of the mast to inspect all the equipment, including the new forestay. They hoisted me up on the bosun's chair with the safety harness fastened to the spare halyard. Up near the top I called down to ask them to roll up the spare halyard a little, and one of them yanked on it too hard and the winch came right off the mast. This is the winch that holds the genoa halyard, and undoubtedly it had worn the bolt holes in the mast after thousands of miles at sea, often in high winds, and it had finally given up. The halyard for the main on which the bosun's chair was attached held firm, so I was in no danger. Everything at the top was fine so they let me down. I was returning to Canada by air in a few days, and decided to leave the winch repairs until after returning, as I did not have the right sized taps to rethread the holes so an oversized bolt could be used to bolt the winch back on the mast. This left me something to do when I returned in January, as if a person needed something else to do on a yacht. Several days later Peter and Craig left the boat and I was very sorry to see them go. They were outstanding young men and were just like sons to me. I do hope I will see them again sometime.

Several days after the departure of the crew, I left for Vancouver, after storing the life raft in the aft cabin and doing all the other closing up jobs including, of course, shutting all 13 through-hull valves so there would be no danger of water getting into the boat. I caught a taxi to the airport terminal, and hoped for the best for *Sea Lure*. This was the second time I had left her and returned to Canada but even without insurance I wasn't unduly worried. I was confident that the yacht would be okay, and I couldn't think of any other precautions I should take. I did phone the marina several times while in Canada and had them confirm that the yacht was okay. My friend who had given up his slip for me must also have checked on it from time to time. He graciously accepted the two bottles of Beefeater gin I presented to him as a thank-you when I returned.

CHAPTER 16

WINTER IN HAWAII

I had been away from Vancouver for nine months this time, and it was good to get back home to my family and also go to Whistler, where we have a ski chalet, to do some skiing.

This was the Christmas Lou and I went to Dauphin, Manitoba to be with my brother and his family, and it was the first time in over 30 years we had been together at Christmas time. We had a very pleasant time.

Denise, our oldest daughter, was due to give birth to her second child just near the end of the year. Shortly after Christmas we flew to Ottawa from Winnipeg and arrived in time for the happy occasion – 29 December 1985 – when Matthew was born. About the middle of January we flew back to Vancouver, and then at the end of January I had to fly back to Honolulu, otherwise my return ticket would have expired. By then I was about the third or fourth day into a very bad flu. I decided to go back and recuperate on board *Sea Lure*. I was very sick for the first two or three days, but then recovered quite quickly.

Sea Lure had been just fine, and was still riding peacefully at the dock tied on the many lines put on it before departure. Even though it did cost a considerable amount (I've forgotten how much) it was worth it, as the marina was very well managed. The fact that the manager lived on his boat with his family just down the dock must have also helped matters. He was quite friendly and helpful later, so I think he liked *Sea Lure* and took a special interest in her. Another marina was right next door, and they had a pub that served food. While I was sick I couldn't cook, so went to the pub for dinner each night. It was such a happy place and so handy that I continued going there until I moved back to the Hawaii Yacht Club on about 8 February. I got to know some of the staff and the regulars that congregated there every evening after work.

In the meantime I went for lunch or dinner at the Hawaii Yacht Club, and lo and behold, there were Dick and Sharon again. This was the third or fourth time we met during the two-year period, and I was very glad to see them. They had just made the voyage from Tonga directly to Honolulu, but had unfavourable winds and some other problems. They had hoped to make it to Honolulu for Christmas, but I think it was close to the middle of January before the passage finally ended – over 40 days at sea – that is a long, long time. They did not carry much fuel on their yacht, and had to rely almost exclusively on the wind. I think it was north or northeast a good part of the time, so their sailing distance was greater than they had anticipated. They had plenty of food and water so that was not a problem. We had a great reunion and several days later Dick offered to help me bring *Sea Lure* back to the Hawaii Yacht Club. We accomplished this easily as it is a run of only about 10 miles, so I was again back at my favourite yacht club.

It was February, and it would be at least May or June before the North Pacific would be suitable for the return voyage, so I decided to do some sailing in the Hawaiian Islands. Manele Bay on the island of Lanai, the Pineapple Island, was the first stop and, as it turned out, was also the last stop.

The next thing to do was assemble a crew for the island hopping. Tom, a friend from Vancouver who owned his own boat, had previously planned to contact me in Honolulu and do some sailing on *Sea Lure*. I called him at his hotel and he came down to the boat, which was docked quite close to his hotel. After several days Tom decided to give up his hotel room and move to *Sea Lure* as I had lots of room. This gave me one crew member. A couple from Canada were holidaying in Honolulu and they were interested in doing some sailing, as they owned a boat and were experienced. So this gave me a crew for the short distance. They were compatible people and shared the boat duties such as cooking meals, etc. After restocking the boat with food for a 10-day period, and filling the fuel and water tanks, we were ready to go.

On 10 February at 1730 hours we departed Honolulu. I chose an afternoon departure so we would have an overnight sail to Lanai and would arrive the following morning. The weather was good, the sea was not as rough as usual, and the winds were about 15 knots from the east. Tom and I took the first watch from 6 p.m. to midnight, which was very pleasant. A ship crossed our route and initially did not alter course, although we were on a collision course. We had all sails up and engine off, so we had the right of way. I was just in the process of altering to avoid him, when he suddenly altered to keep out of our way. The ship was still a mile away so there was no danger. The satellite navigation system was still working, so navigation was no problem. Even if it had not been working there would still be no problem, as the islands and navigation lights are visible from a long distance. Ken and Emma took over at midnight and stayed on watch until 0600 hours. They were experienced sailors, having operated their fish boat on the west coast of Vancouver Island, and had been quite successful in catching fish. Ken was also very knowledgeable when it came to boat repairs. He was most helpful when the bolts holding the compressor in place worked loose, and the threads were stripped. He also replaced the internal water pump with a new one purchased in Pago Pago at great expense, and it is still working. He also tried to repair the autopilot but with less success.

At 0600 hours Tom and I took over the watch again, and everything was okay during the night. We were getting close to Lanai and could still see the light at Palaoa Point. It had been visible for most of the night and was like a beacon for us to steer by. Also the Sat Nav indicated good progress in the right direction. By 1030 hours we were approaching Lanai Island, and by 1130 we were anchored in Manele Bay with the stern tied to the end of one of the six short docks. Manele Bay is quite small, and has space for about 15 or 20 boats in addition to the dock that is reserved for the two or three cruise vessels that come in most days during the week. If all the docks are filled, there is enough space to drop the anchor in the shallow water and go astern to tie to the end of one of the docks. The tide change in this area is only a couple of feet most times of the year, and the docks are not floating. I had a long six-inch wide board in the engine room, so we used it as a gangplank to go down to the dock and then ashore.

Manele is a very pleasant bay about eight miles from Lanai City. There was no bus service to town but there was plenty of traffic and it was quite easy to catch a ride. Fortunately there were no telephones except in Lanai City, so it was nice and quiet and peaceful. There was no swimming in the bay, but just a half mile down the road was another bay for swimming only, no boats allowed, used by the locals and a few tourists who stayed over in Lanai. We took our dinghy around to this bay several weeks later, and were politely told to remove it.

Lanai was the Pineapple Island of Hawaii, and at that time the Dole Pineapple Company ran most operations on the island and provided most of the jobs. Pineapple fields covered most of the island and the company had some very large machines to harvest the pineapple. The main roads were paved and the back roads were kept in good condition. The Dole Pineapple Company has since been bought out by another company. They have built a large hotel where we used to go swimming. We haven't been back to see it but may do so one of these years when we are in Maui.

For the next five days the weather was poor, with lots of rain and high winds. We didn't do much, but when a good day came along we rented a car and went exploring. The island is not very big, so it doesn't take long to drive around and cover most of the roads. Actually there wasn't much to see except pineapple fields and I suppose this was part of its beauty.

On 18 February we decided to sail to Lahaina and anchor for several days and see the sights. The weather by now had improved so we went to Kaanapali first, but decided it wasn't a good place to anchor so we sailed down to Lahaina. We powered through the reef and into the breakwater area looking for a place to tie up. I hadn't been in there with a boat since 1978 when we raced to Maui in the Victoria to Maui Yacht race which takes place every two years. I was the navigator on *Tarun*. At that time, space had been cleared for our boats and all 32 tied up inside the breakwater, but this time all the space was taken on a permanent basis and there was no place for us. So along with a dozen or so other yachtees we anchored just outside the entrance buoys, leaving enough room for the boat to swing. The bottom is sandy and not very good for holding so we put down two anchors off the bow and had no problem.

It was great to get back to Lahaina after nine years and things in the town had not changed much. A considerable amount of construction had taken place; more motels, hotels and houses, but this was mostly out of town. The Pioneer Inn was first in the harbour, and the old Sea Captain was still standing next to the main entrance. The pub next door was busy and the orchestra was playing, so it was a fun place. The Lahaina Yacht Club was basically the same with perhaps a little updating, and the people were still friendly and pleasant. We went there for dinner, and the food was good. It has such a nice location right on the ocean in the middle of town. There were more art galleries in Lahaina now, or maybe I had just not noticed them before, and many have outstanding scenes of Hawaii.

After several nights at anchor and several days seeing the town, it was the consensus that we should go back to the quiet life in Lanai. After shopping for food, we lifted the two anchors and sailed for Manele Bay, arriving late in the afternoon on 20 February. There was still no room at the docks so we anchored again and tied to the end of one of the docks.

When we left Lahaina the sea was rough, and when jumping into the cockpit without taking enough care, I came crashing down on my left knee when the boat lurched at the wrong time. At first it did not seem to be too serious, but as the days passed severe swelling took place and it was necessary to go to a doctor. On the way back to Lanai, Ken and Emma ran the boat and I made sure the navigation was accurate. In the next day or two the leg got progressively worse; the swelling extended from the knee to the foot, giving me considerable pain.

Tom had to make his way back to Honolulu and then to Vancouver. There was a scheduled air service running into the Lanai airport but Tom didn't want to wait for the flight, so he caught a ride to the airport and talked someone who owned an airplane into flying him over to Honolulu.

I continued to struggle with my sore leg, and it wasn't improving. Lou, my wife, was arriving from Vancouver on 25 February, so it was necessary to go back to Maui to pick her up and also drop off Ken and Emma, as they had decided to go back to Canada. Early on 25 February we sailed back to Lahaina, and dropped the hook in the same place we had previously anchored. I had arranged for a U-Drive car, which we picked up, then drove to the airport at Kahului to drop off Ken and Emma and pick up Lou. I was most happy to see her and get a report on how things were going in Vancouver with the family and our various properties. I decided that I needed to see a doctor about my swollen leg. We found one in Lahaina who confirmed that nothing was broken but that with good care and medication it would take several weeks to mend.

Before turning in the car we drove up to the Haleakala Crater, and did some sightseeing on the Island of Maui. We stayed on *Sea Lure* that night, but it was so rough we didn't get much sleep. The wind was blowing one direction and the current was running the other and the boat was pitching like a wild bronco. I have never seen it so rough. This area is undoubtedly one of the worst places to anchor I have ever experienced.

The following day, February 27, we decided to sail back to Manele Bay, as we couldn't put up with that anchorage any longer. Getting the 40 lb. Bruce anchor up with the chain and rope, on a pitching boat, was a real problem with my sore leg. It is normally a job for two men, both in good condition, but there was no one else to help so I had to do it. It was extremely difficult but by taking it in slow stages, and with the help of the engine, I finally got it up. The winch was working so the chain and the Danforth 40 came up considerably easier, and finally after about half an hour we departed for Lanai and Manele Bay.

The next ten days involved getting my sore leg back in shape and being as inactive as possible. With bandages and medication, progress was slow but steady. We would walk down to the swimming beach occasionally but our activities were very much restricted.

After about a week or ten days I had to go back to Lahaina to see the doctor again, so this meant another trip to Lahaina and anchoring again. I was not looking forward to sleeping on a pitching boat and lifting anchors, but this time the sea was much more kindly, and due to the fact that my leg had improved the anchors were not such a struggle. The report from the doctor was favourable.

By this time Marg and Gard Gardiner were holidaying at Waiohuli Beach Hale resort in Kihei, so we called them up and arranged to get together. They very kindly drove down to Lahaina and picked us up and took us back to Waiohuli, where we spent a very pleasant day swimming, lunching and having a good time. They drove us back to Lahaina that night and we went back to *Sea Lure.*

After several more pleasant days in Lahaina, we decided to go back to Manele Bay, as this was my second home. The anchors came up easily and we powered back, as the winds were too light for sailing. I used more than the normal cruising power on the engine, consequently causing the exhaust system to give up. It got us back to the dock in Manele Bay, but the following day when I started up it didn't sound right, and after moving to another dock the engine would not start at all. I checked the fuel filters and determined that the fuel was okay, but was then suspicious that the problem was much more serious. I removed one of the injectors and found water on it, indicating that salt water was getting into the engine. This is extremely serious and if action is not taken promptly the engine can be completely ruined.

I hadn't had any experience with this kind of engine problem, and it had not been covered on the diesel overhaul course I had taken before leaving on the voyage. I talked to the harbour master immediately, and he was most helpful. He knew a diesel mechanic who worked in Maui, but was holidaying at that very moment at Manele Bay. He talked to the chap, and he agreed to help me solve the problem. This was very fortunate for me and was another example of extremely good luck.

The mechanic came on board and first determined how the water was getting into the engine, which turned out to be a corroded plate in the exhaust system. The engine exhaust is mixed with water before going out the stern of the boat, so water is always trapped in the exhaust. Salt water is very corrosive, and after so many hours of powering on the voyage, sometimes with excessive engine temperature, the plate had finally sprung a leak and allowed the salt water to back up into the engine. He turned off the water intake valve, then told me to remove the other five injectors, and said that he would be back when I had finished this work. Sure enough he was back in about 20 minutes. He had me turn the key for the starter and crank the engine. The four batteries on board were all charged up from our run back from Lahaina, so we had lots of battery power. We cranked for about 10 minutes off and on. The engine room was full of exhaust, and there was water all over the ceiling and bulkheads, but this was a small price to pay if we could save the engine. Eventually, after a great deal of cranking, he said, "That should be enough, put the injectors back into the engine, bleed the air out of the fuel line and start the engine. I will be back." It took me about half an hour to get the engine ready and by then he was back. With a few seconds of cranking the engine started and ran, although it was quite rough, which was to be expected with so much salt water in it and on the injectors. He told me to run the engine so most of the salt would be cleared out of the engine, and that the exhaust system would have to be replaced. He knew of a company in Maui that could build a new exhaust system, and offered to take the old one to Maui on his boat that night and deliver it to the company in Kahului. He was an extremely kind fellow and couldn't have been more helpful. Late that afternoon I removed the exhaust system, which is very bulky – about seven feet long. Unfortunately, several of the four bolts that hold the exhaust to the engine could not be removed without breaking off the bolt heads. Had I used heat I might have avoided this problem but I was most anxious to take him up on his offer, and wanted to get the exhaust pipe out of the engine room and carry it down to his boat for loading.

Now we were immobilized and had to rely on public transportation to get us to Lanai City for shopping, phone calls, etc., and aircraft or cruise boats to get us off the island to go to Maui or Honolulu. Fortunately the cruise boats came over to Manele Bay four or five times a week, and as we were considered locals, the fare was very reasonable. Also, the ferry boat from Maalaea ran to Manele Bay several times a week. Over the next two months I was to use these methods of transportation quite frequently.

After about two more weeks Lou's holiday was over, and she had to make her way to Honolulu to catch her flight for Vancouver. Dee, the lady who delivered ice to the boats in Manele Bay and lived in Lanai City, kindly offered to drive her to the airport to catch a local flight to Honolulu. I went along to see her off and then made my way back to *Sea Lure*. Now I had to get the boat in shape for the long voyage back to Vancouver via Honolulu. I also had to return to Vancouver for several weeks because of a problem with a house I owned. I planned to rent it to visitors for short terms, as this was Expo year in Vancouver. But before this, I had to make a trip to Maui to organize the building of a new exhaust.

Getting over to Maui and making my way to Kahului, some 25 miles, at minimum expense, was a project within itself. I didn't know how much the exhaust would cost, but expected it would be quite expensive. Therefore, now was the time to conserve funds, as I would need them later. I took the cruise boat to Lahaina in the late afternoon and stayed over at the Pioneer Inn, then went by bus to Kahului to see the owner of the company that was building the exhaust. My friend had delivered it all right, but the company did not want to do the job. They knew it would be difficult, as they were experienced boaters, and tried to talk me into going to another company. I knew they were the best company in town to do the job, and eventually persuaded the owner to do it. The first difficulty was that he did not have the stainless steel sheeting to make the flex joints. I was on my way to Honolulu for the trip back to Vancouver, so offered to buy stainless steel in Honolulu and have it shipped over to him, which I did.

I flew home and after several weeks called the company to see if the shipment had arrived, and if they were progressing with the job. The sheets had arrived, but they were not suitable and nothing had been done. I phoned again in a week or so and still nothing had been done. Upon my return I went through Kahului again to check on the job. They were at a standstill, and the owner again tried to talk me into going to another company. I guess he eventually felt sorry for me and agreed to go ahead, but the stainless steel flex elbows had to be fabricated on the mainland to the correct size before they could do anything else, and they had a trucking company in Kahului do the ordering. I suppose some of the trucks used a similar exhaust system with flex joints. I took on the job of hastening the supply storesman at the trucking company, who hastened the supplier on the mainland after a week had gone by. Usually spares do not arrive as soon as promised (it is necessary to be patient but keep pushing gently so things will move along at the normal speed). If this is not done, other orders can take priority, and your order left sitting somewhere. I had learned this many years before when in logistics in the RCAF. Every few days I would make my way to Lanai City and phone the trucking company. The chap would give me an update and if necessary he would hasten again. After about two weeks the parts finally arrived, and the welding company was ready to complete the exhaust job. They now wanted to get it out of the yard. Finally, three or four days later, they informed me the job was done and to come and pick it up. So I went to Kahului again by cruise boat and bus, and checked the new exhaust. It was considerably larger than the old one and had a large tank with thicker steel. I think they did this intentionally so it would have a longer life, and after detailed measuring I decided I could make it fit in the engine room. I stayed overnight in a hotel, and the owner of the firm picked me up at 0600 hours the next morning with the exhaust in his truck. He drove me to Maalaea in time to catch the ferry for Lanai, and I paid him $600 U.S. in cash. He helped me load the exhaust on the ferry, and we both agreed that we were happy to see the end of that project. As it turned out I had another surprise when I took it to the boat.

During the trip over to Lanai on the ferry boat, I lined up several young fellows to help me carry the exhaust over to *Sea Lure* after we docked, and they also agreed to help me install it on the engine. All went well until we tried to attach the exhaust to the engine, and then we found that it had been put together incorrectly and was about twenty degrees off centre. This was another frustrating problem, as I expected the exhaust would have to go back to the Company to be rewelded. However, my helpers forced the flex joints sufficiently so it could now be attached to the engine. This solved the immediate trouble, but caused another problem several years later. The vibration of the engine on one of the flex joints eventually caused cracking in one of the flexes but this did not happen until about 1987 when we were cruising the B.C. coast. In the meantime, it worked just fine, the engine started easily and the exhaust worked. Now I had about two weeks to get back to Honolulu, and get the boat and crew organized to be ready for departure to Canada in a month.

More mechanical problems would haunt me before departure for Honolulu. The starter on the engine gave up, and as there was no company in Lanai that could overhaul it, the garage in Lanai City shipped it over to Honolulu for the work. Of course I had to take it off the engine, transport it the eight miles to Lanai City and hope it would come back in good shape. In about a week it was back but hadn't been repaired properly and had to be shipped back to Honolulu a second time. That time it was okay and has done its job without any trouble right up to the present time.

About this time Laine and Janet came in on their yacht *Capello* and tied up right across the dock. Laine was most knowledgeable about boats and mechanical things, and gave me a great deal of help over the next week. The thermostat that controlled the temperature on the engine cooling system had been giving trouble for quite some time, and we had excessively hot water in the domestic water system. The thermostat was sticking and didn't open up as fast as it should. After sitting for so many months while the boat was idle it finally wouldn't open up at all, causing excessive engine heating, so it had to be replaced. The thermostat was held down with three bolts, and one was about 2.5 inches long. They had been in place so long and were so corroded that they would not come out, and unfortunately I broke off the heads of two of them. I doubt if they would have come out with heat, as they were so welded to the other metal. But this meant that the two broken bolts had to be drilled out without destroying the threads. With Laine's help and a little luck we were able to drill directly down the centre, remove the remains of the two bolts, and the threads were still okay. After putting in a new thermostat, we discovered that the new bolts had to have a British fine thread and I did not carry such a thing. Another American yachtee docked close by was able to find several bolts with the right threads among his collection of spares, and even though one was too short it was sufficient to hold the cover over the thermostat in place until I could get to Honolulu and buy the right bolt. Another stroke of good luck.

Now, I had to get a crew together to sail to Honolulu. I had met a musician living in Lanai City who played several times a week with a band in Lahaina. He apparently played in Hollywood with one of the famous bands in some of the major movies. He was a nice fellow, and we became quite friendly. He had done some sailing and was anxious to get some heavy equipment over to Honolulu so he agreed to crew, and I agreed to take his parts. Also one of the American chaps who lived on Lanai offered to crew. He had done an ocean passage on a yacht and was an experienced sailor, so that gave me lots of crew for this short overnight sail.

Shortly before departing on the boat we had a tsunami warning. An earthquake in Alaska had created a tsunami wave and we had about two hours warning before it was due to strike. These waves travel through the water at great speed.

The Civil Defense organization went into action and it is really quite efficient. After the sirens sounded most of the yachts in the harbour departed for sea. It is safer at sea than at a dock when a tsunami wave is approaching. Only *Sea Lure* and another boat remained. My boat was immobilized, and the other boat belonged to the "ice lady" Dee and her husband Ken. She didn't know how to operate the boat, and he was in Honolulu and couldn't make it back in time. So we tied up both boats with extra lines and I dropped an anchor off the stern of *Sea Lure*. This might help if the wave was not too large, otherwise the boat would probably be lifted up on the shore with dock and all. This had occurred a number of years previously when a really large wave came ashore.

Aircraft with loudspeakers were used to warn everyone to go to high ground in plenty of time, and about half an hour before the wave was expected, the police came to the dock to make sure that everyone was up on the high ground up the hill from the dock area. We had portable radios to get the latest news, and someone sent around sandwiches and coffee. It was almost a carnival atmosphere, but with considerable tension for me, as I was the only one present with a boat in the harbour. After some time the wave was reported at the island of Kauai, and it was only about a foot high. This was good news, as it would be down to six inches by the time it got to Lanai and this would not cause any damage. I breathed a sigh of relief and I imagine so did Dee and Ken. Shortly after that, the boats that had gone to sea started coming back into the harbour, and everything went back to normal. In Honolulu the entire Waikiki beach area was evacuated and all buildings up to the 2nd or 3rd floor. Fortunately it was a small earthquake and did not cause much damage, even in Alaska.

A few additional mechanical problems had to be fixed and two batteries sent out for recharging. I tried to get the boat to move at the dock, but without success. It had been sitting for so long the barnacles on the shaft prevented it from turning. Help was required again. One of the yacht skippers, who was also a diver, put on his diving gear and went under the boat and removed the barnacles. Now we were about ready to leave for Honolulu. Ken and Dee had been particularly helpful over the entire period, so I took them out for a nice dinner at the hotel in Lanai City, the only place on the island that had a decent dining room with good food.

The next morning my musician friend brought the charged batteries back to the boat in his car. The other crewman was ready, so at 1400 hours we said good bye to everyone we knew in the area and departed for Honolulu. The Sat Nav had stopped working and didn't work for the rest of the voyage. I suspect someone had been tinkering with it and caused major problems, but I have no proof of this. I didn't need the Sat Nav to get to Honolulu, as only coastal navigation was required. For the long voyage Honolulu to Victoria, I still had my sextant, so the Sat Nav was not required for that passage either. The inconveniences of sending the set back to the Walker Company in England for repairs turned out to be the biggest headache. *Sea Lure* had been in Manele Bay for over three months with only trips over to Lahaina. It was a great place to break down.

After several hours at sea, I decided to check the engine and see what was happening. The engine room had water all over the place, so we closed down the engine and went troubleshooting. The salt water hose that runs to the coils in the refrigerating system had sprung a leak, and was spraying water everywhere. I had spare hose on board, so we put in a new section and the problem was solved. The rest of our passage that night was uneventful, and we were able to run the watch system with three men on board. At 0700 17 May, we powered through the reef at the Ala Wai yacht basin and tied up at the Hawaii Yacht Club again. We were made most welcome – it was our home away from home.

Seventeen days remained before our departure for Canada. There was enough time to complete all arrangements, but no time to waste. The crew had to arrive from Canada, the underside of the boat had to be cleaned, more boat repairs had to be carried out, the food had to be procured, delivered to the boat and stowed away. Fuel and water tanks had to be filled and a multitude of other things completed before departure, including customs clearance.

Several days after I arrived, I spotted *Capella* coming into one of the docks in the harbour. It was Laine and Janet McDaniel again, and we were very happy to see each other. We had a get-together, and the following night I took them out for dinner at a nice restaurant in the harbour as a thank-you for all the help they had given me. We had a very pleasant evening. We were permitted to attend parties at the club at a reasonable price, so we got together several times before my departure.

I was having an electrical problem on the engine and couldn't figure out what it was, so Laine again kindly went to *Sea Lure* and determined the trouble in a short time. I needed a new voltage regulator, which I bought locally

The last time I was in Vancouver, I had arranged for four crewmen to meet me in Honolulu to crew on the return passage. Tony was a farmer/auctioneer from my home town Dauphin, Manitoba, whom I had known for many years. He was not an experienced sailor, but what he lacked in experience he more than made up in enthusiasm and good humour. In fact, he is a born comedian, and we had a lot of laughs during the passage, particularly when he did his tobacco auctioneer patter just like the professionals in the U.S. Paul and Mike lived in Calgary and they arrived first, about a week before departure date. Chris, who came from Vancouver about the same time, was quite an experienced ocean sailor and a very pleasant fellow to sail with.

The last four or five days were very busy. One of the time-consuming jobs was procuring the food, after we had spent two hours discussing the menu and deciding what to buy. After the list and quantities were compiled, we rented a car and again drove out to Pearl Harbour to the Naval Exchange for shopping. We bought everything except the meat, over $400 worth, and had to transport it to the boat with the rental car. The meat was purchased at the Ala Moana Shopping Centre, as it had to be frozen for several days before departure. The deep freeze on the boat would then keep it frozen for the 23 days of the voyage. We had sufficient food for 25 days, considering that I expected to catch fish for at least one dinner a week and possibly more. We succeeded in doing this, and had fresh tuna about six or seven days out, after losing a nice mahimahi the third day out. This was an especially colourful fish, one of the prettiest we caught on the entire voyage. Just as we got it right up to the rail of the boat it flipped the hook, but we did have a good look at it. Just as well it remained in the deep.

On 1 June we powered to the refueling dock in the harbour to fill up the fuel, propane and water tanks. Then we powered back to our same moorage.

One of the yachtees told me about an American chap that had a business doing underwater cleaning of boat hulls. This was a great help, as he gave me a quote of $100 after examining the hull. A previous estimate, just to lift the boat out of the water, was $1000 with the cleaning extra. Several days before departure he agreed to do the job, which turned out to be a good one. The boat was not lifted out of the water for another year for cleaning and painting, and was still in quite good condition.

Previously when departing for Fanning Island I had not bothered to get vessel clearance papers, as this is not required when going from Canada to the U.S. and back. This caused some consternation in Fanning Island with the customs officer, who finally accepted my story but told me to be sure to get clearance papers from him before departure. This I had done, and everything ran smoothly. Ships, yachts, etc., go through customs twice each time they go to a country, once upon arrival and once just before departure. This system keeps track of all the world's ships and controls the movement from one country to another. So this time I decided to get a formal clearance from U.S. customs in Honolulu to avoid any problems. They seemed to be a little confused when I asked for the papers, but finally prepared them for a $25 charge. After a second try I picked up the papers the day of departure. I needn't have bothered, as the Canadian Customs in Victoria didn't know what to do with my clearance papers and some months later sent them back to me. They were more worried about the $600 I had spent on the exhaust system.

While getting everything done that was required before departure, there was still some time for the crew to enjoy themselves, and also do an all-day tour of the island in the rental car. We also went to one or two parties at the Hawaii Yacht Club where we were still welcome. The Royal Vancouver Yacht Club membership card was all that was required and they were kind enough to let the crew participate. The last several days were very pleasant and not busy, as everything seemed to be falling into place.

I had not taken any sights with the sextant, reduced and plotted them for many months, so thought it would be a good idea to practice. Waikiki Beach is a very pleasant area, and a great place to take sights. I must have taken about 20 sights, and reduced and plotted about ten, until I felt comfortable again with the rather complicated procedure. Of course, I had bought the current nautical almanac on my last trip to Vancouver, and still carried all the applicable volumes of HO 229 on *Sea Lure*. The Mercator plotting sheets from the voyage to Hawaii were still on board so I used the same ones for the return voyage. It was necessary to erase the plotting in several instances, but on most occasions the new plot did not interfere with the previous one. This practice was a good idea, as reducing sights when one is tired can cause errors. Several times it was necessary to recheck my work, particularly in the latter part of the voyage when boredom also set in.

CHAPTER 17

HOMEWARD BOUND

Finally 3 June arrived – it was a nice day, but with some wind 15 to 20 knots from the northeast. This was a good wind for our departure, even though it was going to be rough for the first three or four hours. We picked up the frozen meat that we had previously purchased at the store in the Ala Moana Shopping Centre, and the customs clearance papers. Two of the crew returned the rental car while the rest of us stowed the food, filled the water tanks for the last time, and did the rest of the last-minute jobs, including the cleaning of the knot log propeller that turns under the boat to give us boat speed and distance run.

In about an hour the crew returned to the boat, untied the lines, and we powered out past the Hawaii Yacht Club and through the reef. Some of our Hawaiian friends had brought flower leis down to the boat that morning as a farewell gesture, so before hoisting sails we took pictures and had a great half-hour. Just as well, as the next four hours were really rough. I had chosen to go around the east side of the island of Oahu, and it had a reputation of being rough. If I had to do it over again I would go around the west side, as there should have been more shelter. We had come in from the east two years previously and it was very pleasant. The winds were then from the east at 5 knots and we were powering with the waves. This time it was a different story.

We hoisted sails and headed for Makapuu Point, the same point that we had headed for on our voyage from Canada in 1984 after going around the high pressure area north of Hawaii. Because of the wind direction, we had to tack about four times to make our way out past Diamond Head at a safe distance off shore before we could turn north. Each time we tacked, loose items were flying around the forward and main cabin. Tony had never been on a sailboat of this size in these conditions, and he was horrified. He told us later that he was sure that if these conditions continued for the rest of the voyage, he would not be alive when we arrived! The other three crew members were sick almost immediately, so Tony and I had to run the boat. We were the only ones not sick but I have to admit I was not feeling very good for awhile. I couldn't afford to be sick, as someone had to operate the boat. Not having been at sea for many months, except for the short sail from Lanai, one's system takes a little time to again get accustomed to the motion. The brake on the shaft to keep the propeller from rotating while we were sailing was not tight enough, so I went into the engine room to tighten the bolt and then asked Tony to put the brake on again to test it. I didn't get my finger out of the way in time, and got it pinched. Fortunately Tony let the brake off again quickly when I shouted and the damage was minimal, but it didn't help my stomach situation.

We had departed the Ala Wai Yacht Basin at 1400 hours, and it was 5.75 hours later that we had Makapuu Point abeam and could set course for Victoria, Canada. This wasn't a pleasant start. Although three crew members were still sick, they could take their turn at the helm, which helped them recover, but they could not consume any food. Seasickness is most common for offshore sailors, caused by the motion plus the apprehension of departing on a long ocean voyage. The many unknowns, such as the seaworthiness of the boat, the skill of the skipper, the bad weather conditions that could be encountered, plus danger from whales, other vessels, etc., all contribute to the problem. After several days the crew started to get their stomachs back and by the third day they were all fine and eating to make up for the meals they had missed.

It was dark when we set course to go directly north of Oahu, and the ocean had settled down so we had quite a good night. We ran six-hour watches with Mike and Paul on watch until midnight, then Tony and Chris took over until 0600 hours. Mike and Paul then had breakfast and went to bed. I had gone to bed about 2200 hours and was up at 0700 hours, so they could both sleep in the aft cabin which was quiet and dark and a good place to rest. The winds were 20 to 25 knots from the northeast, and we were making good time with a minimum of mechanical problems. In fact we sailed 128 nautical miles that day, which was our best day for the entire passage. I also note from the watchkeeper's log that the winds were 20 knots or better all day and from the right direction.

The crew was settling down into the routine quite well. The boat was being steered properly. The meals were prepared very well and on time, and the dishes washed afterwards. The navigation was working out all right and the weather was still good. A few members of the crew were missing some meals, but their systems were adapting to the motion of the boat and I'm sure their apprehensions were abating. Everything was running too smoothly, and I might have known that this could not last long. Sure enough, the next day, we had a serious problem.

At 1300 hours on June 5th the genoa developed a tear. The genoa is the power sail for the boat, as I said before, and the one that would get us to Canada in a respectable number of days, so it had to be repaired. The boat did have another, but it was made of a light weight material and was several years old. The only thing to do was lower the genoa and repair it, but when we let the halyard off and prepared to take it down, it wouldn't come. It was jammed at the top. We had replaced the wire part of the halyard in Honolulu, as the old one was badly frayed. When putting the new wire on we had somehow let the wire or line tangle at the top of the mast, and the genoa would not come down. This was a major problem, as the only way to get the sail down was send a crewman up to the top, or go myself if I could not find a volunteer. This is a very dangerous operation on a rolling boat, and the crewman going up must be very strong and knowledgeable, as the mast was making an arc of about 10 feet or more each time we went over a wave. The winds were still blowing 15 to 20 knots and the swells were quite high.

Chris, our most experienced young crewman, volunteered to do the job. He deserves a great amount of credit, as he knew the dangers involved but no doubt had the confidence that he could carry out the job and not get hurt. He had undoubtedly been to the top of masts before but not under such difficult conditions. *Sea Lure* had a spare halyard to which the safety harness could be fastened as a safeguard, in case something happened to the main halyard that was fastened to the bosun's chair. I believe this contributed to Chris' decision to go up the mast.

Solving this problem required a max effort by all members of the crew, and they performed very well indeed. The bosun's chair was checked carefully to ensure the extra lines to reinforce it were in place, and that all snap shackles etc., were in first class order. Chris put on my safety harness, which is especially strong, and we attached the spare halyard to it. The best halyard on the boat, which is used to hoist the main sail, was attached to the bosun's chair after Chris was seated in it. The snap shackle was wired after it was closed, to prevent any accidental opening when he was up the mast. He then took a short line and fastened himself to the mast, but with enough slack so we could hoist him up to the spreaders. Then he removed the line and reattached it above the spreaders, so we could hoist him to the top. With two crewmen on the spare halyard on the genoa winch and two of us on the main halyard, we slowly hoisted Chris up the mast. Incidentally, he had a small line 60 feet long in the pocket of the bosun's chair in case we had to send up some tools. He also had a wrench and pliers in the other pocket. The vessel was rolling quite badly, and it is a great advantage to be young, strong and in good condition to cope with such a situation. I'm not sure how I would have made out if a volunteer had not come forward. I know I would have tried and probably would have succeeded, but it would have been a maximum physical effort to stay with the mast when it was making sweeping arcs with every roll of the boat. I had been to the top of the mast many times over the previous two years, but always when the boat was at the dock and not rolling.

Chris and everyone on the crew did their work with great care and concentration and we got him to the top. The halyard was jammed quite badly, but with about five minutes of work he was able to clear it and the genoa was free to come down. But before doing that, we lowered Chris to the deck and gave him a hearty cheer. After that we lowered the genoa and hoisted the old one, so we could continue to sail while the tear was being sewn. We still had sail tape on board along with needles and the proper thread, so for the umpteenth time we were sewing a sail. Fortunately the tear was not very long so we sewed it up in a couple of hours. The winds were a little high and the old genoa was doing the job so we decided to wait until the wind subsided, two days later to be exact. That day, 5 June, we had sailed 119 nautical miles, despite the delay when changing genoas.

The following day, 6 June, we had some rain in the morning and sun in the afternoon. At 1400 hours we caught our first fish on this passage. It was a very colourful mahimahi, about 10 pounds, but the net had not been taken out of the engine room so we attempted to land it with the line only. It flipped the hook just as it was coming over the rail and we lost it! Needless to say, we had the net handy for the next two or three fish caught on the passage, and didn't lose any more. This was also shower day, so we filled the five-gallon shower bag from the special shower water tank and placed it on the deck to warm up. After several hours of sunshine the water was quite warm so we all had a shower. The morale of the crew improved immediately. To drain the shower in the aft cabin, it was necessary to tack the boat for 10 or 15 minutes but this was accomplished with ease.

Since shortly after setting course at Makapuu Point, our true course had been 000 degrees. It is necessary to go straight north from Hawaii when heading for Canada, in order to get around the high-pressure area that wanders around the North Pacific all summer. As the winds blow clockwise in the northern hemisphere, it is best to keep the winds off your starboard beam or quarter unless you want to power for days and days. Usually, at 700 to 1000 nautical miles north of Honolulu, a yacht is in the northwest part of the high-pressure area and it is then possible to alter course for Juan de Fuca Strait in Canada. In our case, the wind started to veer to the east-northeast direction before we were 500 miles north of Hawaii. I didn't alter course immediately, as the winds were rather undecided, but by 7 June the winds had swung around to the east so we altered course for Canada. We were then 525 miles north of our starting point. Our true course was 025 and our compass course 012, as we had 13 degrees of east variation at this point, and 0 deviation. We were getting there slowly but surely. Boat and crew were performing very well and the weather had been good, with winds from the right direction from 10 to 25 knots.

June 8 was the first Sunday on the passage, and it was always a special day on *Sea Lure*. The weather was good, with winds 10 to 15 knots from the east. When cleaning up the boat we noticed that a few strands of wire on the starboard shroud aft were broken, so decided we should reinforce it, as we didn't know what surprises the ocean had in store for us. We had plenty of spare wire on board along with the necessary tool, so we swaged a loop on the wire then hoisted Chris up the mast again, but this time only to the spreaders where he hooked the loop in place. After he came down we hooked up the other end of the wire to the turnbuckle, and the job was finished. It was considerably easier for Chris this time as the boat was not rolling as much, and we were all getting rather skilled at our hoisting jobs.

We had pancakes for breakfast that morning, and it was the skipper's turn to cook dinner. Before dinner we had the usual happy hour. The watchkeeper's log indicated that the steak and wine were good, so it must have turned out all right. Everybody was happy after the drinks and wine. We also sailed 121.3 nautical miles so, all in all, it was a most successful day; I believe the second best day since our departure.

The next morning at 0100 hours the crew sighted a ship. I was in bed, but got up immediately and called on the VHF. After a discussion with their radio operator or officer of the watch, I asked him for his position off his satellite navigation system. He gave me his position and it sounded good according to my recollection of the DR plot before I had gone to bed. The next morning, after updating the plot, the position was only a few miles different from ours and as she was at least a mile away, I was satisfied that the celestial navigation was working out all right.

Several days before this, we caught up to an American yacht about the same size as *Sea Lure*. It was moving very slowly, and it didn't take us long to overtake her. I called the skipper, and he seemed to be having some trouble with his crew. Perhaps they were seasick, or not getting along with the captain. He seemed to be rather vague on the nature of his problem. I asked him if he needed any help but he said, "No, we will manage." We passed them about 50 yards off our starboard side, and about an hour later we were so far ahead we could no longer see them. We never heard from that vessel again. There was considerable discussion on how long it would take them to reach San Francisco at their present speed, but hopefully the skipper would get better organized and make better time.

On 9 June about 1900 hours we were buzzed by three dolphins. They were most active and put on quite a show. Unfortunately they did not stay with us very long as we move too slowly, but it is always nice to have a visit from dolphins. At night their fins light up from the phosphorescence in the water, and they are easily seen. They seem to provide the connection between the sailors at sea and the people on shore, as they normally stay in the vicinity of land, although these dolphins were at least 700 miles out.

At about 2200 hours we sighted another ship. It must have been stopped as we overtook and passed on the port side. We put our spreader lights on so they could see us all right, and I called on the VHF but there was no response. They probably didn't have their VHF radio on or the officer of the watch didn't hear us. It was just a social call so his response was not important.

10 June was our seventh day on the passage, and time we caught another fish. Sure enough we brought in a nice tuna. It was large enough for five hungry crewmen for several meals. As the skipper always grilled the fresh fish, it was his turn to cook the dinner again even though he had cooked two days previously. The cooking days were switched around at times like this, so everyone took their fair share of the cooking duties. The tuna was good as usual with lemon, etc., to improve the flavour, but one of the crewmen did not eat it, which I considered most strange. Perhaps he was not feeling well again, as he had been sick previously, or maybe he just did not like fish. It was the only time on the entire voyage, over two years, that a crewman refused to eat fresh fish. I suppose that is the reason I remember this incident so well. The rest of the crew ate with gusto and finished up all that was cooked.

The winds were light that day from the west and southwest, and we powered for nine hours to keep our boat speed up to five or six knots. By 1900 hours the engine was turned off and we used the whisker pole as we were running wing and wing. Our distance for the day was not spectacular, as we sailed and powered only 107.5 miles. The light winds were the problem and without the engine on it would have been considerably less.

June 11th was more of the same with light winds from the south and southeast, with some from the northwest. During this time we took down the whisker pole, and somehow it fell overboard. We went through our man overboard drill, which we had talked about at some length before departure, and with Tony keeping his eyes on the pole, which was floating, we managed to maneuver the vessel around and come up alongside the pole. Tony reached down and picked it up. Even this is not easy, as the boat has a lot of freeboard. It is difficult to reach down to the water, but Tony was very agile and with great determination he overcame the problem. This was the first and only time that anything went overboard that we could retrieve immediately.

The winds were still very light, so we used the engine again for some hours. This is the advantage of carrying so much fuel – 180 gallons when we started – that it does not have to be conserved. Fuel consumption was less than one gallon per hour, as the engine was normally running at 1000 rpm, with a maximum of 1500 rpm. The weather was getting cool as we were progressing north-

northeast and also that day there was very little sunshine. Our progress for the day was the same as the day before.

At 0300 the following morning the crew got me up as they had sighted a ship. I called on the VHF and they answered immediately. After some discussion I asked them for their Sat Nav position. They gave me their 1252 Zulu position as latitude 33º, 53' North; longitude 152º, 04' West. As we had a 10-hour time change from Greenwich, our local time for their fix was 0252 hours. This was in the ball park for our DR position before I had gone to bed, so I simply recorded it and went back to bed. I would check it out the next morning when the DR plot was updated to 0252 hours. As it turned out, the celestial running fix had been satisfactory and everything was in order. I always confirmed our position by this method, as it was a good morale booster for the crew. The rest of the day was uneventful, cool and overcast with the winds from the northwest at about 15 knots. Our distance for the day was slightly better at 111.6 miles.

The 13th of June wasn't a particularly lucky day for *Sea Lure*, but it was sailing along at its usual speed with few problems. The skipper was sick with a fever and felt miserable, and had no idea why. No one else was sick with the flu, so perhaps I had some food poisoning, though no one else had this problem either. I remained in my bunk for the day, and didn't bother with the daily sights and running fix. It is no problem to go 48 hours without a fix, as all the information was in the watchkeeper's log to update the dead reckoning plot. The error compared to our desired position would probably not be more than five miles. The crew kindly brought some food to me in the aft cabin. The rest seemed to do the job, as the next day I was fine. There were quite a few firsts on this passage and getting the flu was no exception. Fortunately it did not last long, and didn't really inconvenience the operation of the boat. The galley duties I missed that day were made up later and there were no urgent mechanical problems that had to be fixed. Our progress was the same as the previous day, so it was obvious the crew could get along just fine without me. This was good news! The training and the delegation of authority and responsibility were working as they should.

The 14th of June was cold and cloudy, and from 0600 to 1600 hours the winds were up to 25 knots from the west. Early in the morning we caught another tuna. Our distance for the day was 115.5 miles.

Early in the morning on 15 June, about 0200 hours, the crew spotted a large ship ahead of us. It must have been stopped or was moving very slowly as we had overtaken it. The crew got me up and I called on the VHF radio, but there was no answer. Suddenly the crew on the ship turned on all their lights and turned port and came back to have a look at us. I turned on our spreader lights to make sure they could see us, but they must have seen our running lights as the ship passed only 100 yards off our port side. By this time it had lights all the way along the port side. It may have been an aircraft carrier, either Russian or American, but as the crew did not answer my call I presume they did not want to disclose their position, or they didn't have their radio on and after spotting our running lights went back to have a look. If they were on station with not much to do, this kind of thing would break the monotony and help keep the crew awake. We continued to sail on course to Victoria and the ship was soon out of sight. It was indeed strange that they did not answer my many calls on the VHF radio, unless they had something to hide.

The winds were 20 to 30 knots in the afternoon. This meant we were getting into gale conditions. We furled the main as it wasn't very sturdy and we didn't want to tear it. This is the beauty of a ketch, with its mizzen sail. It also became obvious that Tony was having trouble sleeping. He was carrying out his duties satisfactorily, but he wasn't going to bed and sleeping when he should. The main log indicates that the winds were gusting to 45 knots that afternoon, and we reefed the genoa. It was blowing a gale all right, and it looked like we were going into storm conditions. I always considered it a storm when the winds were over 40 nautical miles per hour, especially if there was some rain with it. This is equal to almost 80 kilometres per hour.

Sometime after midnight, when Tony was on the helm, a very large wave hit us. When I woke up I was falling, still in my sleeping bag, on the cushions on the seat and then down to the deck. I was more surprised than hurt. It must have been another seventh wave and it hit us at a bad angle. Chris, the Watch Captain on duty, was thrown from the seat in the eating area in the main cabin over into the galley, but fortunately he was not hurt either. Tony told us later that his feet were up on the side of the cockpit, but he was still hanging onto the helm. Again *Sea Lure* had saved us from a knockdown. This was the only time on the voyage I was thrown out of my bunk. Previously when the big wave hit us in the Tasman Sea out of Sydney, Australia, Louis was thrown out of the bunk on the other side of the cabin and landed on the same cushions. They had saved us both from broken bones. Tony was shaken up a little, but remained on the helm for the rest of his watch and I went back to bed. The rest of the night was uneventful, but the wind continued to blow up to 35 knots from the northwest, and the crew was happy to see the dawn.

It was 16 June; Tony's 30th wedding anniversary. I had known him and his wife Audrey for many years. We had been together in a party of nine people in Hawaii for a two-week holiday in 1977, so we had become close friends. Tony was sad that he could not be at home with his family for this special occasion, but we did celebrate his anniversary in a small way with an extra drink before dinner, several toasts and long discussions.

Despite the high winds and fairly rough conditions, it was a good day. As the sea started to moderate in the evening we gradually rolled out the furled genoa. We had crossed 142°, 30' West longitude, so it was time to advance our watches by one hour from zone description + 10 to zone description +9. This day then had only 23 hours. The watch at the end of the day and the one at the beginning of the following day split the time gained, so each watch got the benefit of 30 minutes. At 2100 hours the crew sighted a ship off our stern and I called on the VHF radio, but there was no answer. We must have been getting closer to land with so many ships sighted. Also we were probably crossing a shipping lane. The moon was up in the daytime, and I was able to get a two-body celestial fix several times, on the moon and the sun. At certain times of the day the angle was right for a fix. This always makes celestial navigation a little more interesting, since reducing the moon is quite different as it moves so much faster than the sun and planets.

Early morning of 17 June the wind had dropped to 20 knots, and by 0900 hours it was down to 15 - 20 knots and the ocean swells were now moderating. The weather was cool and it was still overcast. It was also time for a shower, as we had delayed this luxury during the rough conditions.

When we left Honolulu Paul and Mike had both been growing beards for some years, so Tony, Chris and I decided that we would also grow beards, at least for the duration of the voyage. By this time the beards were getting quite long and unkempt, as we did not trim them. I had never grown a beard before, so this was a new experience and I didn't realize how much it would change my appearance. It also added about ten years to my age. Our beards were to be the source of entertainment for ourselves and our friends and family for quite some time, as I continued to keep mine for several months after reaching Canada. The photograph indicates our unkempt appearance. The beards were trimmed and cleaned up generally after we were able to get to a barber.

At about 2100 hours we sighted a vessel two or three miles off our port quarter. I called on the radio but again, no answer. It was quite difficult to see in the dusk, but it looked very much like a submarine operating on the surface. It soon disappeared.

The 18th of June was Tony's fiftieth birthday, and again this called for some celebrating. We had been on the passage for over two weeks and the days were getting long, so any excuse to break the routine was welcomed. Tony had not been sleeping properly, and his lack of rest was starting to have serious effects. I had seen this problem before, during the Victoria to Maui sailboat race in 1978, when one of the crew almost had a nervous breakdown. Tony was approaching this stage, as he told me he could see shore out there at night, but of course shore was still more than 800 miles away. He was also having trouble keeping the vessel on course. This was significant, as he was a pilot and had his own aircraft, so had lots of practice steering by compass. His birthday gave me an excuse to practice the cure. Tony and I both enjoyed drinking hard liquor, so after lunch that day I got out two bottles I always carried for times like this. I poured him large drinks and myself small portions, and we had quite a birthday party over the next four hours. We discussed many subjects, covered our progress toward Victoria to date, our latitude and longitude at that time, the distance to go, and day we should arrive. Initially Tony got quite high, and I must admit I was feeling good, but still under control should an emergency occur. Then he got very tired and sleepy, and soon went to my bunk in the aft cabin where he would not be disturbed. Tony slept that evening and all night without waking up. I took his turn on watch so he could sleep right through, and I believe he slept for 12 or 14 hours. When he woke up he was fine. His problem had disappeared. All he needed was a good sleep, and he was fine for the rest of the passage.

The watchkeeper's log indicated eight more days to go, with a question mark, but this was accurate as we arrived on June 26. The wind had dropped to 5 - 10 knots, so the engine was running for at least eight hours that day. That kept us moving along and we sailed and powered 110.6 miles.

The next day, 19 June, the watchkeeper's log reads "a very damp morning and Tony's hung over." By 0700 hours the sun was shining and everything picked up on *Sea Lure*. I was able to get some sun sights and plotted a running fix at 1106. Our position was latitude 40°, 33' North and longitude 137°, 38' West. By 1400 hours we had caught another tuna. It is recorded in the log as 30 lbs. Probably the actual weight was about 20 lbs., but it was plenty big enough for several meals. Fresh tuna was on the menu for dinner that night, courtesy the skipper, who had to gut, scale, cut it up, and cook it. I was getting tired of this routine after so many fish, but I was never able to get a crew member interested in the first part of this process. It was not easy, as it was all done in a bucket of salt water and did require some practice. The only thing to do was persevere and be thankful that we were still catching fish. Other ocean mariners were not always so lucky. The rest of the day was uneventful, but we did travel 123.9 miles in the day with 10 to 20 knot winds from the west – not a bad day.

June 20th was uneventful, with light winds from the southwest and northwest, and we were sailing wing and wing. At 1700 hours we had 567 miles to go according to the watchkeeper's log, and the crew were now counting off the miles. I got a running fix at 1143 hours and the day's travel was 108 miles. We were getting there slowly, and *Sea Lure* and the crew were still performing very well.

Saturday 21 June was a nice day. The ocean was calm with winds from the southwest, and west at 10 to 14 knots. The barometric pressure was 1033 most of the day, so we must have been in a high-pressure area. It was a good time for pictures, so we had a photo session. By 2000 hours it was cold and wet according to the log, despite the high-pressure area, but the rain did not last long. Early that morning the winds were so light we had all sails furled and the engine running, but by 1300 hours the sails were up again. It was not a very productive day from a sailing point of view as we only covered 102 miles. The light winds were the problem.

On 22 June the winds were still light and the sea calm. At 0300 hours the crew on watch sighted a cargo ship, but they did not wake me up to operate the radio. Just as well, as I'm sure I was in a deep sleep at that time. The boat speed was not much over four knots and some hours it was less. By noon we started the engine and powered for the next 36 hours – a good workout for the engine, and it performed without a problem. When crew are trying to sleep the noise of the engine can be disconcerting, but after you get tired enough nothing will keep a person awake. It is surprising how fast a human will adapt to the environment (i.e. engine noise) and actually rest quite well. We then followed our usual Sunday routine. The sea condition was favourable for all this work and pleasure, but the engine noise was always present. The crew must have had the broadcast band on the radio on as they reported that a station from Portland, Oregon (1190 on the dial) was coming in loud and clear at 2300 hours. Unfortunately, I hadn't thought to use the RDF radio with the broadcast band to pick up radio stations on the mainland. This was an oversight on my part, as this radio will pick up stations with high wattage up to 1000 miles out at night, and this can be quite a morale booster. Also, I could have been taking rough radio bearings in the past few days, but I was tired and the celestial navigation was still working out all right. At 0900 hours I recorded in the main log that the light on Tatoosh Rock, the entrance to Juan de Fuca Strait, was 391 nautical miles away. This was four days of powering and sailing at our present speed to get to Victoria as it is about 80 miles beyond Tatoosh. Our distance for the day was 111.3 miles – quite satisfactory.

23 June started out as a very calm day, but little did I know what surprises were in store. The wind was very light from the southwest and the engine was still running. At 0800 we had fog and the visibility was reduced to one mile, which was still no problem. We knew we must be getting close to Canada, as fog was practically unknown for the previous two years of the voyage. I think the last time I had seen it was in the Bay of Islands in New Zealand and then it was very light. The crew on watch had hoisted the radar reflector on the flag halyard, as we only put it up when it is needed. The fog cleared in about an hour, and the radar reflector was taken down. It is noted in the watchkeeper's log that the RPMs on the engine were reduced from 1500 to 1200. This could have been significant on this particular day, in hindsight.

At 1500 hours I was working on the navigation plot in the main cabin when Chris called to me and said we had whales as company, and one was just off the port side of the boat. I would have preferred to have been advised much earlier, but perhaps he didn't see the whale earlier, although its waterspout should have been visible from miles away. I immediately jumped up and rushed into the cockpit. I had had considerable experience that winter with the whales that calve in the Maui area in Hawaii. My experience, was that even when they were accompanied by a calf, whales would not come within ¼ mile of the boat if the engine was running, which ours was, but at low RPM. This visit was most unusual, and I wondered what the whale had in mind. Chris saw it do a shallow dive down the port side of the boat heading toward the stern. I immediately rushed to the stern, and in 5 or 10 seconds I could see the whale coming toward the stern at a good speed, only about 5 feet under the surface. I had read several stories of yachts being sunk by friendly or not so friendly whales, and this flashed through my mind. I ran forward to the helm and took over from Chris and put on full power. Thank goodness the engine was running, and full power brought our speed up in a hurry. All this took about 4 or 5 seconds, and as the boat was gaining speed the whale came right up out of the water. It was longer than the 46 feet of *Sea Lure*, and its big head with the barnacles on the nose was so close I could have touched it with the boat hook. It was on our starboard side. Since it had come that far forward in such a short time, it must have been travelling at a good speed. It had a good look at me and the boat with its big eye, and fortunately for us decided that it wasn't interested in *Sea Lure* anymore. The roar of the engine at 3000 RPM, and the boat speed increasing to over eight knots must have been a deterrent. Also the whale had a mate about a mile behind the boat, and it turned and went back to its friend. I really don't know what the whale might have done, but I wasn't waiting around to find out. They don't know their own power, and a flip of that massive tail, even in jest, could have put a gaping hole in *Sea Lure* and we would have sunk in a few minutes. I heaved a sigh of relief when the crew reported that the whale was not following us.

This was probably the most dangerous few minutes of the entire voyage, including the three days in the hurricane and the near knockdown. I apologized to Chris for taking over in such a fashion. A less experienced sailor might not have understood. There was very little discussion about the close call with the whale, other than my remarks. Either they didn't realize the danger, or may have been concerned that they did not take action sooner to forestall the close call. I suspect that very few ocean sailors have much experience with whales. I suppose it was fortunate that *Sea Lure* had wintered in Lanai, and I had gained some knowledge of their behaviour. We will never know what that whale had in mind.

This turned out to be quite an eventful day, in fact, the most eventful of the remaining days before reaching Victoria. At 1700 hours, just two hours after our experience with the whale, we were buzzed by an aircraft from the American coastguard. I knew from experience two years previously that they had the emergency marine channel on their VHF radio, so I gave the captain a call. He answered immediately and we had a little chat, then I asked him for his latitude and longitude position according to his instruments. He said he was not allowed to give it to me, as there was a possibility the coastguard could be sued if he gave me the wrong information. This sounded very strange, and if it is a coastguard regulation it should be changed. Consequently he wouldn't give me a position, so as he flew around I quickly updated my plot and told him my dead reckoning position. He said that sounded pretty good, so that was the best I could do. We were now getting in close enough to shore that the radio direction finder on the boat would provide a backup for my celestial navigation, so I was not too concerned. It was important, however, to make sure we arrived at the Strait of Juan de Fuca, and not mistake it for another inlet, etc. Some years ago, the crew of a large ship thought they were coming into the Columbia River entrance in Oregon, but it was actually an inlet many hundreds of miles north on the Canadian coast. The shipwreck remained on the beach for many years and may still be there. I was going to make sure this didn't happen to *Sea Lure.*

Our mileage for the day was 112 miles, and it had been quite a day. I was thankful not to be in the life raft, with *Sea Lure* at the bottom thanks to a whale. Had the worst come to the worst, I was confident we could have launched the life raft successfully. The ocean conditions were good, we would have taken the emergency personal identification radio to the raft, and its transmissions would have been picked up quickly by other vessels or aircraft flying over. If there had been time to transmit an emergency on the VHF or ham radio, then our chances for an early pickup would have been that much better.

The following day, 24 June 86, was really quite uneventful compared to the previous day. At 0800 hours the sun was shining and the winds were 22 knots from the northwest. I got a running fix at 0945 and by 1500 hours we had 160 miles to go to Tatoosh light. The winds were good all day, and in the latter part of the day 25 - 30 knots, but we were not making very good time. Everyone was tired, and didn't concentrate too much on the sailing. The distance for the day was only 99 miles.

Late that night, the winds picked up some more to 25 - 30 knots. It was a rough night, and I reported in the main log that winds were gusting to 35. One of the crew reported a wet bunk. I think that was Tony, as we had a water drip on the small berth in the main cabin when the sea water washed over the deck. This was to be a good day, nevertheless, and at 0800 hours some dolphins came out to meet us. According to my navigation, and in particular a RDF bearing on a beacon on the Washington coast, we were a little too far south to come right in on Tatoosh Rock. I called for an alteration of course to 000 compass, so we could run almost parallel to the coast, but gradually go in towards land. At 2200 hours we could see some lights on land. According to *Sea Lure* tradition, this called for a drink all around. Shortly after that, at midnight, the light on Tatoosh Rock came into view, only about 20 miles away.

When making a landfall, day or night, I always stay up to do the navigation, and there is considerable excitement at times such as this. At 0215 we had the light on Tatoosh off our starboard. I took a bearing and checked the Morse code identifier, and it agreed with the information in the radio book that identifies all radio beacons on the North American west coast. The book was only two years old so it still had reliable information. This was definitely the Strait of Juan de Fuca. At 0325 hours, when well clear of Tatoosh and the other rocks close by, we altered on to 080 compass and started up the strait. We had 80 miles to go to the customs dock in Victoria, and would complete our voyage that day, the 26th of June 1986.

We were proceeding up the American side of the Strait of Juan de Fuca. My plan was to go 20 or 30 miles, and then gradually power across into the Canadian side of the channel. Early that morning the sun was shining, it was warm, and the sea was absolutely calm. It was a very pleasant way to return to Canada, when it could have been foggy, cold and raining. The morale of the crew, especially Tony, was high. He had had enough of the ocean, and was anxious to get back to Dauphin to his family and his farm.

At about 1030 hours we were progressing towards the Canadian side of the channel. Nobody on the crew had noticed that an American coastguard boat was following us. Things on board were very relaxed, and the helmsman had not checked behind *Sea Lure* every 20 minutes as required by the rules. Probably the coastguard helmsman had put on lots of power to catch up quickly, when he saw us proceeding towards the Canadian side. They would not have any jurisdiction once we crossed into Canadian waters. The first thing I knew, I had a call on the VHF on channel 16 from the coastguard boat directly behind us. He asked me to switch to a working channel, and put an Alpha after the channel number. I had not used the Alpha button on the VHF in the past two years. In fact, I hadn't used it at any time in the past, as this VHF radio had been purchased shortly before I left Canada. I did not switch to the American channel number and after a delay, the coastguard radio operator came back on channel 16, and he agreed to use a Canadian working channel. After this minor delay, he directed me to stop *Sea Lure*, and advised that they were going to put a party on board my boat. I wasn't too happy about this, but after delaying for a few minutes I could see some guns on the coastguard boat, and they were pointed in our direction, so decided it was a good idea to comply with the request. After we stopped *Sea Lure*, there was another delay of probably 15 minutes while the coastguard crew launched their small boat. In the meantime both vessels were drifting with the tidal current, but our rate of drift was about the same. Eventually four crewmen came alongside in their inflatable boat, and we caught their lines and put down the ladder to make it easier for them to come on board. The man in charge gave me a speech about how they were authorized by American law to search my boat, as I was still in American waters. They then proceeded for the next 40 minutes to search *Sea Lure*. They were undoubtedly looking for drugs, and anything else that we might be smuggling to into Canada. At this point I was quite sure that we did not have any drugs aboard, except morphine in the main medical storage box. I had questioned the crew on this point before leaving Honolulu, but one cannot be 100% sure, so I was on tenterhooks while they did the search. The four men did an extremely thorough search of the boat. They emptied the clothing, etc. from all the bags, and checked each item in detail. They sniffed the ashtrays, even though they had not been used in weeks, to try to determine if any hash had been smoked. They looked in the bilge and most of the storage areas. Undoubtedly they had a lot of experience searching vessels, and knew where to look. To my relief nothing was found – this was as it should be, as I never carried illegal drugs.

After they were finished, the man in charge became quite friendly, and said they had observed us coming in from the ocean very early that morning, and started following us after we passed Neah Bay on the Washington side of the strait. I suppose we were going too slow for them, so they stopped a ship going out and searched it. Then when they saw us heading for the Canadian side of the channel, they put on lots of power and caught up before we had crossed into Canada. They seemed to be relieved that nothing was found on board *Sea Lure*. I suppose this cut down their workload for the day, and the crew may have been on a quota of vessels to be searched each month. They finally boarded their inflatable and went back to their vessel, after advising us that we were free to proceed to Canada and Victoria. This was the one and only time I have ever been searched by any coastguard. Since it had taken over an hour of our time, this meant that we would arrive in Victoria an hour later than estimated. It didn't matter, as it turned out, as customs in Victoria were open well into the evening due to the heavy summer traffic into Canada from the U.S. at that time of year.

At 1300 hours I called the Canadian coastguard radio, and had them patch me through to my home in Vancouver. I talked to Lou about our arrival time in Victoria, and she agreed to fly over that evening to meet us.

We proceeded up the strait, through Race passage, and docked in Victoria, in the inner harbour at the customs dock, at 1845 hours.

We had been 23 days at sea since leaving Honolulu – a long time. I had also been away from Canada two years and four days, since leaving Bellingham, Washington in 1984. Even though I had flown back three times, *Sea Lure* had been out of the country the entire time.

Customs clearance was no problem, although they questioned me in some detail about the $600 expenditure on the exhaust systems in Hawaii, but finally decided that it was not important. I couldn't have sailed home without the engine. At least I didn't want to, as the freezer and the batteries required powering every day for at least an hour. After about half an hour, the customs clearance was completed and we moved over to the government dock, and managed to squeeze into a spot on the outside of the main dock. It was really too small, and the davits on the stern were touching another vessel, but we stayed there for the night.

It was traditional that I take the crew out for dinner after docking, as a thank-you. I invited them to the Keg Restaurant directly above the docks for dinner that night. There was a delay until I met Lou at the Empress Hotel, a few blocks away, after she flew to the Victoria airport and taken a taxi to the hotel. The crew went to the pub at the Keg and hoisted a few in the meantime.

We were all still wearing our beards – 23 days growth, except for Paul and Mike, who had already had beards. They were all badly in need of a trim. I hadn't mentioned my beard to my wife when I called on the marine telephone. I had never grown a beard in our 36 years of married life. I was standing at the side entrance to the Empress Hotel when she arrived in the taxi, but she did not know me at first sight. It was a cool evening and I was wearing a sweater, and she said she recognized the sweater first. We had a good laugh, but she was in a state of shock for some time. It took her several days to get used to the beard, which added about 10 years to my age. I did have a lot of fun with it after returning to Vancouver, as my old friends had plenty to say. Some liked it, some didn't, and some didn't say anything, so I presumed they didn't like it either. But it was a good conversation piece, and I didn't have it shaved off until several months later. We went to the Keg Restaurant, joined up with the rest of the crew and had a very pleasant dinner.

Mike and Paul departed the next morning for Calgary, so I did not see them, as they were gone before Lou and I returned to *Sea Lure*. Tony stayed on and sailed back to Scott Point on Saltspring Island and then to Vancouver. By chance we met the Gardiners at Scott Point, as they docked a few minutes after us. We had a great reunion as they had been involved over the past four years starting with the purchase of *Sea Lure* in 1982.

It was great to be united with my family again and I think they all breathed a sigh of relief that we had made it back safely.

Although I was tired and on edge after 23 days on the ocean, it was a great feeling of accomplishment having completed the voyage successfully, and with *Sea Lure* still in reasonable shape requiring only minor repairs, some varnish and a new stove.

The end of the voyage was somewhat of a letdown too. I was no longer free to sail the oceans with my crew as I saw fit, but must face all the problems of everyday life in Vancouver, with properties to manage, a family, a horse and a multitude of other things. Also, I could no longer escape the telephone. I was exchanging one set of problems for another. I expect most ocean skippers go through this adjustment when they settle down again. A few do not, as they just keep sailing for 10 – 15 years only stopping to earn some money from time to time. I did meet several of them.

It was indeed unfortunate that Bob Dormer was unable to complete the adventure, but on the other hand two years may have been more than our compatible relationship could have survived. We did get together in Ottawa some months later.

One or two yachts disappear each year in the South Pacific. A yacht may be swamped by a rogue wave, run over by a ship unbeknown to the ship's crew, or holed by a large fish. Despite such hazards, the adventure is still highly recommended. Chances of success are very good as long as a suitable vessel is selected and the preparation is thorough. As well, the captain and crew must be adequately trained.

Many sailors are going offshore in yachts these days, and it is still an experience of a lifetime.

GLOSSARY

ANCHOR RODE – a chain or line attached to the anchor.

ANCHOR WINCH – a mechanism to bring in the anchor rode.

ANEMOMETER – an instrument to measure wind speed and direction.

ASTERN – to go backwards in a boat.

BACKSTAY – wire supporting the masthead which attaches to the back part of the boat.

BILGE PUMP – pumps water etc. from the inside lowest part of the boat.

BLOCK – a pulley used for lines on a boat.

BOSUN'S CHAIR – a chair for going up the mast when hooked to a halyard.

BOW CLEAT – boat fitting on which to secure a line.

BOWSPRIT – extension to the bow to which the forestay is attached.

COPRA – a product of the coconut shell.

D.R. (Dead Reckoning) – calculation and plotting of a position on a plotting sheet based on direction and distance travelled.

FURLING GEAR – mechanical system for rolling a sail in or out.

FURLING HALYARD – a line used to operate the furling gear.

GALLEY – area on boat where food is prepared and dishes washed.

GIMBALLED – a stove, etc. attached on each side so it will have the same heeling angle as the boat.

GPS (global position system) – determines boat's position using satellite and calculation on the boat's computer.

HAM RADIO – used by Amateur Radio Society for long distance radio communication.

HARDSTAND – area in a marina where boats are stored.

HEAD – toilet on a boat.

HEEL – angle that a boat leans when sailing, compared to level conditions.

KNOT LOG – boat instrument to record boat speed and distance travelled.

MAYDAY – international distress call sign.

MERCATOR PROJECTION – a navigational chart where course lines are all straight lines.

MIZZEN – a sail attached to the mizzenmast, which is closer to the boat's stern on a ketch.

PORT – the left side of the boat when facing forward. Boat bow light is red.

RAFT – to tie alongside another boat.

REEF – to roll a sail partly in or reduce the sail area.

SAT NAV (Satellite Navigation System) – uses satellites and boat equipment to determine latitude and longitude.

SEA COCKS – boat valves under the water line to drain areas of the boat.

SEVENTH WAVE – the cycle of wave action after the wind has been blowing for some time is that frequently the seventh wave is higher than the preceding six waves.

SEXTANT – instrument to determine angle between celestial body and horizon, used to calculate a boat's latitude and longitude.

SHROUDS – wire supports usually attached near the spreaders and the top of the mast.

SPREADERS – short struts between the mast and the shrouds to support the mast.

STARBOARD – right side of boat when facing forward. Bow light is always green.

VHF RADIO – (Very High Frequency) radio for short range communication not over 100 miles. Operates on line of sight.